To Follow

The Frontiers of Theory

Series Editor: Martin McQuillan

To Follow

The Wake of Jacques Derrida

Peggy Kamuf

Edinburgh University Press

First published in hardback by Edinburgh University Press 2010

Edinburgh University Press Ltd
22 George Square, Edinburgh EH8 9LF

www.euppublishing.com

Typeset in Adobe Sabon
by Servis Filmsetting Ltd, Stockport, Cheshire, and
printed and bound in Great Britain by
CPI Antony Rowe, Chippenham and Eastbourne

A CIP record for this book is available from the British Library

ISBN 978 0 7486 4154 3 (hardback)
ISBN 978 0 7486 5509 0 (paperback)

Contents

Acknowledgments

Most often written in response to invitations, the chapters of this book are indebted first to all those who conceived and hosted congenial contexts for initial presentation of work then in progress: Deborah Lesko Baker, Karyn Ball, Roger-Daniel Bensky, Thomas Dutoit, Simon Glendinning, Christopher Johnson, Kir Kuiken, Dragan Kujundžić, René Major, Martin McQuillan, Steven Miller, Michael O'Driscoll, Eric Prenowitz, Philippe Romanski, Marta Segarra, Ashley Thompson, and Massimo Verdicchio.

Many of these same friends (Tom, Simon, Chris, Dragan, Philippe, and Marta) also edited journal issues or essay collections in which earlier versions of some of the chapters appeared, for which I want to thank them again, as well as: Thomas Eaglestone, Lawrence Kritzman, Michel Lisse, Marie-Louise Mallet, Dawne McCance, Ginette Michaud, and Julia Simon.

My longest-standing debts are to incomparable friends and readers of Derrida: Geoff Bennington, Pascale-Anne Brault, Hélène Cixous, Ted Jennings, Elissa Marder, Michael Naas, Elizabeth Rottenberg, Nick Royle, Brigitte Weltman-Aron, David Wills, and Sarah Wood.

I am grateful to the publishers for permissions to reprint a number of the chapters.

Chapter 1, "Tape-Recorded Surprise: Derrida Interviewed," first appeared in *Nottingham French Studies* 42, 1 (Spring 2003), pp. 87–96, in an issue titled *Thinking in Dialogue: The Role of the Interview in Post-War French Thought*, edited by Christopher Johnson.

Chapter 2 is a translation of "*Bartleby*, ou la décision, une note sur l'allégorie," published in *Derrida d'ici, Derrida de là*, edited by Thomas Dutoit and Philippe Romanski (Paris: Galilée, 2009), pp. 125–36.

Chapter 3 is a translation of "Traduire dans l'urgence," published in *Le Magazine Littéraire* 430 (April 2004), p. 49, a special issue on Derrida edited by Michel Lisse.

Chapter 4 is a translation of "Venir aux débuts," in *Derrida* [see infra, "Works Cited], pp. 329–34.

Chapter 5, "To Follow," was first published in an earlier version in *Differences: A Journal of Feminist Cultural Studies*, 16, 3 (Fall 2005), pp. 1–15.

Chapter 7, "One day someone . . .," was first published as an untitled contribution to "Forum: The Legacy of Jacques Derrida," *PMLA* 120, 2 (March 2005), pp. 479–81.

Chapter 8, "The Affect of America," was published in an earlier version in *Derrida's Legacies: Literature and Philosophy*, edited by Simon Glendinning and Robert Eaglestone (New York: Routledge, 2008), pp. 138–50.

Chapter 9, "From Now On," was first published in *Epoché*, 10, 2 (Spring 2006), pp. 203–20.

Chapter 11, "*Aller à la ligne*," is a translation from an earlier version published in *L'Événement comme écriture: Cixous et Derrida se lisant*, edited by Marta Segarra, Paris: Campagne Première, 2007, pp. 73–84.

Chapter 12, "Composition Displacement," was published in an earlier version in *MLN* 121 (2006) edited by Lawrence Kritzman, pp. 872–92.

Chapter 13, "The Ear, Who?", was first published in *Discourse* 30, 1–2 (Winter–Spring 2008), edited by Dragan Kujundžić, pp. 177–90.

Chapter 14, "To Do Justice to 'Rousseau,' Irreducibly," appeared in an earlier version in *Eighteenth-Century Studies* 40, 3 (Spring 2007), pp. 395–404, a special issue titled "Derrida's Eighteenth Century."

Chapter 15, "The Deconstitution of Psychoanalysis," appeared in *Mosaic* 42, 4 (December 2009), edited by Dawne McCance, pp. 35–44.

Works by Jacques Derrida Cited

The following list gives full publication information for all works by Jacques Derrida quoted or cited in these chapters. Works are in alphabetical order of their title in the published English translation when one is available, followed by the citation of the original French edition. Untranslated works are listed only by their French titles. Short titles used to refer to the works throughout are given in parentheses. Unless otherwise indicated, all quotations are from the published English translations, which have occasionally been modified.

(*Acts*) *Acts of Literature*. Edited by Derek Attridge. New York and London: Routledge, 1992.

("Afterword") "Afterword: Toward an Ethic of Discussion." Translated by Samuel Weber. In *Limited*; "Postface: Vers une éthique de la discussion." See *Limited*.

(*Alibi*) *Without Alibi*. Edited and translated by Peggy Kamuf. Stanford: Stanford University Press, 2002.

(*Animal*) *The Animal that Therefore I Am*. Edited by Marie-Louise Mallet. Translated by David Wills. New York: Fordham University Press, 2008; *L'Animal que donc je suis*. Edited by Marie-Louise Mallet. Paris: Galilée, 2006.

("Ants") "Ants." Translated by Eric Prenowitz. In *Oxford Literary Review* 24 (2002); "Fourmis." In *Lectures de la différence sexuelle*. Edited by Mara Negrón. Paris: Éditions des femmes, 1994.

("Aphorism") "Aphorism Countertime." Translated by Nicholas Royle. In *Psyche* II; "L'Aphorisme à contretemps." In *Psyché* II.

(*Archive*)   *Archive Fever: A Freudian Impression*. Translated by Eric Prenowitz. Chicago: University of Chicago Press, 1996; *Mal d'archive, une impression freudienne*. Paris: Galilée, 1995.

("As If")   "As If It Were Possible, 'Within Such Limits' . . ." In *Paper*. "Comme si c'était possible, *'within such limits'* . . ." In *Papier machine* (see *Paper*).

("Autoimmunity")   "Autoimmunity: Real and Symbolic Suicides." Translated by Pascale-Anne Brault and Michael Naas. In *Philosophy in a Time of Terror: Dialogues with Jürgen Habermas and Jacques Derrida*. Edited by Giovanna Borradori. Chicago: University of Chicago Press, 2003; Derrida and Jürgen Habermas, *Le "Concept" du 11 septembre: Dialogues à New York (octobre–décembre 2001)*, *avec Giovanna Borradori*. Paris: Galilée, 2003.

("Avances")   "Avances." Preface to Serge Margel, *Le Tombeau du dieu artisan*. Paris: Minuit, 1995.

("Barthes")   "The Deaths of Roland Barthes." In *Work*; "Les Morts de Roland Barthes." In *Chaque fois*.

(*Beast*)   *The Beast and the Sovereign*, Volume I. Edited by Michel Lisse, Marie-Louise Mallet, and Ginette Michaud. Translated by Geoffrey Bennington. Chicago: University of Chicago Press, 2009; *La Bête et le souverain* I, 2000–2001. Edited by Michel Lisse, Marie-Louise Mallet, and Ginette Michaud. Paris: Galilée, 2008.

("Before")   "Before the Law." Translated by Avital Ronell and Christine Roulston. In *Acts*; "Préjugés: Devant la loi." In Derrida et al., *La Faculté de juger*. Paris: Minuit, 1985.

("Book")   "The Book to Come." In *Paper*; "Le Livre à venir." In *Papier machine* (see *Paper*).

(*Chaque fois*)   *Chaque fois unique, la fin du monde*. Paris: Galilée, 2003 (see *Work*).

(*Cinders*)   *Cinders*. Edited and translated by Ned Lukacher. Lincoln: University of Nebraska Press, 1991 [bilingual edition]; *Feu la cendre*. Paris: Éditions des femmes, 1987.

(*Circumfession*)   *Circumfession*. Translated by Geoffrey Bennington. In Geoffrey Bennington and Jacques Derrida. *Jacques Derrida*. Chicago: University of Chicago Press, 1993; *Circumfession*. In Geoffrey Bennington and Jacques Derrida, *Jacques Derrida*. Paris: Seuil, 1991.

(*Counterpath*)   Catherine Malabou and Derrida, *Counterpath: Traveling with Jacques Derrida*. Translated by David Wills. Stanford: Stanford University Press, 2004; Catherine Malabou and Derrida, *La Contre-allée*. Paris: La Quinzaine Littéraire and Louis Vuitton, 1999.

(*Demeure*)   *Demeure: Fiction and Testimony*. Translated by Elizabeth Rottenberg. Stanford: Stanford University Press, 1998; *Demeure, Maurice Blanchot*. Paris: Galilée, 1998.

(*Derrida*)   *Derrida*. Edited by Marie-Louis Mallet and Ginette Michaud. Paris: Cahiers de l'Herne, 2004.

(*Dissemination*)   *Dissemination*. Translated by Barbara Johnson. Chicago: University of Chicago Press, 1981; *La Dissemination*. Paris: Éditions du Seuil, 1972.

(*Ear*)   *The Ear of the Other: Otobiography, Transference, Translation*. Edited by Christie V. McDonald. Translated by Avital Ronell and Peggy Kamuf. New York: Schocken Books, 1985; *Otobiographies: L'enseignement de Nietzsche et la politique du nom propre*. Paris: Galilée, 1984.

(*Eyes*)   *Eyes of the University: Right to Philosophy 2*. Translated by Jan Plug and others. Stanford: Stanford University Press, 2004; *Du droit à la philosophie*. Paris: Galilée, 1990 (see also *Philosophy*).

("Faith")   "Faith and Knowledge: The Two Sources of 'Religion' at the Limits of Reason Alone." Translated by Samuel Weber, in Derrida, *Acts of Religion*. Edited by Gil Anidjar. New York: Routledge, 2002; "Foi et savoir: Les deux sources de la 'religion' aux limites de la simple raison." In Derrida and Gianni Vattimo, *La Religion*. Paris: Seuil, 1996.

("*Fichus*")   "*Fichus*: Frankfurt Address." Translated by Rachel Bowlby. In *Paper*; *Fichus: Discours de Francfort*. Paris: Galilée, 2002.

("Forgive")   "To Forgive: The Unforgivable and the Imprescriptible."
Translated by Elizabeth Rottenberg. In *Questioning God*.
Edited by John D. Caputo et al. Bloomington and Indianapolis:
Indiana University Press, 2001. "Pardonner: l'impardonnable et
l'imprescriptible," in *Derrida*.

("Fors")   "Fors: The Anglish Words of Nicolas Abraham and Maria
Torok." Translated by Barbara Johnson. In Nicolas Abraham and
Maria Torok, *The Wolf Man's Magic Word*. Edited and translated
by Nicolas Rand. Minneapolis: Minnesota University Press, 1986;
"Fors. Les mots anglés de Nicolas Abraham et Maria Torok." In
Nicolas Abraham and Maria Torok, *Cryptonymie: Le Verbier de
l'homme aux loups*. Paris: Aubier-Flammarion, 1976.

("Freud")   "Freud and the Scene of Writing." In *Writing*; "Freud et
la scène de l'écriture." In *L'Écriture et la différence* (see *Writing*).

(*Geneses*)   *Geneses, Genealogies, Genres and Genius: The Secrets
of the Archive*. Translated by Beverley Bie Brahic. Edinburgh:
Edinburgh University Press, 2006; *Genèses, généalogies, genres et le
génie*. Paris: Galilée, 2003.

("Geopsych")   "Geopsychoanalysis 'and the rest of the world.'"
Translated by Peggy Kamuf. In *Psyche* I; "Géopsychanalyse '*and the
rest of the world*.'" In *Psyché* I.

("*Geschlecht*")   "*Geschlecht* I: Sexual Difference, Ontological
Difference." Translated by Ruben Berezdivin and Elizabeth
Rottenberg. In *Psyche* II. "*Geschlecht* I: Différence sexuelle,
différence ontologique." In *Psyché* II.

(*Glas*)   *Glas*. Translated by John P. Leavey, Jr. Lincoln: University of
Nebraska Press, 1986; *Glas*. Paris: Galilée, 1974.

(*Grammatology*)   *Of Grammatology*. Translated by Gayatri
Chakravorty Spivak. Baltimore: Johns Hopkins University Press,
1974, 1976; *De la grammatologie*. Paris: Minuit, 1967.

(*H.C.*)   *H.C. for Life, That Is to Say* . . . Translated by Laurent Milesi
and Stefan Herbrechter. Stanford: Stanford University Press, 2006;
H.C. pour la vie, c'est à dire . . . Paris: Galilée, 2000.

("Hand")   "Heidegger's Hand (*Geschlecht* II). Translated by John P. Leavey, Jr. and Elizabeth Rottenberg. In *Psyche* II; "La Main de Heidegger (*Geschlecht* II)." In *Psyché* II.

(*Heading*)   *The Other Heading.* Translated by Pascale-Anne Brault and Michael B. Naas. Bloomington: Indiana University Press, 1992; *L'Autre cap*. Paris: Minuit, 1991.

("Illustrate")   "To Illustrate, He Said . . ." Translated by Peggy Kamuf. In *Psyche* I; "Illustrer, dit-il . . ." In *Psyché* I.

("Journalists")   "Above All, No Journalists!" Translated by Samuel Weber. In *Religion and Media*. Edited by Hent de Vries and Samuel Weber. Stanford: Stanford University Press, 2001.

("Justices")   "'Justices.'" Translated by Peggy Kamuf. *Critical Inquiry* 31, 3 (Spring 2005).

("*Khōra*")   "*Khōra.*" Translated by Ian McLeod. In *Name*; *Khôra*. Paris: Galilée, 1993.

("Lacan")   "For the Love of Lacan." Translated by Peggy Kamuf. In *Resistances of Psychoanalysis*. Stanford: Stanford University Press, 1998; *Résistances, de la psychanalyse*. Paris: Galilée, 1996.

("Law")   "The Law of Genre." Translated by Avital Ronell. In *Acts*; "La Loi du genre." In *Parages*.

(*Limited*)   *Limited Inc.* Translated by Samuel Weber. Evanston: Northwestern University Press, 1988; *Limited Inc.* Edited by Elisabeth Weber. Paris: Galilée, 1990.

("Living")   "Living On: Borderlines." Translated by James Hulbert. In Harold Bloom et al., *Deconstruction and Criticism*. New York: Continuum, 1979; "Survivre: Journal de bord." In *Parages*.

("Me")   "Me—Psychoanalysis." Translated by Richard Klein. In *Psyche* I; "Moi—la psychanalyse." In *Psyché* I.

(*Memoirs*)   *Memoirs of the Blind: The Self-Portrait and Other Ruins.* Translated by Pascale-Anne Brault and Michael Naas. Chicago: University of Chicago Press, 1993; *Mémoires d'aveugle:*

L'Autoportrait et autres ruines. Paris: Réunion des Musées Nationaux, 1990.

(*"Mochlos"*)   "*Mochlos*, or the Conflict of the Faculties." Translated by Richard Rand and Amy Wygant. In *Eyes*; "*Mochlos, ou le conflit des facultés.*" In *Du droit à la philosophie.* Paris: Galilée, 1990.

(*Monolingualism*)   *Monolingualism of the Other; or, the Prosthesis of Origin.* Translated by Patrick Mensah. Stanford: Stanford University Press, 1998; *Monolinguisme de l'autre, ou la prothèse d'origine.* Paris: Galilée, 1996.

("Mourning")   "By Force of Mourning." In *Work*; "À force de deuil." In *Chaque fois*.

(*Name*)   *On the Name.* Edited by Thomas Dutoit. Stanford: Stanford University Press, 1995.

(*Negotiations*)   *Negotiations: Interventions and Interviews, 1971–2001.* Edited and translated by Elizabeth Rottenberg. Stanford: Stanford University Press, 2002.

("No Apocalypse")   "No Apocalypse, Not Now: Full Speed Ahead, Seven Missiles, Seven Missives." Translated by Catherine Porter and Philip Lewis. In *Psyche* I; "*No Apocalypse, not now,* à toute vitesse, sept missiles, sept missives." In *Psyché* I.

("Oreille")   "L'Oreille de Heidegger: Philopolémologie (*Geschlecht* IV)." In *Politiques de l'amitié* (see *Politics*).

(*Paper*)   *Paper Machine.* Translated by Rachel Bowlby. Stanford: Stanford University Press, 2005; *Papier machine.* Paris: Galilée, 2002.

(*Parages*)   *Parages.* Paris: Galilée, 1986.

("Parjure")   "'Le Parjure,' *Perhaps*: Storytelling and Lying ('abrupt breaches of syntax')." In *Alibi*; "Le parjure, peut-être ('brusques sautes de syntaxe')." In *Derrida*.

(*"Pas"*)   *Pas.* In *Parages*.

("Passe-Partout")   "Passe-Partout." In *Truth*. "Passe-partout." In *La Vérité en peinture* (see *Truth*).

("Passions")   "Passions: 'An Oblique Offering.'" Translated by David Wood. In *Name; Passions*. Paris: Galilée, 1993.

("Pharmacy")   "Plato's Pharmacy." In *Dissemination*; "La Pharmacie de Platon." In *Dissémination*.

(*Philosophy*)   *Who's Afraid of Philosophy?: Right to Philosophy 1*. Translated by Jan Plug. Stanford: Stanford University Press, 2002; *Du droit à la philosophie*. Paris: Galilée, 1990 (see also *Eyes*).

(*Points*)   *Points . . .: Interviews, 1974–1994*. Edited by Elisabeth Weber. Translated by Peggy Kamuf et al. Stanford: Stanford University Press, 1995; *Points de suspension: Entretiens*. Edited by Elisabeth Weber. Paris: Galilée, 1992.

(*Politics*)   *Politics of Friendship*. Translated by George Collins. London: Verso, 1997; *Politiques de l'amitié*. Paris: Galilée, 1994.

(*Positions*)   *Positions*. Translated by Alan Bass. Chicago: University of Chicago Press, 1982; *Positions*. Paris: Minuit, 1972.

(*Post Card*)   *The Post Card: From Socrates to Freud and Beyond*. Translated by Alan Bass. Chicago: University of Chicago Press, 1987; *La Carte postale, de Socrate à Freud et au-delà*. Paris: Aubier-Flammarion, 1980.

("Psyche")   "Psyche: Invention of the Other." Translated by Catherine Porter. In *Psyche* I; "Psyché: Invention de l'autre." In *Psyché* I.

(*Psyche*)   *Psyche: Inventions of the Other*, volumes I and II. Edited by Peggy Kamuf and Elizabeth Rottenberg. Stanford: Stanford University Press, 2007 and 2008; *Psyché: Inventions de l'autre*, tomes I et II. Paris: Galilée, 1998 and 2003.

("Qual Quelle")   "Qual Quelle: Valéry's Sources." In *Margins of Philosophy*. Translated by Alan Bass. Chicago: University of Chicago Press, 1985; "Qual quelle, les sources de Valéry." In *Marges—de la philosophie*. Paris: Minuit, 1972.

("Racism")   "Racism's Last Word." Translated by Peggy Kamuf. In *Psyche* I; "Le Dernier mot du racisme." In *Psyché* I.

("Rams")   "Rams: Uninterrupted Dialogue—Between Two Infinities, the Poem." Translated by Thomas Dutoit and Philippe Romanski. In *Sovereignties*; *Béliers, Le Dialogue ininterrompu: entre deux infinis, le poème*. Paris: Galilée, 2003.

("Rhetoric")   "The Rhetoric of Drugs." Translated by Michael Israel. In *Points*; "La Rhétorique des drogues." In *Points*.

("Restitutions")   "Restitutions: Of the Truth in Painting." In *Truth*; "Restitutions, de la vérité en peinture. In *La Vérité en peinture* (see *Truth*).

(*Rogues*)   *Rogues: Two Essays on Reason*. Translated by Pascale-Anne Brault and Michael Naas. Stanford: Stanford University Press, 2005; *Voyous: Deux essais sur la raison*. Paris: Galilée, 2003.

("Salut")   "'Dead Man Running': Salut, Salut." In *Negotiations*; "'Il courait mort': Salut, salut." *Les Temps Modernes* 587, Mars–Mai, 1996.

("*Sauf*")   "*Sauf le nom* (Post-Scriptum)." Translated by John P. Leavey, Jr. In *Name*; *Sauf le nom*. Paris: Galilée, 1993.

(*Signéponge*)   *Signéponge/Signsponge*. Translated by Richard Rand. New York: Columbia University Press, 1984 [bilingual edition]; *Signéponge*. Paris: Éditions du Seuil, 1988.

("Silk Worm")   "A Silk Worm of One's Own." Translated by Geoffrey Bennington. In Hélène Cixous and Derrida, *Veils*. Stanford: Stanford University Press, 2001; "Un ver à soie." In Hélène Cixous and Derrida, *Voiles*. Paris: Galilée, 1998.

(*Sovereignties*)   *Sovereignties in Question: The Poetics of Paul Celan*. Edited by Thomas Dutoit and Outi Pasanen. New York: Fordham University Press, 2005.

(*Specters*)   *Specters of Marx: The State of the Debt, the Work of Mourning, and the New International*. Translated by Peggy Kamuf. New York and London: Routledge, 1994; *Spectres de Marx: L'État de la dette, le travail du deuil et la Nouvelle Internationale*. Paris: Galilée, 1993.

("Speculate")   "To Speculate—on 'Freud.'" In *Post Card*; "Spéculer—sur 'Freud.'" In *La Carte postale* (see *Post Card*).

(*Speech*)   *Speech and Phenomena and Other Essays on Husserl's Theory of Signs*. Translated by David B. Allison. Evanston: Northwestern University Press, 1973; *La Voix et le phénomène*. Paris: Presses Universitaires de France, 1967.

("States")   "Psychoanalysis Searches the States of Its Soul." In *Alibi*; *États d'âme de la psychanalyse*. Paris: Galilée, 2000.

("Structure")   "Structure, Sign and Play in the Discourse of the Human Sciences." In *Writing*; "La Structure, le signe et le jeu dans le discours des sciences humaines"; In *L'Écriture et la différence* (see *Writing*).

("Telepathy")   "Telepathy." Translated by Nicholas Royle. In *Psyche* I; "Télépathie." In *Psyché* I.

("This Work")   "At This Very Moment in This Work Here I Am." Translated by Ruben Berezdivin and Peggy Kamuf. In *Psyche* I. "En ce moment même dans cette oeuvre me voici." In *Psyché* I.

(*Time*)   *Given Time: 1. Counterfeit Money*. Translated by Peggy Kamuf. Chicago: University of Chicago Press, 1992; *Donner le temps: 1. La Fausse monnaie*. Paris: Galilée, 1991.

(*Tomorrow*)   Derrida and Elisabeth Roudinesco. *For What Tomorrow: A Dialogue*. Translated by Jeff Fort. Stanford: Stanford University Press, 2004; Derrida and Elisabeth Roudinesco, *De quoi demain: Dialogue*. Paris: Fayard and Galilée, 2001.

("Tone")   "On a Newly Arisen Apocalyptic Tone in Philosophy." Translated by John P. Leavey, Jr. In *Raising the Tone of Philosophy: Late Essays of Immanuel Kant, Transformative Critique of Jacques Derrida*. Edited by Peter Fenves. Baltimore: The Johns Hopkins University Press, 1993; *D'un ton apocalyptique adopté naguére en philosophie*. Paris: Galilée, 1983–2005.

(*Touching*)   *On Touching—Jean-Luc Nancy*. Translated by Christine Irizarry. Stanford: Stanford University Press, 2005; *Le Toucher, Jean-Luc Nancy*. Paris: Galilée, 2001.

(*Tourner*)   Derrida and Safaa Fathy. *Tourner les mots: Au bord d'un film*. Paris: Galilée, 2000.

("Tout")   "Du tout." In *Post Card*; "Du tout." In *La Carte postale* (see *Post Card*).

(*Truth*)   *The Truth in Painting*. Translated by Geoff Bennington and Ian McLeod. Chicago: University of Chicago Press, 1987; *La Vérité en peinture*. Paris: Flammarion, 1978.

("Ulysses")   "Ulysses Gramophone: Hear Say Yes in Joyce." Translated by Tina Kendall and Shari Benstock. In *Acts*; "Ulysse gramophone: ouï-dire de Joyce." In *Ulysse Gramophone: Deux mots pour Joyce*. Paris: Galilée, 1987.

("Unconditionality")   "Unconditionality or Sovereignty: The University at the Frontiers of Europe." Translated by Peggy Kamuf. *Oxford Literary Review* 31, 2 (2009); "Inconditionnalité ou souveraineté: L'Université aux frontières de l'Europe." Athènes: Éditions Patakis, 2002.

("University")   "The University Without Condition." In *Alibi*; *L'Université sans condition*. Paris: Galilée, 2001.

("Witnessing")   "The Poetics and Politics of Witnessing." Translated by Outi Pasanen. In *Sovereignties*; "Poétique et politique du témoignage." In *Derrida*.

(*Work*)   *The Work of Mourning*. Edited and translated by Pascale-Anne Brault and Michael Naas. Chicago: University of Chicago Press, 2001; see *Chaque fois*.

(*Writing*)   *Writing and Difference*. Translated by Alan Bass. Chicago: University of Chicago Press, 1978; *L'Écriture et la différence*. Paris: Éditions du Seuil, 1967.

Since its inception, Theory has been concerned with its own limits, ends and after-life. It would be an illusion to imagine that the academy is no longer resistant to Theory but a significant consensus has been established and it can be said that Theory has now entered the mainstream of the humanities. Reaction against Theory is now a minority view and new generations of scholars have grown up with Theory. This leaves so-called Theory in an interesting position which its own procedures of auto-critique need to consider: what is the nature of this mainstream Theory and what is the relation of Theory to philosophy and the other disciplines which inform it? What is the history of its construction and what processes of amnesia and the repression of difference have taken place to establish this thing called Theory? Is Theory still the site of a more-than-critical affirmation of a negotiation with thought, which thinks thought's own limits?

"Theory" is a name that traps by an aberrant nomial effect the transformative critique which seeks to reinscribe the conditions of thought in an inaugural founding gesture that is without ground or precedent: as a "name," a word and a concept, Theory arrests or misprisions such thinking. To imagine the frontiers of Theory is not to dismiss or to abandon Theory (on the contrary one must always insist on the it-is-necessary of Theory even if one has given up belief in theories of all kinds). Rather, this series is concerned with the presentation of work which challenges complacency and continues the transformative work of critical thinking. It seeks to offer the very best of contemporary theoretical practice in the humanities, work which continues to push ever further the frontiers of what is accepted, including the name of Theory. In particular, it is interested in that work which involves the necessary endeavor of crossing disciplinary frontiers without dissolving the specificity of disciplines. Published by Edinburgh University Press, in the city of Enlightenment, this series promotes a certain closeness to that spirit:

the continued exercise of critical thought as an attitude of inquiry which counters modes of closed or conservative opinion. In this respect the series aims to make thinking think at the frontiers of theory.

Martin McQuillan

Introduction: Watchwords

in order to watch over the future, everything would have to be begun again . . .

(Specters of Marx)

I: Cryptography

While this book was "in progress" it remained unoriented, its progression having no overarching idea. It was only very late, after all these pieces had been written, that the thought of aligning them in the order of their composition took over somewhat. This is a circumstance that I hasten to confide to the reader of this introduction, who rightfully expects some accounting for what is to follow.

Each of the steps in this non-progression were taken within the compass of the work of Jacques Derrida. This repeated reference was, for the large majority of pieces collected here, dictated by a context, occasion, or event. Before the fall of 2004, these contexts always varied. After Derrida's death in October, 2004, each context was, whether or not this was made explicit, a frame of some sort thrown around the disarray that so many then experienced. At many public gatherings in the weeks and months that followed, often at institutions with which Derrida had been associated, a few of his colleagues, friends, or students spoke or tried to speak, thought or tried to think aloud in some manner of response to the loss.

More than five years have now passed. In addition to memorial issues of numerous journals, a number of monographs have appeared whose signatories have likewise been jolted by the sudden disappearance of someone whose work and whose friendship had long accompanied them.[1] *To Follow*, then, may be getting ready to fall into some category or genre, a general idea of a kind, a kind of writing, for example, or a kind of book. It is perhaps becoming a risk for such books, the risk of seeming to confirm the view that there is such a kind, genre, or category, which subsumes the different exempla under its general heading or name.

This is less a risk of unoriginality or repetition, however, than a risk taken with the very name of this category, the name of Jacques Derrida. For it is, of course, Derrida who gives the category its name, his name. What all of these writings or collections must share is his name in their titles. But this shared trait can become the mark of a genre only by dividing the mark of the proper name that allows it to function, at least for some time yet, as also the name of the no-longer living friend, author, thinker. This division puts at risk the name as proper name that can call the friend, living, himself, call him, for example, on the telephone in Ris-Orangis or Laguna Beach.

But, of course, this is not a risk for it is what has happened, once and for all. These, then, are writings from the place where what is called mourning must be undertaken, where one must become an undertaker, burying the other somewhere in oneself until he or she has been absorbed into memory. Because we should not forget that mourning is also a way of forgetting. There, perhaps, is the greatest risk run with books that have been impelled by the divided trait of mourning. They may also be working to forget.

No one has undertaken to question in a more unflinching manner the aporetic and finally *unreadable* condition called mourning than Jacques Derrida. In "To Follow," the essay included here that most proximately registers the ultimate division of Derrida's name, I underscore that this analysis underlies all of Derrida's mature thought, beginning with *La Voix et le phénomène* (1967). What is called mourning? What do we think we are naming thus? Derrida questions, very acutely, the supposition that there can be any certain feature that divides so-called normal mourning from its pathologies, where normal mourning has gone awry somehow. Distinctions made between normal and pathological would have only heuristic, diagnostic, or clinical value, but, absent that demand, there is no *general* concept of mourning. Likewise, there can be no *genre* of mourning-writing, subsuming all exempla under its indivisible trait. Because mourning registers the experience of the division of names and traits, the undivided mark of its genre is impossible.[2] What is called mourning is the experience of an inescapable divisibility; because its proper trait is irretrievably divided, it is generalizable only as ungeneralizable.

One of the texts in which Derrida pursues most probingly the division of mourning's trait is "Fors," which was published in 1976 as a foreword to Nicolas Abraham and Maria Torok's *Cryptonymie: Le Verbier de l'homme aux loups*.[3] Nicolas Abraham was a psychoanalyst who practiced in Paris beginning in the 1950s and, until his death in 1975, he did so without a strong affiliation to any one of the then mostly warring French psychoanalytic societies. But Abraham was also a philosopher, trained in Husserlian phenomenology, who set out to elaborate what he called a "transphenomenology" that would throw a bridge to the discoveries of psychoanalysis. One can easily understand, therefore, the affinity that Derrida developed with Abraham, after the two met for the first time in 1959.

The circumstances of this meeting—at the Cerisy-la-Salle colloquium on *Genèse et structure*—are recounted, in a parenthesis, by Derrida in "Fors,"[4] but what is nowhere disclosed in this longish text is from which side of his mourning-friendship relation with Abraham Derrida is then writing. There is no unequivocal reference in "Fors" to Abraham's death, which was on 18 December 1975, thus almost 1976, the year "Fors" would see publication. As a consequence—and this may seem extraordinary—it is possible to read "Fors" as written either *just before* or *just after* the death of the one whom Derrida here associates, writing either in 1975 or 1976, with "the breath of living friendship" ("Fors," 40).

This suspension of certainty is extraordinary, however, only to the extent that one assumes mourning begins on a certain date (18 December 1975 or 9 October 2004). But all of Derrida's thought, bolstered here by Abraham and Torok's analysis of a famous case of "failed" mourning, follows from the insight that mourning will have begun with the friends' or lovers' first encounter. It is fatally inscribed when Juliet meets her Romeo, who can henceforth never not be called Romeo, by this name destined to survive him.[5] From the very first, every name, anyone's name, names a site of mourning to come.

Derrida's thought, I said, follows from this insight. But the term "insight" must also be read as the sight that has to divide between inside and outside so as to continue seeing the other, himself or herself, living, but now only within: in memory, in dreams. Like the other's name, the visibility of the other, the possibility of seeing the other, of catching sight of him or her, divides and where it divides a limit is traced between an outside and an inside space. Or rather "space" as well has to divide its trait between outside and inside on a limit that is both traced and effaced by the divisibility of all marks. This dividing movement is what Derrida has called the iterable trace, the minimal element of any language or inscription, something like the DNA of writing.

The generalization of mourning's divided trait thus traverses Derrida's whole work, but doubtless "Fors" situates one of the most concentrated nodes in its elaboration. A key deconstructive lever Derrida activates throughout the text is the non-situability of this or any writing. Where does it take place? What takes place? On which surface? On which division between inside and outside, that is, between the terms of a distinction that is the very possibility of general concepts, names, and thus language? This de-situating has already begun with the essay's title, "Fors," which points the reader in a plurality of directions and thus away from any single location: toward that inside that is the *for intérieur*, the "tribunal of conscience," but also toward the outside of the public and political forum, as well as toward that outside of the inside Abraham and Torok called a crypt where someone is kept safe, *fors le reste*.[6]

The first lines of the text perform this becoming-unlocatable of writing with its two opening questions:

> What is a crypt?
> What if I were writing on one here? [*Et si j'écrivais ici sur elle?*] ("Fors," xi)

When taken together in their minimal sequencing, these become strange, estranging questions. For "What is a crypt?", as Derrida will proceed to point out, does not ask what is "*the* crypt *in general*, but *this* one, in its singularity" ("Fors," xiii). The question thus detaches itself from the fund of common or general knowledge of a language in which the word "crypt" is anchored by a concept. Instead, the reader is marooned at the indeterminable location of a singularity, "this one." The second question narrows down the coordinates of this location but only by plotting them at and with the conjunction of writing. It now asks: what is a crypt if I could be writing on one here, now? It is the concrete and not just the abstract sense of "writing on" that has then to be reckoned with, that is, not just the idea of writing on a subject or topic, for example crypts, but also of writing *on* a support, a surface, or the outer face of some construction, for example, the wall of a crypt, this one here. What if the support of writing could be a crypt, which is always singular, always a "one," as the translation says, or as Derrida writes using the feminine objective pronoun, "elle"? "What if I am writing on it—on her—here?" What—or who—is this crypt? And what is writing if its support, the very condition of its becoming readable for another, may be each time such a singular location?[7]

Where will all this writing *on* Jacques Derrida—his work, his friendship, his teaching, his mourning—have taken place?

II: Exemplarity

Before or after, before and after the death of the friend: the dated occasions for each of the pieces to follow seem fixed in relation to this event. Yet, just as mourning works also to forget, chronology imposes homogeneous order on experience that otherwise leaps out of time under the impulse of encounter with a heteronomous time, the time of the other.

The encounter with the teacher Jacques Derrida was such an experience. Although I was fortunate to have known it "in person," as we say, the space of reading—that virtual space framed by an *as if* or *what if?*—can be at least an equally fertile ground for the kind of surprising interruption that causes to tremble the referential certainties of "time," "self," "other," "my life," or "my death."

Early in "Envois," the long epistolary fiction that opens *The Post Card*, Derrida's narrator and principal post-card writer (who resembles the author in just about every way) recounts something that happened one day after a seminar he had conducted at Balliol College, Oxford:

> Afterward, on the lawn where the discussion continued, which aimlessly followed switch points as unforeseeable as they were inevitable, a young student (very handsome) thought he could provoke me and, I think, seduce me a little by asking me why I didn't kill myself [*me suicider*]. In his eyes this was the only way to "forward" [*"faire suivre"*] (his word) my "theoretical discourse," the only way to be consistent and produce an event. Instead of arguing, of sending him back to this or that, I responded with a pirouette . . . (*Post Card*, 19)[8]

This scene has always struck me as paradigmatic not only of the ambiguously aggressive response that Derrida often attracted and of the kind of grace with which he was able to deflect it, but as well of the underlying motive, which is here spoken aloud, of the response to Derrida the teacher. That young student, I imagine (for it is a fiction and one is free to elaborate on it), had read or heard Derrida enough to know that death, his, yours, or mine, is never far from his thoughts; indeed it is the closest, the most imminent and intimate certainty leaving its mark of finitude on every experience. Sensing this proximity, his young interlocutor on this occasion feels at once provoked and seduced, an unsettling response that he settles by projecting it toward the older (very handsome) man and teacher in the form of a question: "Why don't you kill yourself?" he asks with a sly smile. The teacher's response to this response is a "pirouette" inasmuch as it sends the question back to the questioner:

I responded with a pirouette, I'll tell you about it, by signifying to him, that he must have been savoring, along with me, the interest that he visibly was taking, at this very moment, in this question that I moreover concerned myself with along with others, among them myself. And what proves to you, I said to him if I remember correctly, that I do not do so, and more than once.

This strange teaching moment says something about the effect that Derrida's example had on those who followed him into and out of lecture halls all over the world. For the exemplarity of the example, as he frequently pointed out, always obeys an aporetic logic: "The example is not substitutable; but at the same time the same aporia always remains: this irreplaceability must be exemplary, that is, replaceable. The irreplaceable must allow itself to be replaced on the spot" (*Demeure*, 41). The pirouetting exchange with the young man turns on this replaceable irreplaceability of the teacher's example, the example that the young man was essentially asking him to be by killing himself. Derrida's response draws out this substitutability from that singular experience that seems to be the most irreplaceable, the event called "my death." He does so both by mirroring back to his interlocutor the interest "he visibly was taking" in "my death," that is, his own *as* the other's, but also by dangling before him the figure of that event's repetition in the "more than once."

The heart of Derrida's example lies in this divisible, substitutable because unsubstitutable relation to "my death." In countless encounters, and whether or not they occur face-to-face as did apparently this one in the exemplary teaching space of an Oxford college lawn, a seductive provocation takes place when "my death" loses its bearings in reference to an only future occurrence to be anticipated (or precipitated) and assumes the guise of the condition of possibility—and impossibility—of whatever passes between us.

After he was provoked in this manner to muster proof that his living interlocutor was not a survivor of suicide "and more than once," we do not learn if the young man said anything more that day. I am tempted to think that he fell silent while the axis of his world shifted to accommodate the thought of such a survival.

III: Wakefulness

The Post Card, then, was another one of several texts I reread to try to overcome the inertia of an introduction to this ten-year span of essays and what are called in French "interventions." As regards "Fors," however, it was also the word "wake" that awakened the urge to return to a text which, soon after I initially encountered it in 1976, prompted my first attempt to register in print the impact of Derrida's writing. Of that essay I recall now little more than the title, "Abraham's Wake," which is memorable for me at present only because of the partial recurrence here in the title *The Wake of Derrida.*[9] It would seem that the thing called in English a "wake" has lent its name to this thirty-year experience of attempting to write about Derrida's work. It has been, it will have been a wake.

But what is it, a wake—or to wake? Here are portions of relevant entries from the *Oxford English Dictionary* (*OED*):

> **wake,** n^1: **2.** Abstinence from sleep, watching, practised as a religious observance: often coupled with *fasting*. Also, an instance of this; a night spent in devout watching; . . . a watch, vigil. **3.** The watching (*esp.* by night) of relatives and friends beside the body of a dead person from death to burial, or during a part of that time; the drinking, feasting, and other observances incidental to this. Now chiefly *Anglo-Irish* or with reference to Irish custom. Also applied to similar funeral customs in other times or among non-Christian peoples. **4.** The vigil of a festival (and senses thence derived).
> **wake,** n^2: **I. 1.** The track left on the water's surface by a ship (in the sea often marked by a smooth appearance). **2.** *transf.* Anything compared to the wake of a vessel. **a.** The disturbance caused by a body swimming, or moved, in water. **b.** The air-currents behind a body in flight. **3.** A course, or general line of direction, that a ship has taken, or is to take. **4. in the wake of. a.** *Naut.* or quasi-nautical. *in the wake of* (*a vessel*); *in her* (*its*) *wake*, etc.: immediately behind, and (properly) in the actual track made by, a vessel; immediately backward and along the track made. **c.** *transf.* and *fig.* (*a*) With nautical metaphor (often jocular): Following close behind (a person compared to a ship). (*b*) In wider use (cf. 2): In the train or track of, behind (a moving person or object); in imitation of; following as a result or consequence.

As for the current intransitive and transitive uses of the verb "to wake," a complex history has left there a number of traces. The *OED* remarks that "to wake" was formed when "two distinct but synonymous verbs from the same root coalesced in early ME." This could account for the odd oscillation that the verb continued to harbor for a long time, wavering its senses between becoming awake (or waking up as we would more likely say today) and being awake. Today the absolute form "to wake" survives only when it is said of those keeping wake: they wake, that is, they keep watch. "The sense 'to remain awake, watch' gave rise to a transitive use = 'to watch (over)'; but in the modern Eng. period the static sense, both intr. and trans., has become almost obsolete, the usual meanings of the word being 'to become or cause to become awake'." This might explain why, in modern English (although not necessarily

Irish English, but certainly American English), the phrase "to wake the dead" is today often understood in the sense more or less of "to make enough racket to wake (up) the dead." If one follows the dictionary, however, to keep watch over (the dead) and to wake (the dead) with reveling and noise-making are, or ought to be, two distinct meanings of the verb, roughly distributed between the ideas of being and becoming/causing to become awake. Today, this difference is distributed between the two expressions: to be awake and to wake up.

While noun[1] is thought to derive from the verb, noun[2] is most likely unrelated etymologically to either of them. It also appears to follow an altogether more straightforward path that branches by way of transference and metaphor. Rather than a confused or half-waking state between being and becoming, it is more like a thing, although a passing thing that does not linger long in place: a mark drawn on water or through the air, a sign of something's passage, a readable trace—and marine navigation depends a lot on reading wakes. The nautical meaning given as the proper or literal sense, albeit one that is "writ in water," would then be transferable to anything that can, as the venerable dictionary puts it laconically, "be compared to the wake of a vessel." The possibility of this comparison hangs, in all the occurrences quoted by the dictionary, on the relation of something coming or being close *behind* something or someone else, "(a person compared to a ship)," whether this proximity is spatio-temporally actual or, again, a figure, thus a figure for a figure (a metalepsis), a proximal relation close "behind" the way an imitation follows the original. This sense of following behind is indeed the principal trait on which the transfer turns, so that in its fullest extension, the expression "in the wake of" has become synonymous, more or less, with the preposition "after,"[10] but also with the logical conjunction "because of," for example: "In the wake of the crash of the home mortgage market, the economy fell into recession." *Post hoc ergo propter hoc.*

Our reference says nothing, however, of the wake's churning turbulence. And it records no occurrences in which what is transferred is the wake's mark made on a surface by the force of something or someone passing. As if, in its transfer from the sea, the wake left nothing behind but an after-figure. What, then, about the wake as *mark or trace* and thus a possible figure for what is called writing (or reading)?

Unless it is the other way around and it is writing, some writing, that tells us what *a* wake is, and whose it is, this one. In other words, and to repeat:

What is a wake? What is a wake if it can also be a crypt?
And what if I were writing on one here?

As with the questions that open "Fors," in the space between them, the one in the wake of the other, a swerve takes place. Something happens to divert the question about a crypt or a wake into a question about writing. (You think you hold a book in your hands, but what if I could persuade you it is a crypt over which a watch, a wake, must be kept?) This swerving or veering movement pulls one into the wake (or the crypt) of this writing here, that is, the one *on* which, as we say, I am writing, the writing of Derrida, who is himself always writing on another('s) crypt, in another('s) wake.

IV: Wake writing

The homophonic nouns can fuse or become confused. The *OED* even wonders if the sense of the vessel's wake did not form through some connection with its homophone. Perhaps it is the trait of a certain afterness that fosters the exchange between one wake and the other, each a kind of following that marks a passage, of a life or a vessel but, precisely, the one can always be a metaphor for the other. Drawn into the play between wake and wake is a potential for the suspension of sense in which what comes after can also come before, in which the trace of a passage keeps watch for what may come. To wake, in the sense of to keep watch, and to leave a wake behind: these wakes apparently pull in opposite directions and yet writing in our language can always forge their convergence.

Indeed, Herman Melville, for one and not surprisingly, did not overlook the idea that the wake is a kind of writing:

> like as this pilot stands by his compass, and takes the precise bearing of the cape at present visible, in order the more certainly to hit aright the remote, unseen headland, eventually to be visited: so does the fisherman, at his compass, with the whale; for after being chased, and diligently marked, through several hours of daylight, then, when night obscures the fish, the creature's future wake through the darkness is almost as established to the sagacious mind of the hunter, as the pilot's coast is to him. So that to this hunter's wondrous skill, the proverbial evanescence of a thing writ in water, a wake, is to all desired purposes well nigh as reliable as the steadfast land.[11]

Writing that a wake is (like) writing, Melville also lets one read how writing is (like) a wake drawn through the invisible medium of thought, following "through the darkness" as the hunter tracks the whale. What converges here, then, is also the written wake with the night and thus with the other wake that keeps watch so as to anticipate the "future wake." This wake—but which one?—is written in advance, as it were, ahead of "the proverbial evanescence of a thing writ in water."

V: Wakefulness (again)

The state of vigilance, wakefulness, or alertness is one to which Derrida consistently assigns a positive value; it is the name, if you will, of one of the most highly-prized and praised virtues in his vocabulary.[12] To be sure, this evaluation is hardly unique to him for, to a great extent, it is the legacy of modern philosophy at least since the Enlightenment. Especially since Kant, vigilance (from *vigilo, vigilare*: to watch, to be wakeful) is allied and nearly synonymous with the light of critical reason that dispels obscurantist shadows. It was Kant, after all, who famously confessed that reading "David Hume was the very thing which many years ago first interrupted my dogmatic slumber and gave my investigations in the field of speculative philosophy quite a new direction."[13] This wake-up call to critical, non-dogmatic philosophy has continued to resonate ever since and, I would argue, nowhere in a more thought-provoking fashion than in Derrida's writings of the last half century.

An inheritance, as Derrida has explained most insistently perhaps in relation to the legacy of Marx and Marxism, "is always the reaffirmation of a debt, but a critical, selective, and filtering reaffirmation" (*Specters*, 91–2). It would seem difficult to extend this description to the reaffirmation of vigilance itself, which is less a legacy from any one thinker than the very condition or possibility of critical reception and inheritance. Nevertheless, Derrida's principal act in *Specters of Marx* of reasserting the Marxist legacy in deconstruction is highly pertinent here and not only because Marx himself bequeaths an exemplary vigilance in the face of all the slumbering dogmatisms of political economy, social theory, or religious ideology. To be sure, Marx as well was necessarily an inheritor of "a spirit of the Enlightenment which must not be renounced" (*Specters*, 88). But the hyper-vigilance of Marxism's "*radical* critique, namely a procedure ready to undertake its self-critique" (ibid.), does not yet situate the pertinence I had in mind for assessing Derrida's own critical *and* deconstructive reaffirmation of this Enlightenment legacy. This pertinence attaches, rather, to another "spirit of Marxism" that, Derrida professes, "I will never be ready to renounce":

> Now, if there is a spirit of Marxism which I will never be ready to renounce, it is not only the critical idea or the questioning stance (a consistent

deconstruction must insist on them even as it also learns [or teaches: *apprend*] that this is not the last or first word). It is even more a certain emancipatory and *messianic* affirmation, a certain experience of the promise that one can try to liberate from any dogmatics and even from any metaphysico-religious determination, from any *messianism*. (*Specters*, 89)

It is as regards this "experience of the promise" that the vigilance Derrida prizes departs from a solely critical, even hyper- or self-critical tradition. But the point is, of course, Marx does likewise because the emancipatory, messianic affirmation is the very "spirit of Marxism" that its heir deconstruction receives and *reaffirms*. Nevertheless, no one would ever simply mistake a vigilant, deconstructive posture for its Marxist antecedent. That posture has thus fundamentally shifted something in the vigilant stance or gaze, turned it not only back upon itself in self-critique (which would be "in principle and explicitly open to its own transformation, re-evaluation, self-reinterpretation" [88]) but emphasized how it also pivots to watch for what may be coming from the other direction and the direction of the other.

Specters of Marx takes its point of departure in this pivotal vigil of the watch for the spirit—the ghost—that comes back, for the revenant that opens the play by showing itself once again to those who "watch the minutes of this night." *Hamlet* Act 1, scene 1 stages the watchfulness for what the posted vigils have already twice seen and still they are surprised when it returns to interrupt their colloquy:

> *Marcellus*: What, has this thing appeared again tonight?
> *Bernardo*: I have seen nothing.
> *Marcellus*: Horatio says 'tis but our fantasy,
>   And will not let belief take hold of him
>   Touching this dreaded sight twice seen of us.
>   Therefore I have entreated him along
>   With us to watch the minutes of this night . . .
> *Bernardo*: Last night of all,
>   When yon same star that's westward from the pole
>   Had made his course t'illume that part of heaven
>   Where now it burns, Marcellus and myself,
>   The bell then beating one—
>   *Enter the Ghost . . .*
> *Marcellus*: Peace, break thee off. Look where it comes again.

The watch watches for—it knows not what may come. This vigilance does not anticipate or expect an arrival that will put an end to or interrupt its waiting, but nonetheless it watches for another's coming to interrupt it. There is thus alertness tensed in advance toward that which will all the same surprise, overcome, and interrupt it.

Derrida has more than once described this state of readiness for interruption, for example in the essay titled "Rams: Uninterrupted Dialogue—Between Two Infinities, the Poem," which, among other things, is a meditation on interruption in memory of Hans-Georg Gadamer. Having just cited the latter commenting on a certain indecision in a poem by Celan, he declares:

> More than the indecision itself, I admire the respect Gadamer shows for the indecision. This indecision seems to interrupt or suspend the decipherment of reading, though in truth it ensures its future. Indecision keeps attention forever in suspense, breathless, that is to say, keeps it alive, alert [*éveillé*], vigilant, ready to embark on a wholly other path, to let come, listening faithfully, giving ear, to that other speech. Such indecision hangs upon the breath of the other speech and of the speech of the other—right where this speech might still seem unintelligible, inaudible, and untranslatable. Interruption is indecisive, it undecides. It gives its breath to a question that, far from paralyzing, sets in motion. Interruption even releases an infinite movement. ("Rams," 145–6)

More than just a description, these lines declare admiration for Gadamer's readiness to let the poem interrupt and "undecide" his reading. As such, they declare as well that this vigilance, "ready to embark on a wholly other path," is the attention that the reader Derrida himself seeks to bring to bear, "listening faithfully, giving ear" to an interruption. "Giving ear" translates here "tendant l'oreille," to prick up one's ears, to listen for a sound or a voice, more literally, to stretch out or tense the ears in some direction. The admired vigilant alertness is thus a matter of ears turned or held out toward the other speech, which has come to interrupt a too certain decipherment of meaning.

I underscore this auditory sense because vigilance or wakefulness may otherwise suggest above all watching for something visible, as it does initially in the master example from *Hamlet*, where the watchmen watch again for "this dreaded sight twice seen of us," the Ghost who, at least while within their hearing, comes and goes in silence. For Derrida, vigilance is no less, and perhaps it is indeed more, a matter of what may be heard, picked up by ears pricked up by the interruption coming from the other's direction. And yet, since the vigilance also in question here is that of a reading that lets its deciphering movement be interrupted or suspended by the other *parole* (speech or word, rather than discourse), it is also apparent that the faithfully listening ear is attuned to a virtual inner voice, sound, or (as Derrida will stress in another text to which we will turn in a moment) tone, in other words, that which "does not let itself be recovered by the analysis—linguistic, semantic, or rhetorical— of speaking" ("Tone," 166).

Whether it is configured as auditory or visual, however, Derrida reckons with and appeals to a vigilant space that occupies what is commonly represented as the interiority of a subject. That representation has traditionally supposed the condition of an intrapsychic relation that remains between me and myself, consciously or unconsciously. With his earliest writings on Husserl's analysis of signs, speech, and language, Derrida has contested this supposition of immediate, unmediated presence of a self to itself in "solitary mental life."[14] On the contrary, he argues, self-relation is possible and interiorizable as an effect only through differing from and deferring of some exterior "non-selfness," that is, only through what he then began to refer to as differance. Giving differance its due has fundamental consequences for how one may thereafter represent and describe, so as to account for, the experience of interiority as a space of relation to some non-self, alterity, some other, indeed more than one other.

And these others within us keep watch, they are vigilant. Writing, for example, of Henri Thomas's novel *Le Parjure*, whose central character appears to have been based on the early life of Paul de Man, Derrida comments:

> For, however trembling and undecidable, however suspended remained and still remains today the novel's and the fictional "character"'s reference to our friend de Man, we could not not be haunted at the same time by the memory we still had of him. We could not not know that we were in some way being observed internally by him, by the spectral vigilance of his gaze, even if this quasi "presence" in no way limited our freedom. In truth, it even sharpened our responsibility. ("Parjure," 171)

These remarks could take us back onto the ramparts of Elsinore as revisited in *Specters of Marx* where, we read, "[t]his Thing meanwhile looks at us and sees us not seeing it when it is there" (*Specters*, 6). Interiorized spectral vigilance is asymmetrical from the moment that the other's look can no longer be met, where "no longer" marks the temporality of interruption and mourning. It reminds us that the vigil or the wake—*la veille*—names as well the watch kept over the dead, over all those whose image and gaze will from then on observe us internally while sharpening our responsibility.[15]

VI: Following

"To follow" is a possible translation of "à suivre," although "to be continued" is more usual. Derrida often uses the expression as a way of holding out the promise to pursue further some topic or question in another place at another time.[16] The whole of *The Animal that Therefore I Am* is placed under or after a certain "à suivre" that follows the titling phrase when it is reprised as the title of the book's first chapter.[17] As if to say that everything to follow is a reflection on what it means "to follow," "to be followed," "to be following," especially in a language that marks no difference for eye or ear between the verbs "to be" and "to follow" when it is I who am or who follow in the present indicative: *je suis*. In this idiom, I do not affirm my presence in the present without also marking the other animal's who comes before me and who I am after, whose wake I am or keep.

I am a wake, I follow.

VII: Wakefulness (to be interrupted)

Be wakeful so as to listen for a difference within the apocalyptic tone that calls: "Wake and watch: the end is near." In "On a Newly Arisen Apocalyptic Tone in Philosophy," Derrida addresses the "enigmatic desire for vigilance, for lucid wakefulness [*la veille lucide*], for elucidation, critique, and truth" that is called up or called to by *both* apocalyptic discourse, which promises imminent and final revelation of the truth, the truth of the end and as the end, *and* any discourse that, like this one, would "deconstruct apocalyptic discourse itself and with it everything that speculates on vision, imminence of the end, theophany, parousia, last judgment" ("Tone," 148). The deconstruction of apocalyptic discourse passes by way of vigilant attention to all that interrupts the unity of tone or voice and pluralizes the routes along which meaning is sent. To characterize this general derailment of destination or end, Derrida proposes the German word *Verstimmung*—disgruntlement, out-of-tuneness, upset—which keeps the trace of *Stimme*, voice. The apocalyptic tone would be but

> the effect of a generalized derailment, of a *Verstimmung* multiplying the voices and making the tones shift [*sauter*], opening each word to the haunting memory of the other in an unmasterable polytonality, with grafts, intrusions, interferences [*parasitages*]. Generalized *Verstimmung* is the possibility for the other tone, or the tone of another, to come at no matter what moment to interrupt a familiar music . . . suddenly, a tone come from one knows not where renders speechless, if this can be said, the tone that tranquilly seemed to determine (*bestimmen*) the voice and thus ensure the unity of destination, the self-identity of some addresser or addressee. *Verstimmung*, if that is henceforth what we call the derailment, the sudden change [*saute*] in tone as one would say *la saute d'humeur*, "the sudden change of mood," is the

disorder or delirium of destination (*Bestimmung*), but also the possibility of all emission. The unity of tone, if there were any, would certainly be the assurance of destination but also death, another apocalypse. ("Tone," 150)

This passage can recall the indecision that, as we already read, "keeps attention forever in suspense, breathless, that is to say, keeps it alive, alert, vigilant, ready to embark on a wholly other path, to let come, listening faithfully, giving ear, to that other speech." Listen faithfully for the *Verstimmung* of the *Stimme*, the delirium of destination within the tone, voice, discourse: this is the watchword of deconstructive vigilance.

And it is called into action with the first sentence of this text, which reads: "Je parlerai donc d'un ton apocalyptique en philosophie." This is a thoroughly ordinary, regular sentence in its grammar and syntax, and yet it cannot be translated, at least into English, without some supplement or artifice to mark the derailing division that takes place there between more than one destination of sense. It says both "I will speak then *of* an apocalyptic tone in philosophy," in other words, it will be the subject *of* my discourse or the topic *on* which I will speak; and it announces at the same time and with the same words "I will speak then *in* an apocalyptic tone in philosophy."[18] It thus pulls off a remarkably economical demonstration of at least two things at once. By plotting the overlap between apocalyptic discourse and the discourse that would deconstruct it, the sentence becomes the audible stage of the haunting or parasiting of one speech by another that divides the whole scene of destination between more than one speaker, addressee, and sense. Moreover, this haunting is reciprocal for neither discourse can prevent its being haunted by and suspended from the other in the general condition of a-destinality, which is also the condition of any emission of sense.

One thus imagines that when the sentence was initially read out, it was followed by a pause, however slight, to allow its first addressees a moment to hear it repeat silently and to listen faithfully with more than one ear, letting the resonance disperse in the space of the difference between them.[19] As Derrida would later write, apropos of Nietzsche: "everything comes down to the ear with which you can hear me" (*Ear*, 4).[20]

VIII: Dream writing

The figure of the vigilant wake may be working to disavow what strikes me, after rereading all these chapters, more like the logic of a dream writing. Not only do dreams and dreaming, blindness and the blind spot come back frequently in these pages, but often one chapter picks up where the preceding has left off, without this continuity or progression—this sense of following—taking deliberate, conscious, wakeful charge of the direction. Instead there is a wavering between dream and wakefulness, which has been left to stand (or waver) here in the wake of this reminder from the end of *Grammatology*, a passage quoted only late in this dreamlike progression: "Is not the opposition of dream to wakefulness [*la vigilance*] a representation of metaphysics as well? And what must the dream be, what must writing be, if, as we now know, one can write while dreaming? And if the scene of dreaming is always a scene of writing?" (*Grammatology*, 315–16).

More than thirty years after they were formulated thus, these questions will still resonate for Derrida as the one who would think—or dream—the "possibility of the impossible." For such a thinking cannot oppose its wakefulness to dreams; instead, it must watch over dreams so as to overcome them without betraying them, as Adorno remarked about Walter Benjamin, a remark that draws Derrida's admiration:

> *Overcoming* the dream without *betraying* it . . .: to wake up, to cultivate awakeness and vigilance, while remaining attentive to the meaning, faithful to the lessons and the lucidity of a dream, caring for what a dream lets us think about, especially when what it lets us think about is the *possibility of the impossible*. The possibility of the impossible can only be dreamed, but thinking, a quite different thinking of the relation between the possible and impossible, this other thinking . . . perhaps has more affinity than philosophy itself with this dream. Even as you wake up, you would have to go on watching out for the dream, watching over it. ("*Fichus*," 168)

Il faudrait, tout en se réveillant, continuer de veiller sur le rêve: in order to watch over the future, expect the unexpected, listen for the change of tone, ready oneself for interruption.

IX: No denial

> There is some complacent self-satisfaction, already in the gesture that consists in publishing. Simply in publishing. This first complacency is elementary; no denial could erase it. What then should be said of the gesture that gathers up previous writings, whether or not they are unpublished? (*Psyche* I, xiii)

There is no denying that, to justify collecting these writings on the work, teaching, and friendship of Jacques Derrida, I have to confront the contradiction that complacent display lodges in the tribute. This is an exquisite irony, perhaps, since it is Derrida's own example, as indexed in the quotation above, that denies me the denial of complacency. The irony, however, would be merely an acute, undeniable version of the vigilance that, for Derrida, should oversee all acts of reading, writing (and publishing), interpreting, translating, in short, all these transactions where the ruses of narcissism are put to the test of another's language or speech.

So, yes, there is no denying that Derrida keeps watch from the innumerable watchtowers that are his texts and from the countless memories that continue to awaken to the future. The essays to follow all attest to this watchfulness of the other, the friend.

Notes

1. Among these: Hélène Cixous, *Insister of Jacques Derrida*, trans. Peggy Kamuf (Stanford: Stanford University Press, 2007); Jean-Luc Nancy, *À plus d'un titre: Jacques Derrida* (Paris: Galilée, 2007); Michael Naas, *Derrida From Now On* (New York: Fordham University Press, 2008); J. H. Miller, *For Jacques Derrida* (New York: Fordham University Press, 2009); Nicholas Royle, *In Memory of Jacques Derrida* (Edinburgh: Edinburgh University Press, 2009); Sean Gaston, *The Impossible Mourning of Jacques Derrida* (London: Continuum, 2006); Max Genève, *Qui a peur de Derrida?* (Paris: Anabet, 2008); Geoffrey Bennington, *Not Half No End: Militantly Melancholic Essays of Jacques Derrida* (Edinburgh: Edinburgh University Press, 2010). The list is doubtless not exhaustive.
2. On the dividing mark of genre, see Derrida, "The Law of Genre" ("The Law").
3. Barbara Johnson's translation of "Fors" first appeared separately in *The Georgia Review*, 31, 1 (Spring 1977), pp. 64–116.
4. The full parenthesis reads: "(in my memory, restricted here to a kind of parenthetical shorthand, this period is called 'la rue Vézelay,' two years after our meeting at a colloquium where we began a dialogue that went on for almost twenty years between us, along various paths—parallel, tangential, intersecting—and through many transverse translations, within which was maintained, like a living breath of friendship, that mobile reserve that I would describe in a word dear to Maria Torok and Nicolas Abraham, as can be seen in their writing: the 'authentic' [and all its synonyms] as opposed to the 'alienated,' to 'empty words,' to the 'hollow words that move the ideologues, the utopians, the idolators')" (xxx). The quotation is from Abraham, *Le Cas Jonas*. Although the translation here suggests a term to the friendship ("a dialogue that went on for almost twenty years"), the original French verb tense allows one also to understand it continues in the present: "dont l'*a parte* s'est poursuivi près de vingt ans entre nous" ("Fors," 40).
5. For an analysis of this survival of names in *Romeo and Juliet*, see Derrida, "Aphorism."

6. On the title "Fors," see the translator's note in the *Georgia Review* edition of Johnson's translation: "The word *fors* in French, derived from the Latin *foris* ('outside, outdoors'), is an archaic preposition meaning 'except for, barring, save.' In addition, *fors* is the plural of the word *for*, which, in the French expression '*le for intérieur*,' designates the inner heart, 'the tribunal of conscience,' subjective interiority. The word *fors* thus 'means' both interiority and exteriority, a spatial problematic which will be developed at great length here in connection with the 'crypt'" ("Fors," 64). This note is omitted in *The Wolf Man's Magic Word*.
7. For a very suggestive and probing engagement with "Fors," especially its reframing by the American translation, see Elissa Marder, "Mourning, Magic and Telepathy," *Oxford Literary Review*, 30, 2 (2008).
8. In his *Someone Called Derrida: An Oxford Mystery* (Brighton and Portland: Sussex Academic Press, 2007), John Schad speculates at length on this anecdote.
9. Peggy Kamuf, "Abraham's Wake," *Diacritics* (Spring 1979).
10. On the several senses of this preposition, see Nicholas Royle *After Derrida* (Manchester: Manchester University Press, 1995), esp. pp. 1–7.
11. Herman Melville, *Moby-Dick, or the Whale* (London and New York: Norton, 1967), p. 453.
12. To take just a few examples: "He applies an extraordinary vigilance, a faultless erudition to the measure of the desire of the unconscious" (on Roger Laporte); "With a vigilance one could probably say operates at every instant . . ." (on Emmanuel Lévinas); "For example, to analyze a genre or discursive code, or the rules of a particular social arrangement, and to do so with his meticulousness and vigilance . . ." (on Roland Barthes) (*Psyche* I, 81, 166, 282); "A joy to rediscover, to discover in another way, the force and the exigency, the uncompromising vigilance, of a faithful thought" (on Philippe Lacoue-Labarthe; *Psyche* II, 201); "while reading himself, while analyzing vigilantly his *selftaste* . . ." (on J. H. Miller; "Justices," 715); "her friendly vigilance" (on Peggy Kamuf; *Alibi*, xxv).
13. *Prolegomena to Any Future Metaphysics*, ed. Lewis White Beck (New York: Macmillan, 1950), p. 8.
14. See *Speech,* esp. chaps. 3–5.
15. On this interiorized gaze of the other, see Derrida, "The Deaths of Roland Barthes": "Roland Barthes looks at us (inside each of us, so that each of us can then say that Barthes's thought, memory, and friendship concern only us), and we do not do as we please with this look, even though each of us has it at his or her disposal, in his own way, according to her own place and history. It is within us but it is not ours; we do not have it available to us like a moment or part of our interiority" ("Barthes," 44), and "By Force of Mourning": "We are all looked at, I said, and each one singularly, by Louis Marin. He looks at us. *In us*" ("Mourning," 161); see also, infra, "To Follow," pp. 56–8.
16. See, for example, footnote 32 to "The Double Session" (*Dissemination*, 220) where Derrida refers to Freud's "Das Unheimliche," "of which we are here, in sum, proposing a rereading." Then, after two quotations from Freud's text, the note breaks off with a parenthetical "(*à suivre*)."
17. David Wills translates this "à suivre" as "more to follow" (*Animal*, 1).

18. John Leavey translates "I will speak then of/in an apocalyptic tone in philosophy" ("Tone," 117).
19. Both the original edition and the translation format this pause as a blank line after the initial sentence.
20. For another reading of this line, see, infra, "The Ear, Who?", pp. 154–5.

Chapter 1

"Tape-Recorded Surprise": Derrida Interviewed

As far as I know, there is no accurate count of all the interviews Derrida has granted, in one circumstance or another, since 1968, the date cited in many bibliographies for his first published interview in a now vanished journal.[1] These were, in any case, very rare throughout the 1970s, and began to proliferate only after 1980. In 1992, *Points de suspension: Entretiens*, a collection of twenty interviews assembled and presented by Elisabeth Weber, included in appendix a list of an additional sixty-seven interviews then published or broadcast. In the more recent *For What Tomorrow*, a book that itself has the subtitle of "Dialogue," Derrida's interlocutor, Elisabeth Roudinesco, estimates in a note that he has "taken part in about a hundred interviews (*Tomorrow*, 14).[2] This figure probably falls well short of any thorough count, presuming one could be made that included all the interviews Derrida has frequently granted to newspapers when he travels abroad, to obscure journals, or even student publications. Above all, any such accounting—a hundred, two hundred, five hundred—presumes that the genre "interview" is a self-evident one, and therefore easily discernable from every other genre of writing, speaking, or engaging with interlocutors. But this assumption and its attendant or supporting presuppositions encounter serious challenges in all of Derrida's work, challenges that are not only theoretical, as we say, but quite practical. Just to point provisionally to one symptomatic indicator of the challenge, there is the dialogic or polylogic form of texts published under Derrida's name alone, for example "Restitutions" in *The Truth in Painting* or "Droit de regards," which often proceed as most interviews do: through questions and responses, with the "interlocutors" sending the ball back and forth.[3] For the moment, however, and before saying more about plurivocality in Derrida's thought in general, I will rely first on fairly standard, conventional markers of the interview in order to make some initial remarks about Derrida's practice of that genre or mode.

From the first this practice has called the conventions of the interview into question and has rarely missed an opportunity to remark on them or to make apparent the constraints that are usually left outside the frame of such printed exchanges. This is perhaps the most constant feature of Derrida's interviews: the remarking of framing devices within the frame, the retracing of the interview's conditions within the space those conditions make possible but also, of course, constrain and limit. There is thus almost always in Derrida's interviews an explicit meta-interview in which the interviewee switches the machine's gears or rather points to the gears of the interview mechanism that is usually kept out of sight, whirring offstage, like the two reels of a tape recorder.

I will take the first examples of this insistent trait from the long two-part interview published in the journal *Digraphe* in 1976. Near the beginning of the first installment, which was given the title "Between Brackets," Derrida refers to the interview he is then engaged in as only the second time he has accepted, as he puts it, "to expose myself to the risks of this tape-recorded surprise."[4] In the course of the replies that follow, Derrida will develop at some length the motif of the tape recorder's two reels and cross it with the double-band motif of *Glas*, which had been published the previous year, 1974, and to which the interlocutors here have referred in their first question. But before this intricate contrivance of the double-band, double-reeled machine is set rolling to draw the conversation toward a discussion of *Glas* or other works of his, Derrida, as it were, pushes the pause button on that machine and begins to record a meta-interview. I excerpt a long passage:

> Here and now an "interview" is taking place, what is called an "interview," and it implies all kinds of codes, demands, contracts, investments, and surplus values. What is expected from an interview? Who requests interviews from whom? Who gets what out of them? Who avoids what? Who avoids whom? There are all sorts of questions and programs that we should not run away from, here and now. "Political" questions (economic, editorial, academic institutional, theoretical, and so forth). . . . Perhaps we should have begun there. I wonder if it is not necessary to begin with these kinds of questions. They are, finally, the ones that have always interested me the most and the most consistently. . . .
>
> Here, for example . . . is there anyone who does not expect me to defend, justify, consolidate things that I have done these last years and about which you have asked me certain questions . . .? And even if I were to indicate, in an autocritical mode, such and such a limit, or negative aspect, or strategic weakness, would anyone be duped by the maneuver of reappropriation?
>
> The fact that I have accepted—for the second time—to expose myself to the risks of this tape-recorded surprise, that I have agreed to pay the price (simplification, impoverishment, distortion, displacement of argument by symptom, and so forth), now here is right away a singularity which I would

like to insist on, rather than on what I have written and which is a little bit somewhere else, somewhere else for me, somewhere else for others. Okay, you are going to think I am piling up the protocols in order to run away from an impossible question. So running away is a bad thing? And why is that? Does one have to be noble and brave? What if all the questions put to me about what I write came down to fleeing something I write? Okay. I give in . . . (*Points*, 9–11)

I have quoted at such length because this early interview about interviews, or meta-interview, introduces many of the notes Derrida as interviewee has continued to sound throughout the years, in vastly different circumstances where nevertheless the same or similar programs and expectations are in place. As one can hear, these are being neither overturned nor abandoned here, but questioned, interrogated, pointed out, with a gesture that might be compared to that of an actor who, before going on with his role in the play ("Okay. I give in . . ."), draws back the curtain covering the machinery in the wings or beneath the stage, all the "codes, demands, contracts, investments, and surplus values" implied in "what is called an 'interview'." As we will see, the sort of "political" questions alluded to here can be made quite pointed when the interview is being staged by a large-circulation press, and in particular the French press. But even here, where the scene is not at all adversarial but collaborative—the journal *Digraphe* was very open to Derrida's work, unlike *Le Monde* or *Le Nouvel Observateur*—there is some chiding of the tendency to evade questions about the set and silently running program of the interview-with-the-author. With meta-interview remarks like these, which return regularly throughout these two early, if not strictly the first, interviews, Derrida seems to want to set a sort of benchmark for any and all future engagements of the sort, even when these are conducted, as here, with friends and collaborators, in the best of circumstances.[5] Exposed here in uncompromising terms is the expectation that an interview will, precisely, expose the writer in the defense of his work, catch him out in a gesture of reappropriation of the sort Derrida would elsewhere have to identify with a disavowal of the force of dissemination. So, when he refers to the "risks of the tape-recorded surprise," these would seem to be especially high for this thinker of dissemination and of the deconstruction of the proper, who also must take the risk of giving himself as example of the very thing he would let deconstruct.

That interviews are about exposing the writer himself, or his thought itself, without the cover of the complexities of writing, in a presentation through the naked voice that allows no delay: all of this seems to go without saying, which is precisely why it needs to be said and exposed, although that does not mean that the expectation is thereby left simply unfulfilled. But by making explicit rules of a game that are commonly unacknowledged as such, the game itself may be allowed to shift onto a slightly different field of play and risk. That, at least, is what can be discerned in Derrida's practice of this risky genre as he proceeds over the years to give more and more interviews.

In these benchmark interviews or meta-interviews conducted in 1975 and published in 1976, the resistance to or defense against this exposure mechanism takes the form of exposing it to the light of questions, for example, questions about the desire or compulsion driving it. "What if," Derrida asks, "all the questions posed to me about what I write came down to fleeing something I write?" (*Points*, 10–11). In other words, what if interviews-with-the-writer sought above all to avoid an encounter with writing? The suggestion seems hardly farfetched; it says out loud what everyone can already easily suspect. And it cannot be surprising coming from Derrida, the "thinker of writing," as he was then positioned especially at this time. And yet, such a simple positioning or opposition between writing and *viva voce* interview is not sustainable, and not only because, doubtless with very few exceptions, all Derrida's interviews will have been written or rewritten. On the contrary, the idea that there is an opposition here, that an interview takes place or has its place outside writing, that therefore one can avoid writing or flee it, take refuge from it in "what is called an 'interview'," all this is part of the construct or the program that has to be exposed and allowed to deconstruct.

To take just one more indicator of this deconstruction from what I am calling the benchmark interviews, I will cite a segment from the long development on improvisation, on, in other words, that mode of speaking *sur le vif* without the calculating delay of writing, which is supposed to characterize the interviewee's response. The passage is from this meta-interview's second installment, given the untranslatable title "Ja, ou le faux-bond":

> What is important here is the improvisation—contrived like all so-called free association—well anyway, what is called improvisation. It is never absolute, it never has the purity of what one thinks one can require of a forced improvisation: the surprise of the person interrogated, the absolutely spontaneous, instantaneous, almost simultaneous response. . . . A battery of anticipatory and delaying devices, of slowing-down procedures are already in place as soon as one opens one's mouth—even if there is no microphone or electric typewriter present—in order to protect against improvised exposition. And yet, even if it always already does this, it never succeeds. . . . The use one may make of all these apotropaic machines will always end up forming a place that is exposed, vulnerable, and invisible to whoever tries out all the clever

ruses; it is a blind spot. . . . There always remains improvisation, and that is
what counts here. . . . Someone is interrogated who has taken, who thinks he
has taken (up to a certain point) the time to write and to elaborate coded,
supercoded machines, and so forth. . . . Then he is asked some questions.
These are of a kind that, in any case, he will not be able to answer at leisure
and in a manner as closely controlled as in a published text where he can
correct galleys and page proofs. The interesting thing, then, or at least the
pertinent thing is not *what* he says . . . but what he selects, what selects . . .
itself in the rush as he clips out clichés from the more or less informed mass of
possible discourses, letting himself be restricted by the situation, the interlocutors. This is what will betray his defenses in the end. . . . It is another way of
remaining an exhibitionist around the edges. But whoever decided that all of
this deserved to be published or that anything deserved to be published . . . ?
(*Points*, 49–51)

The deconstruction of the interview construct: this is what is at stake,
at risk, or in play in what I am calling the meta-interview, which would
be an inadequate or misleading designation if it causes one to overlook
that it also *responds* to an expectation for the interview, that is, it also
accepts to play the game according to common rules, even as it exposes
both the rules and expectations to shifts and even to surprises. The
quality or experience of surprise, however, affects not only the ordinary expectation of an interview, interviewer, or those who publish
and read them, but as well and first of all the one who submits to the
questions even "in order to protect against improvised exposition." In
the end, these defenses will be betrayed, surprised, and this is what is
interesting, if anything at all is interesting in an interview. But in order
to surprise in this manner, the interview's drive to expose must also be
defended against, resisted, displaced. The one who is exposed cannot see
himself or herself exposed, cannot calculate the place of exposure: "it
is a blind spot." The blind spot is the surprise given up or given over,
but without any possible calculation, to the other: interviewer, reader,
listener.[6] In this sense, the meta-interview is no less a response to the
expectations of an interview; it responds to them even as it seeks to
displace them; it takes the expectation by surprise from an unexpected
place.

I have so far talked about only this one benchmark interview, which
was conducted in a manner meant to give the interviewee wide latitude to
respond as he wished and at length (its two parts are over seventy pages
long). Obviously, these are not at all the conditions of the standard press
interview, in which there are not only rigid constraints on space and
time, but also an always implied and sometimes explicit demand to simplify. (In French, the difference I am pointing to is implicitly marked by
the distinction between the imported English word, *interview*, restricted

in its use to the journalistic interview, and *entretien*, used for any kind of conversation, discussion, exchange.) Derrida has had extensive practice of press *interviews*, and adjusts his meta-interview tactics to its strictures. He takes also, as one could expect, a "higher defense posture," to borrow from the language of strategic analysis, since the risks of exposure are exponentially greater in the mass-circulation media. In these interviews, therefore, he invariably turns questions back upon the media themselves, remarking their framing apparatus within the frame.

Here is an example of what I am talking about from a relatively long interview that appeared in *Le Monde*, January 1982. Toward the end, after a series of topic statements about his work that provoke Derrida each time to respond with a few more sentences,[7] the journalist, Christian Descamps, turns to what he calls "the political field" and states: "As regards the political field, you have never taken up noisy positions there; you have even practiced what you call a sort of withdrawal [*retrait*]." This statement draws out the longest reply in the interview, which begins by quoting back to the journalist his own phrase: "Ah, the 'political field'!" Derrida then goes on to signal his trouble identifying himself with what are taken to be, precisely in and by the media, the features of the intellectual "playing his political role according to the screenplay you are familiar with." And then he remarks:

> This is one of the most serious problems today, this responsibility before the current forms of the mass media and especially before their monopolization, their framing, their axiomatics. For the withdrawal you spoke of does not at all mean in my view a protest against the media in general; on the contrary, I am resolutely for their development (there are never enough of them) and especially for their diversification, but also resolutely against their normalization, against the various takeovers to which the thing has given rise, which has in fact reduced to silence everything that does not conform to very determinate and very powerful frames or codes, or still yet to phantasms of what is "receivable." But the first problem of the "media" is posed by what does not get translated, or even published in the dominant political languages, the ones that dictate the laws of receivability, precisely, on the left as much as on the right. (*Points*, 86–7)

This exchange remarks the conditioning device whereby the media limits the "political field" to that which they cover or place between their covers, determined as a space of "receivability." It is typical of Derrida's press interviews to press these limits to unconceal themselves as what he calls here "phantasms of what is 'receivable'." In the process, the newspaper will have had momentarily to expand those limits or redraw the lines between what it imputes to the other's "withdrawal" and what it excludes from the bounds of "receivability."

I will take another example where this tactic is even more pointedly articulated, although the points are made or scored with the help of a fiction. It is another "interview" with *Le Monde* that appeared the same year, 1982, in a Sunday series on issues in philosophy. Derrida was asked to write the first of the series, a page on language. These circumstances are recorded in a text that simulates a telephone interview with *Le Monde*'s representative, presumably Christian Delacampagne, who at the time wrote on philosophy for that newspaper. This text, which is dialogic in form, begins: "Hello? Could you write an article on language for *Le Monde Dimanche* . . ." Playing himself, Derrida immediately takes up this question by turning it back on the questioner: "Are you asking me whether *I am capable of it*, which is doubtful, or whether *I would accept to do it*?" This repartee launches a brief and eminently pedagogical exposition of the constative/performative distinction in speech act theory to which the interlocutor from *Le Monde* contributes quite sensibly. But Derrida's simulacrum does not merely stick to the program of airing for a large public debates in philosophy; he also insists on remarking the conditions of this airing. After the newspaper's representative has explained the project, he (or she, for there is in fact no gender marking) specifies that "the majority of your readers will not be trained philosophers . . ." With this implicit reminder to "keep things simple," the Derrida character interrupts and one hears some impatience as he says:

> I'm familiar with that warning. But you have to admit that it remains obscure, even cryptic. In whose name and of what readers are you speaking? What are you holding, what secret? To whom *do you want me* to address myself? For centuries now, I have been waiting for statistical arguments on this subject. Does this addressee exist? Does he or she exist *before* a reading which can also be active and determinant (in the sense that it is only then that the reader *would determine himself or herself*)? How do you construct the image and the program of these readers, selecting what they can decipher, receive, or reject? (*Points*, 172–3)

The rest of this faux interview interweaves questions to the journalist about the framing conditions under which a newspaper proposes to expose its readers to philosophical discourse and a discourse that would all the same do just that, if indeed it were possible. The tactic of reflecting back to the newspaper its own conditioning limits, so that, as I put it earlier, it momentarily at least oversteps or uncovers them as such, this tactic is wittily employed here by having the journalist speak lines that Derrida could have signed himself, which of course he did: "One could thus never know," reflects the newspaper's representative, "to what extent the media produce or reproduce their addressee, always needing, toward that end, to maintain the simulacrum of an addressee." But then, in his next intervention, the Derrida character warns that

> if I wrote this article, I would strongly underline the conditions of the thing: why such an article in *Le Monde* at this particular moment? Why me? By whose intermediary, in view of whom and of what? How does this or that framing (for example 225 lines) come to constrain each of my sentences from within? (*Points*, 174)

In effect, these lines doubly mark the question to these conditions: they both say that these questions will be posed, and thereby they also pose them, now and for the future, they promise to pose them again and again.

Given its fictional provenance, one may be tempted to dismiss this "interview" from our survey. But fiction does not necessarily mean parody or exaggeration. Moreover, a note added to the text when it was collected in *Points* indicates that the simulacrum was realistic enough to fool some of *Le Monde*'s readers: "The remarks attributed to Christian Delacampagne are obviously fictive, and since certain commentators at the time thought otherwise, it is better to make clear that their author is Jacques Derrida" (*Points*, 468). The giveaway that this is indeed a fiction is obviously not couched in the role the journalist is made to play here. For this is the role played by journalists everywhere whenever they filter, frame, and "simplify" for the benefit of a readership that is conceived, or phantasized, as already given before reading, instead of allowed to be, as Derrida puts it, "active and determinant." It is, moreover, quite clearly what journalists presume to do when they undertake to interview philosophers and other intellectuals whose work is said to be "difficult." They interpose themselves as representative spokespersons of a public who has given them the assignment to extract accessible, "receivable" replies to questions this public wants to ask, or so it is supposed. This is massively obvious; it is a prime operation of the mass media. And we know that the leverage needed to shift such a massive construction is almost unimaginable.

Yet, who could disagree with Derrida that "this responsibility before the current forms of the mass media" is the most serious *political* problem for "intellectuals" today, and not just for intellectuals? As he has also insisted, responsibility is taken in or as a movement of response. I think one should understand his engagement with the massiveness of the mass media interview, his response and responsiveness to this construction, as accepting a responsibility to act there, if possible, to shift, displace, or at least expose the conditions of its reproduction, to expose it to and for the chance of another readership, an actively determinant one.[8]

I will take one last example of the media interview that illustrates well, I believe, both its massive construction and a response or responsibility that engages with it deconstructively.

Catherine David, a journalist for *Le Nouvel Observateur*, begins her September 1983 interview with almost a caricature of the journalistic assignment I have just recalled. Her first words quote no one in particular, just people who delegated her to bring back a version of Derrida-light:

> "An interview with Derrida? At last maybe we're going to understand something about him!" That's what some people said when I announced I was preparing this work with you. It is said [*On dit*] your texts are difficult, on the limit of readability. Some potential readers are discouraged in advance by this reputation. How do you live with that? Is it an effect you are seeking to produce or, on the contrary, do you suffer from it? (*Points*, 115)

This could have gotten the conversation off to a bad start. In fact, however, Derrida will proceed to respond that he does indeed suffer from the reputation of unreadability, but also, and so as to explain why the "difficulty" in question is not avoidable, he cites once again "philosophical and political reasons" for which "this problem of communication and receivability, in its new techno-economic givens, is more serious than ever for everyone" (*Points*, 116). The interview is thus engaged on the issue of difficulty. Derrida points out the different standards applied to philosophers or innovative writers, on the one hand, and to scientists, on the other, whom no one expects to be accessible to a general public. At one point he says: "I believe that it is always a 'writer' who is accused of being 'unreadable,' as you put it, that is, someone who is engaged in an explanation with language, the codes and the channels of what is the most receivable" (ibid.). David's questions then begin to elicit from her difficult interviewee some rather intricate remarks about idiom and idiomaticity, as if he were defying the demand to "keep things simple." After Derrida has said "The living desire to write keeps you in relation to a terror that you try to maneuver with even as you leave it intact . . . in that place where you may find yourself, understand yourself, you and whoever reads you, beyond any partition, thus at once saved and lost," David thinks of nothing better to ask than a question about "your destiny as a philosopher." This provokes from her interlocutor a first movement of resistance, refusal, almost rebuke, which is also of course a response. Responding by not responding, Derrida remarks the conditions in which he is being asked to answer such a question. He asks: "Do you seriously want to get me to speak about my 'destiny' under these conditions? No." And yet, in a next moment he will translate

David's impertinent question into a pertinent one, which saves things once again: "But if by destiny one means a singular manner of not being free, then what interests me is especially that, precisely and everywhere" (*Points*, 118).

David will next have recourse to straight biographical questions, and again this all-too-predictable gambit is heavily underscored as such by the response. David: "You mentioned a moment ago Algeria. That is where it all began for you." Derrida: "Ah, you want me to say things like 'I-was-born-in El Biar-on-the-outskirts-of-Algiers-in-a-petit-bourgeois-family-of-assimilated-Jews-but . . .' Is that really necessary? I can't do it. You will have to help me . . ." David: "What was your father's name?" Derrida: "Ok, here we go." And then there follow a few lines, in which Derrida points to the encrypting of his father's names in *The Post Card*, but David will not take the hint and continues in the same vein: "How old were you when you left Algeria?" To which Derrida replies "*Décidément*" [which I translated as "You really are persistent"] before complying with this persistent urging to "get autobiographical," which he finally does by recounting his experience under the application of Vichy's laws excluding Jews during the non-occupation of Algeria (*Points*, 119–21). This reflection on the experience of French anti-Semitism is kept going by more questions from the interviewer, to which Derrida responds in part by at one point inserting a parenthetical observation about what is happening right then in this *interview*: "But during adolescence, it was *the* tragedy, it was present in everything else (for there was everything else, and it was perhaps just as determinant: you see, we give in to facileness or a certain kind of curiosity when we select out this sequence; why are you leading me first of all in this direction?) . . ." (*Points*, 121).

"Why are you leading me first of all in this direction?" Is such a question receivable in "what is called an 'interview'?" A question about the interview's very *conduct* and where it is leading one? What would happen if, instead of pretending not to hear it, choosing not to respond to it, or opting not to take it seriously, as David does here, the interviewer, the media, summoned themselves, let themselves be summoned to respond? What would happen, in other words, if the interviewer, the media, could be interviewed? An interview as meta-interview, or vice versa?

One could pursue very far this micrological analysis of what is a most symptomatic *interview*, symptomatic above all of a certain relation between the media in France and figures cast there as "intellectuals." But symptomatic as well, I think, of Derrida's response to these media when he chooses to engage with them. For it is true that this engagement, while very extensive, sustained, and differentiated, has also been very selective. If the media (and obviously not just in France) persist in applying to him the label "difficult," it is also because he, unlike many others, has posed difficulties to easy assimilation by the programs that run their operations when it comes to intellectual, political representations.

I mentioned at the outset that Derrida's interviews or *entretiens* were very rare until around 1981. Likewise, there were also almost no published photographs of him. Hence the figure of "retrait" to which Christian Descamps referred in his 1982 interview for *Le Monde*. In the subsequent interview with *Le Nouvel Observateur*, Derrida recounts what may have been one turning point in the decision to give up resisting the capture of his image by the media. It would not, however, have been a calculated decision on his part alone, but more like a response to a moment in which he was summoned to respond, live on camera, stripped, as it were, of any resistance to the media's demand to make himself and his experience "receivable," accessible, not difficult. This turning point is narrated and commented upon at the end of a long, richly detailed reply to a question from David about the experience of his arrest on false charges of drug possession in Prague, in 1981, after traveling there to give a clandestine seminar to a group of blacklisted philosophers. I will conclude with a long quotation from this reply, which draws a certain lesson about difficulty and the media.

Derrida has just evoked the experience of his imprisonment in Prague and then remarks that, since it is such a common experience, it would be indecent for him to narrate it "unless I could capture some absolute singularity, which I cannot do while improvising in front of a microphone." This allusion to the microphone switches the scene, from the present one of his interview with David, to another, singular event: its singularity is that of a "very first time," *la toute première fois*, the absolutely singular moment that occurred when a French TV crew intercepted him somewhere in Germany, at night, on the train bringing him back to France after his release from the Czech prison. Derrida recalls how, when he was placed before camera and microphone, he felt he should say something about what only he could testify to of this experience but how, in those circumstances, he "had to be satisfied with broad stereotypes of the sort: 'I-went-there-out-of-solidarity-with-those-who-are-struggling-for-the-respect-of-human-rights, etc." And then he continues:

> This was all true . . . [b]ut how can you expect me, in that situation, to say to someone from Antenne 2 who puts a microphone in front of me: "You know, I am asking myself certain questions about the State, the foundations and the function of the discourse on human rights today"? Or else: "The essential thing is what was said there in the outlawed seminar about the political

question of the 'subject' and other related things"? Or else: "What I really lived through there would demand a completely different form of narration, another poetics than that of the evening news"? . . . Just imagine the look on the faces of the reporters and the TV viewers. But the *difficulty* I felt in the most acute way at that moment is permanent . . ."(*Points*, 129)

The difficulty is permanent; the very first time is never the first time that the difficulty is felt and at the turning point, the decision has already been made by another, long ago, in my place. Remains the "tape-recorded surprise" of singularity, no doubt even on television.

Notes

1. "Culture et écriture. La prolifération des livres et la fin du livre," *Noroît*, 132 (November 1968).
2. See also *Negotiations*, which collects five interviews.
3. On these questions, see Elisabeth Weber, "Upside-Down Writing," her fine introduction to *Points*.
4. In a translator's note in *Points* (459, n13), I rather hastily identified the allusion here to the first interview as *Positions*, published in 1972. But the book by that title in fact collected three interviews, given between 1967 and 1971, with different interlocutors and initially published in different reviews. In a brief prefatory note dated May 1972, Derrida writes that these three interviews are "the only ones in which I have ever participated" (*Positions*, 7), a remark that still leaves one wondering which of these three—or which other from the same period (see Bibliography in *Points*, 495)—was the first exposure to "tape-recorded surprise." Once again, it is difficult to know how to count Derrida's interviews.
5. By this I mean that manifestly few if any constraints were imposed on either the length or the manner of response, which even appears at points to be deliberately and provocatively "digressive." Derrida also makes the point of remarking his freedom to rewrite what was initially recorded: "What happens," he asks, "when . . . a tape recorder records that which—such is the implicit contract of this interview—I will certainly reread, which I may even transform here and there, perhaps even from beginning to end, before publication?" (*Points*, 9). It is likely that most or even all of Derrida's print interviews have observed a similar condition—the written revision of a transcribed recording—when they were not produced in writing from the outset.
6. In another interview from 1986, Derrida makes this point with an analogy to photography: "whether one likes it or not, there is an *effect of the idiom for the other*. It is like photography: whatever pose you adopt, whatever precautions you take so that the photograph will look like this or like that, there comes a moment when the photograph surprises you and it is the other's gaze that, finally, wins out and decides" (*Points*, 200–1).
7. The interviewer, in other words, conducts the interview by strictly avoiding the interrogative form for his "questions." This tactic seems itself to be a defensive one, the interlocutor appearing thus less naïve, merely stating

what is "known" or said to be the case, rather than posing questions out of a possible ignorance.

8. In this, Derrida remains close to Walter Benjamin's insistence, in "The Author as Producer" (1934), on "the decisive difference between the mere supplying of a productive apparatus and its transformation" and on the fact "that the bourgeois apparatus of production and publication can assimilate astonishing quantities of revolutionary themes, indeed can propagate them without calling its own existence, and the existence of the class that owns it, seriously into question" (Benjamin, *Reflections: Essays, Aphorisms, Autobiographical Writings*, trans. Edmund Jephcott [New York: Schocken Books, 1978], pp. 228–9).

Chapter 2

"Bartleby," or Decision: A Note on Allegory

Let us approach Melville's incomparable short work and ask it to decide the question of decision. How is it, according to "Bartleby the Scrivener," that a decision is possible—assuming that it is ever possible? What happens when someone decides or, as one says in French, *se décide*? Let us see.

> At last I was made aware that all through the circle of my professional acquaintance, a whisper of wonder was running round, having reference to the strange creature I kept at my office. This worried me very much. And as the idea came upon me of his possibly turning out a long-lived man, and keep occupying my chambers, and denying my authority; and perplexing my visitors, and scandalizing my professional reputation; and casting a general gloom over the premises; keeping soul and body together to the last upon his savings (for doubtless he spent but half a dime a day), and in the end perhaps outlive me, and claim possession of my office by right of his perpetual occupancy: as all these dark anticipations crowded upon me more and more, and my friends continually intruded their relentless remarks upon the apparition in my room; a great change was wrought in me. I resolved to gather all my faculties together, and for ever rid me of this intolerable incubus.[1]

In the retrospective narration, this passage recounts a well-calculated and weighed act of decision. The narrator calculates, then he decides, he resolves on a course of action. His calculation is rapid and approximate, but it is enough for him to estimate how long the other might live. It is thus on the basis of Bartleby's ghost, of his possible and even probable survival beyond the calculator's own lifetime that the "great change" of the decision begins work in him. To this calculation of probabilities is added the knowledge of a man of the law whose particular specialty is overseeing the goods of property owners and inheritance rights.[2] Alone in his chambers, where he frightens himself with the specter of a Bartleby who might very well enter into possession of his property, the lawyer seeks counsel with himself and, so as to conjure away the specter, he decides: "I resolved . . . to for ever rid me of this intolerable incubus."

In numerous places, Jacques Derrida has pointed out that the concept of decision, which is indispensable for any reflection on ethics or politics, requires a thorough recasting and deconstructing to the extent that it presupposes the identity and the presence to itself of a subject. Melville's tale, I would argue, convokes us to such a deconstruction. The fact that it is precisely a narrative which does this is not insignificant, as we will confirm later more patiently. But first let us take our bearings from a text of Derrida's, where he wonders if

> a decision that I *am able* to make, the decision that is *in my* power and that indicates the passage to the act or the deployment of what is *already possible* for me, the actualization of my possible, a decision that depends only on me: would this still be a decision? Whence the paradox without paradox that I am trying to accept: the responsible decision must be this impossible possibility of a "passive" decision, a decision of the other-in-me that does not exonerate me of any freedom or any responsibility. ("As If," 357)

A decision, if there is any, would be of the order of that ordeal or experience of the im-possible that Derrida proposes here and elsewhere as another name of deconstruction:

> the ordeal of an im-possible that would not be negative. Such a test implies another thinking of the event, of the *avoir-lieu*; only the impossible takes place. The deployment of a potentiality or a possibility that is already there will never make an event or an invention. What is true of the event is also true of the decision, therefore of responsibility. (Ibid.)

What the lawyer–narrator of "Bartleby" recounts as the "great change" that happened in him and gave rise to his decision seems to be an exercise in the pure calculation of the possible and of possibilities. To recall Derrida's terms, it would be but "the deployment of what is *already possible* for me, the actualization of my possible." The narrator says so rather exactly, in his way: "I resolved to gather all my faculties together," that is, I resolved to gather my strength, my knowledge, in short, all that was already possible for me, all that was in my power, so as to deploy it against the other inhabitant *chez moi*. The narrator's calculation would thus seem to refrain from letting the other decide, the other whom he seeks to expel.

But if one reads more closely, Melville's text provides much to think about regarding this figure of the im-possible that is the passive decision. In this narrative where Bartlebian passivity leaves its mark on everything it touches, this is not at all surprising. At work is a principle of communication or contamination that the narrator illustrates with the repetition of Bartleby's preferred word. Twice he qualifies this use as involuntary: "Somehow, of late I had got into the way of involuntarily using this word 'prefer' upon all sorts of not exactly suitable occasions. And I trembled to think that my contact with the scrivener had already and seriously affected me in a mental way" (31). Hearing one of his other scriveners use the word, he remarks: "It was plain that it involuntarily rolled from his tongue. I thought to myself, surely I must get rid of a demented man, who already has in some degree turned the tongues, if not the heads of myself and clerks" (31). It is the proper will of the lawyer and his clerks that is breached, infiltrated, contaminated by the unyielding preference of the other to remain where he is, without any occupation. In the face of these proliferating signs, the narrator does not doubt that he must act to rid himself of the altogether passive agent of this illness of contagious involuntarism. He determines, resolves, decides within himself to do so, he encourages himself to do so: his entire will to action remains enclosed in this circle or this counsel that he forms with himself. So long as he alone decides within himself to be rid of the other, the decision has no effect and Bartleby remains where he is.

Because he cannot manage to decide, because all his decisions are suspended from Bartleby's passive immobilism, the narrator, one might say, undergoes the ordeal of the im-possible decision. In this respect, Melville's tale would resemble an allegorical configuration of the deconstructive analysis of the deciding subject. Here "allegorical" would not mean a mode of figural representation of abstract qualities, but rather a spacing or displacing of the act of the other's deciding in me, the impossibility of passive decision. What the narrative displaces and defers is the necessity that it be the other in me who decides.

To confirm this, and as so often in Melville, one must read how space and spacing come to signify. Upon Bartleby's first appearance or apparition at the lawyer's chambers, his placement is carefully detailed: "a motionless young man one morning, stood upon my office threshold, the door being open, for it was summer" (19). Bartleby having crossed this first threshold, the narrator will have him cross a second one within the chambers that glass doors divide into two compartments, "one of which was occupied by my scriveners, the other by myself" (ibid.). It is in his own compartment that the narrator decides—"I resolved," he says—to install his new employee, as he explains in a paragraph that lays out a minute description of this placing of Bartleby according to the narrator–employer's desire: "I resolved to assign Bartleby a corner by the folding-doors, but on my side of them . . ." (ibid.). What is thereby constructed, according to the narrator–employer's desire, is an interior space that is interior to that interior that is an office in a Wall Street building. There, in a corner of his separate office, the narrator installs Bartleby between a large screen on one side and on the other a window that looks out on the exterior only to show a brick wall three feet away (which can recall the second title of the story: "A Story of Wall-Street").

Careful readers have often underscored this curious arrangement whereby the lawyer encloses himself with Bartleby, brings him into his own space even as he keeps the scrivener apart, closed off. Gilles Deleuze, for example, sees there the bizarreness of the lawyer even before the preferred formula, which will drive him a little mad, has been pronounced for the first time.[3] Philippe Jaworski, whose remarkable study of Melville I would especially like to acknowledge here, has also pointed to this description in his reading of the Melvillian city.[4] Calling attention to itself, this complex topology places an outside within, but also an inside without, according to a structure of enclavement or enfolding of the border between the external and the internal. In his corner, invisible, Bartleby will thus be the figure of the outside within, interiorized in the self but always apart from the self, on the invaginated border of the relation to the other.

This enfolding of the other within/without oneself happens in the blink of an eye, it seems. According to the narrator's discourse, the decision to hire Bartleby right away speculates on the supplementary benefits for the lawyer's business of "a man of so singularly sedate an aspect" (19). The lawyer employs this sedative, speculating on the beneficial effect it will have on the body of his copyists.[5] Here once again the narrator is calculating a profit before deciding. But, in fact in the order of the narrative, this self-interested reasoning takes place *après coup,* after the *coup* of the other's unforeseeable arrival.

So, what happened? What came about?

Standing for the first time in front of the door, Bartleby would have presented himself as *already* within. How is that possible? Well, it is precisely the im-possible arrival of the other that happens. There, on the threshold, it is indeed a matter of a decision that the narrator has to allow the other to make in him, *already in him,* even before this other has come through the door. The impossibility of this "already" can be read when the narrative jumps in time in order to present Bartleby the way he appeared "one morning" on the threshold: "a motionless young man one morning, stood upon my office threshold, the door being open, for it was summer. *I can see that figure now*—pallidly neat, pitiably respectable, incurably forlorn! It was Bartleby" (19; emphasis added). The figure that he says he can still see *was* Bartleby, already. Already in the past this figure presented himself as having passed or being past, thus as his own ghost. It is *as if* he were saying that Bartleby stood there dead, already dead in the past present, figuring his future death as having already passed, *as if* he were saying that he had seen the coming of that figure, that morning. The narrator affirms: "I can see that figure now" and the figure of an impossible present tense lets speak as well the impossible decision to take into one's abode the other who must already be there, within, within him, in order to make the decision.

Beyond what can be laid to the account of his possible subject, the narrator gives us this figure in narrative. By figuring the act of no possible subject, the narrative or the *récit* differentiates itself from the discourse of the narrator even as it remains inseparable from that discourse. By remarking this difference, one recalls that there is indeed reason and room to distinguish them, and this "room" is the narrative itself as the spacing of a repetition. In this placeless place, which is a narrative without narrating subject, the impossible comes to trace and archive itself, like Bartleby coming to take up his place among the copyists. Narrative, fiction, literature: Philippe Jaworski has described well why the figure of Bartleby could also be called "literature":

> To know if we can live with literature: with what, one fine summer day, appears—the door is open—on the threshold: a pale shadow that we have desired, and concerning which we soon notice that it is waiting to be saved or chased away. . . .
>   It is a matter of questioning oneself. . . .
>   The instant of decision . . . (20)

This instant of im-possible decision of the other already within creates a hole that will be covered over only *après coup* by the discourse of the one who then begins to speculate on his own account. But it is the narrative, the *récit*, that gives one to read this hole as what the other, by arriving, does to *time*, to the instant, instantly, of the decision. With the other the impossible arrives, happens; the instant is divided and a decision will have taken place in that place that does not properly belong to any subject. The subject of the decision *already* absents himself in the other. This is what comes about. The discourse of the narrator can say this only backwards, by way of the narrative told starting from the death of the one who already stood as a dead man from the first step onto the threshold: "After a few words touching his qualifications, I engaged him, glad to have among my corps of copyists a man of so singularly sedate an aspect, which I thought might operate beneficially . . ." (19).

One could pursue much further this allegorical configuration of the narrative, that is, its spacing or displacing of the im-possible decision. But I will consider just one other episode, which seems to stand in opposition to the im-possible decision just outlined.

As the other edge of the tale approaches, the narrator recounts the manner in which Bartleby was expulsed or disenclaved:

> a note from the landlord lay upon the desk. I opened it with trembling hands. It informed me that the writer had sent to the police, and had Bartleby removed to the Tombs as a vagrant. . . . The tidings had a conflicting effect upon me. At first I was indignant; but at last almost approved. The landlord's energetic, summary disposition, had led him to adopt a procedure which I do not think I would have decided upon myself; and yet, under such peculiar circumstances, it seemed the only plan. (42)

The narrator, in fact, lets another decide—the new owner of his former chambers—and this other seems indeed to stand outside the one who recounts this act and its effects. This other is anonymous, unknown, named only by the legal titles of property-owner or his profession: here it is the "landlord," elsewhere he is identified also as a lawyer. Thus, this anonymous other would have decided the thing somewhere outside of the one who recounts. It is a decision according to the law, or rather, the landlord acts in such a way that it will be finally the law that "decides," by sending its police. As we have just read, the narrator insists on this energetic act of the other property-owner, the other lawyer, the one who puts a certain "procedure" in motion. All of this, of course, brings out more clearly the passivity of our narrator.

But what about this passivity? By which paths does it pass? By whom? Who lets whom decide what? I said that this decision to transfer Bartleby to the Tombs stood in an apparently clear opposition, at least on the level of the story, to the decision taken on the tale's threshold to engage Bartleby. Yet, it is less than certain that these acts can be simply opposed in their structure of passive decision. The relation between the two decisive moments would be instead one within the im-possible time of decision, this time of the other in me that divides the instant and the present.

If, with Bartleby's first arrival, the mark of this im-possible time is a certain "already," then his departure is signaled no less by a time and a tense without possible present. In order better to hear this, one may compare several French translations of the sentence in which the narrator situates himself in time when he assumes his passivity in the face of the energetic activity of the law: "The landlord's energetic, summary disposition, had led him to adopt a procedure which I do not think I would have decided upon myself; and yet, under such peculiar circumstances, it seemed the only plan." Notice, among other things, the play among the verbal tenses: pluperfect, present, past conditional, imperfect. The three translations I consulted (by Michèle Causse, Pierre Leyris and, most recently, Jean-Yves Lacroix) give quite different readings especially when one compares the tense of "decide" as conjugated in the relative clause: "which I do not think I would have decided upon myself." Michèle Causse translates it with a past conditional: "que je n'aurais jamais pu prendre sur moi"; "which I never would have been able to take upon myself."[6] This choice substitutes an absolute negation for the original's more nuanced negation that lets one hear the extent to which the narrator can only hesitate still in the present to say, with certainty, whether or not he would have decided thus and on his own. Pierre Leyris and Jean-Yves Lacroix, by contrast, translate better this present state of uncertainty, the former when he adopts the pluperfect subjunctive ("que je ne me fusse sans doute jamais résolu à prendre"),[7] and the latter by inserting a "je pense" to muffle somewhat the absolute negation of the verb in the past conditional: "une procédure à laquelle, je pense, je ne me serais pas résolu de mon propre chef"; "a procedure upon which, I think, I would not have resolved on my own."[8]

This comparison brings out what remains unresolved in the decision that no doubt would not have been made by the one speaking. But what does he affirm in this manner if it is not once again his experience of the im-possible decision since it comes down to another already, still within him? This condition of possibility is at the same time a condition of impossibility, that of deciding "upon myself," as he says in a syntax that can be understood several ways. One hears first, perhaps, the sense of a simple emphasis on the subject: "myself, as for me, I would not have acted thus, I myself would not have decided upon this procedure." But the same grammar allows other readings. There is, for example, an echo of the idiom "to take it upon oneself," to take the responsibility for something. The narrator would thus be sounding or implying a rather unconvincing denial of responsibility. But in another, less idiomatic syntax, he might seem to be saying: I would not have decided thus by myself, myself alone, and on my own account. This is what would have been impossible for him and in him. Him, that is to say, already the other, another, himself acting and from the threshold *like and as* the wholly passive Bartleby. No, he says as the other and speaking always from or in the place of the other, "I do not think I would have decided upon myself." "I would have preferred not to," the other would no doubt have said, and already within him.

* * *

I will not pursue any further the allegorical configuration that I believe one may read between Melville's text and deconstructive thought. Since this mode has been so powerfully rethought by Walter Benjamin, Paul de Man, Samuel Weber, and still others, it is no doubt rather presumptuous to invoke allegory as I have just done, and especially so as to speak of an allegory of deconstruction. All the more so since deconstructive thought does not allow one to situate allegory, this speaking-in-the-place of the other, as one mode among others. On the contrary, this thinking calls one to question any discourse that would affirm its essentially *anallegorical* status, in other words, that would affirm to be speaking solely for itself, without responsibility for and before the other in whose place its speech acts take place. The recasting of the concept of decision, but also of responsibility, hospitality, gift, and still so many other experiences that must pass by way of the ordeal of aporetic impossibility, is thus part of an opening to the fundamental allegoricity generally neglected or denied by discourses—political, scientific, or even ethical—of the sovereign subject. As recent works by Jacques Derrida confirm, the deconstruction of anallegorical sovereignty has been on the agenda of deconstruction for a long time.[9]

To conclude this brief note, I want to let a single sentence resonate against the background of what I just called fundamental allegoricity, which Melville's bottomless tale will have helped us sound to a certain depth. The sentence I have in mind was heard and repeated throughout the world. First uttered in English, it affirmed in a few words a dogmatic doctrine of sovereign decision. Here it is: "The course of this nation does not depend on the decisions of others." The orator was then US president George W. Bush and the sentence had its place in the annual State of the Union speech, delivered to the United States Congress, and before the world's media, in January 2003, two months before an invasion of Iraq that had certainly already been decided by then. Before a world that was all ears, this is what was announced by the head of state of the country that is taken to be or takes itself to be, that makes itself be taken to be or would like to make itself be taken to be the most powerful on the planet. The sentence proclaims the sovereignty that gives one the right to self-determination. As sovereign, one affirms there that "others" cannot decide in the place of the sovereign nation itself. These "others" are not further specified, which allows the word to float and to generalize its reference to every other, indeed to the very idea of alterity, within or without, in relation to "this nation." The sovereign decider would be constituted as sovereign precisely inasmuch as it is one with itself and without difference, without other.

As for its mode, which is negative declarative, the sentence is indeed a constative, but a performative force is inseparably bound up there with the constative declaration itself. To pose sovereign independence, in this context, comes down to imposing it; to say what is the case comes down to a performative act. This performative force, which goes without saying, has to do with the conditions of the sentence's utterance: by a head of state, speaking officially in the name of his nation. With the support of this context, the performative force poses and imposes itself as without limit, not stopping in the face of anything that might bid to oppose it. Nothing can oppose it, the course of the sovereign nation being unopposable as soon as it does not depend on the decision of any other, as soon as the nation *can decide* for and by itself (but can it? is this possible?) or, which comes down to the same thing, as soon as the decision is made by the one who utters the sentence and is alone in speaking for the head of the sovereign, in its name. Speaking in the place of the sovereign, he says its absolute sovereignty, without dependence, without tie, ab-solute and ab-solved of what could link it to any other.

"The course of this nation does not depend on the decisions of others." And one heard, one still hears the force behind this constative-performative, a force that, in January 2003, was massing on several foreign borders where this nation alone was led in its self-determining course to go travel the world. Now, precisely, in these grave conditions, what is one to think of everything just said about the impossible passive decision? What is the pertinence of this notion on the stage of the world where the idea of the sovereign, self-determined, and independent decision is being reinforced so massively?

The pertinence, that is to say, what brings one thing to touch another. The questions just asked touch on the very pertinence of events in their happening in the world, to everyone, and to each and every world. What happens is what manages to touch the world somewhere and the whole world at the same time, a time that begins right away to repeat. Trace of the event, a mark left on each one. It is deconstructive thought that has always traced the pertinence of this structure of trace-event. It thus touches on what makes for the very experience of the world, of what "n'arrive qu'à se répéter," to echo an untranslatable syntax that Derrida has exploited and that grasps so economically the condition of possibility in the condition of impossibility. With its undecidable syntax—what happens only by repeating itself/what manages only to repeat itself and thus fails to happen for the first time—the event signifies that it is still arriving, not yet arrived, or else it has been repeating itself for a long time.

And this is always a chance for it to arrive or not manage to arrive, *pour que cela arrive ou n'arrive pas à arriver*. President Bush's sovereign sentence also sounds this chance, indeed the quasi certainty, that it will not be able to impose itself and, thus, that its performance or its performative will be "infelicitous," unhappy. By the very fact that the gap in the truth that it claims merely to state must remain visible, readable, sensible, the performative force of sovereignty declares itself everywhere to be unhappy. Perhaps this is even what is happening: the "unhappiness" of sovereignty. Perhaps, but it is certain that others will decide.

Notes

1. "Bartleby the Scrivener: A Story of Wall-Street," in Harrison Hayford et al., eds, *The Writings of Herman Melville*, vol. 9 (Evanston and Chicago: Northwestern University Press and the Newberry Library, 1987), p. 38.
2. In his admirable reading of "Bartleby," J. Hillis Miller does not fail to underscore the term "conveyancer," which is the narrator's legal title. Miller quotes and comments on the passage where the narrator presents himself under this title: "The narrator's 'original business,' as he tells the reader, was 'that of a conveyancer and title hunter, and drawer-up of recondite documents of all sorts'. The narrator [. . .] 'conveys' property and money, especially property, from one place to another or from one owner to another" (J. Hillis Miller, *Versions of Pygmalion* [Cambridge: Harvard University Press, 1990], p. 148).
3. Gilles Deleuze, "Bartleby; or, the Formula," in Deleuze, *Essays Critical and Clinical*, trans. Daniel W. Smith and Michael A. Greco (Minneapolis: University of Minnesota Press, 1997), p. 75.
4. Philippe Jaworski, *Melville, le Désert et l'empire* (Paris: Presses de L'École Normale Supérieure, 1986), p. 271. Since the first version of this essay, I have also learned greatly from the far-reaching and provocative study of Melville by Branka Arsić: *Passive Constitutions, or 7½ Times Bartleby* (Stanford: Stanford University Press, 2007).
5. More precisely he imagines that the sedating effect will act to moderate the opposite humors of his two other copyists. The narrator has already described this opposition at length before Bartleby enters the narrative scene.
6. Melville, *Les Îles enchantées,* trans. Michèle Causse (Paris: Flammarion, 1989), p. 53.
7. Melville, *Benito Cereno et autres contes de la Veranda*, trans. Pierre Leyris (Paris: Gallimard, 1951), p. 82.
8. Melville, *Bartleby, le scribe, une histoire de Wall Street*, trans. Jean-Yves Lacroix (Paris: Allia, 2003), p. 77.
9. See especially *Rogues*.

Chapter 3

Urgent Translation

He held out the book to us, saying "You've got to read this." The book was *De la grammatologie*, and the young professor of French literature who exhorted us in this manner had just brought it back from Paris. We did not waste any time before obeying.

This scene took place in 1971, at Cornell University, but no doubt something similar was happening in those years at other American university graduate schools. Derrida's books were being transmitted there under the sign of a very particular urgency because they upset everything and gave rise to an experience of thinking that one did not easily get over. This urgency was also political: the American university had just been badly shaken by the events at Kent State in 1970, where four students had been gunned down by National Guard troops during a demonstration against the American bombing raids on Cambodia, which had extended the ravages of the war in Vietnam. With his books, Derrida called on readers to reflect on everything that connected this unavowable violence of the fathers toward their own sons and daughters. He thus gave us the means to re-establish links between current politics and the metaphysics of presence that he showed to have been long at work in the philosophical tradition. And he summoned us to think this thing—and to respond to it.

But this urgency had first to pass by way of translation if it was to broadcast its call beyond the very small milieu of readers of French in US universities. In 1973, six years after its publication in France, *La Voix et le phénomène* appeared in English translation; as for the translation of *De la grammatologie*, one had to wait until 1975. Thereafter, the rhythm accelerated, but there would always be a palpable delay, owing at once to the cumbersome machinery of publication at American university presses, where the majority of these translations appeared, and to the formidable difficulties attending the translation of a practice of writing that is as inventive and crafty as Derrida's.

Because Derrida ruses cunningly with the French language and shakes it up, asking it to render always more meaning. Each sentence harbors a plurality of other sentences. No text of Derrida's is simple; all shelter an incalculable crowd of other texts beneath the appearance of their unicity. That such an irreducible and inevitable pluralization characterizes any text as the very condition of its readability: this is what Derrida thinks and analyzes in works that are theoretical insofar as they are performative.

About twenty-five years ago, I attempted for the first time to translate one of these pluralizing texts. Since then, I have often repeated the experience although the repetition has not brought me much closer to a solution of the dilemma that Derrida poses to all his translators in every language. What haunts us and keeps us in suspense is that he often borrows from the simplest, most ordinary language, which is familiar in its tone and rhythm, recognizable by whoever understands French, so as to slip in something unheard-of, extraordinary, and unrecognizable. These sleights of hand can be altogether disconcerting, stimulating, exhilarating, and very often hilarious. One laughs at the surprise of hearing a piece of language fold up its plainest face with an unexpected and still unknown face. The idiom emerges from these tricky spins like a newborn and yet, at the same time, one receives it like the oldest of friends. One is unable to distinguish finally the one from the other. This is the joy that makes translators weep if they cannot find ways to produce similar miracles in their own language.

But one does not find them often and even, at least in my experience, very rarely. Perhaps if one were not always pressed for time one would have the leisure to wait for unhoped-for coincidences to spring to mind; but, even when publishers or the circumstances leave you alone, there is still the urgency that forces you to let translations go when they are still in search of their miracles. You weep for them, but especially for the readers who may never know the extent to which Jacques Derrida, reputed to be a "difficult writer," writes so easily in his idiom.

And yet, to translate quickly is not necessarily a fault, and it can even be indispensable. When Jacques Derrida gave the long lecture that became the stunning book *Specters of Marx*, he had to deliver it first in English. As the chosen translator for the occasion—I was in California near the place where the conference was going to be held—I had to work very fast to keep up with the number of pages Derrida was passing along to me as he finished drafting the lecture. It was rather comical despite the very serious stakes of this book. When this translation had to be sent off to the publisher a few months later, I did not weep for it even as I feared that my haste had left many traces of awkwardness. For these traces as well were responses to urgency and said, however well or ill, "you've got to read this."

Chapter 4

Coming to the Beginning

Let us imagine him: he sits down before a keyboard, stretches his hands over the keys, and, after a slight hesitation, begins to strike them very quickly. Other than the noise of keys being struck, there is silence and no one else is nearby. There is nothing happening in the room with the exception of this movement of fingers above the little plastic cubes each bearing some kind of mark.

What is he doing? Manifestly, he has begun to write. To confirm this, one has merely to look at the screen (or, some time ago, the sheet of paper): appearing there are the first strings of letters, words, phrases. It is indeed he, is it not, and those are indeed his gestures causing the impression or inscription on a support, which will carry the words toward the common readability of what is ordinarily called writing, a piece of writing. So why make a mystery of it? The question "what is he doing?" is uncalled-for because it is so obvious. Perhaps, however, one should look more closely at what has thus begun to appear as the clear evidence of writing. Is it certain that one can recognize the beginning beginning with the first written words?

So let us start again at the beginning, the beginnings. Let us proceed a little in the manner of a catalog of indexed poems or songs, of which only the first lines, the incipits, will be cited. (Let this also be, on the present occasion, our manner of tribute to Marian Hobson. *Opening Lines* is the title of her remarkable and singularly thoughtful book on the writings of our honoree.)[1] The order followed in what follows will not be a conventional one (for example, chronological or alphabetical), but will be uncovered, precisely, as we advance. We will be looking for a few motifs that return in the first sentences of written works that are very dissimilar as regards their principal subjects, their occasions, and their formal or rhetorical strategies. All of this (everything essential, therefore) will be left out of account, as if these sentences came to us already detached, isolated from whatever might accompany them.

For example:

But who is talking about 'living'? ("Living")

Or else:

Someone comes, not me, and pronounces: "I am interested in the idiom in painting." ("Passe-partout")

Or again:

Someone, you or me, comes forward and says: *I would like to learn to live finally.* (*Specters*)

These are all incipits that begin only by echoing "someone" who is unnamed and unnamable, without name or face, a "someone" who speaks, utters, or says in silence enough to set the machine in motion. Offstage or with what is called in French a *voix-off* (voiceover), he or she calls forth the first words that appear on the page or screen, which would thus come along in second place to awaken the impression of what the other has let be heard but without sound or sign. Before any sign, there is a speaking or saying that comes forward, advances, and takes place, thereby giving place and giving rise to the beginning of writing. Before the beginning, there will have been the advance. By inscribing itself after the advancing other who gets out in front of it, writing can take the measure of this advance only by taking down, as if in dictation, the opening of the consigned speech. For right away there is more than one speaking, at least two and therefore more than two.

So many texts deliver themselves over to this appearance of a polylogue from the beginning, for example, the text that takes the title or lets itself be called "Avances," "Advances," and whose first words are inscribed by the advance of the one who begins by pronouncing:

Once more the Timaeus, but another Timaeus, a new Demiurge, it's a promise. ("Avances")

"Once more the Timaeus" recalls the long lineage of commentary on Plato's dialogue, including an earlier text signed by this same writer. Here is how, a few years in advance of "Advances," this earlier text, "*Khōra*," had begun:

Khōra reaches us [*nous arrive*], and as the name. And when a name comes, it immediately says more than the name: the other of the name and quite simply the other, whose irruption the name announces. ("*Khōra*")

Upon reading a little further on this page, one recognizes something like the unexpectant announcement of the principal thread to be followed later through "Advances," namely, the thread of that which will forever suspend the possibility of the promise from the threat. After the arrival of these first words, "*Khōra*" continues:

> This announcement does not yet promise, no more than it threatens. It neither promises nor threatens anyone.

So one would have to back up and find elsewhere the beginning of "Advances," which would have been beaten to the starting line by this other text, "*Khōra*," the text that itself opens with the irruption of the other who always gets there first. This "reference" is not pointed out as such, which leads one to think that it is a matter of something else altogether than a scholar's reference back to an earlier piece of writing. One imagines instead a scene of the return of what had let itself be inscribed once in this form of a neither promising nor threatening announcement: "the other of the name and quite simply the other, whose irruption the name announces."

By isolating and serializing these irruptive debuts, one could almost see them as thematizing this figure of a beginning that always begins elsewhere and in advance of itself. Consider for example the following sequence of four opening lines:

> At the moment of beginning, even before beginning, while slowing down, *adagio*, and even *lento, lento*, one knows, yes, one knows that it will always be necessary to begin again. (*H.C.*)

> Despite the delay of what is beginning here, it will not, one suspects, be a matter of some last word. ("As If ")

> Let us not begin at the beginning, or even at the archive. (*Archive*)

> *In the beginning, there will have been speed.* ("No Apocalypse")

One hears the first words of *Genesis* and of the Gospel of John in echo (and if he has devoted a number of stunning pages to the Ovidian figure of Echo, it is no doubt because he puts himself in the place of the one who can only speak after the other). This last opening line—"In the beginning, there will have been speed"—echoes as well the first two words of an earlier text. On this other occasion, there is a turn toward the absolute fiction of a writing that would be at the beginning of writing:

> In the beginning, that's the fiction, there would be writing. Thus, a fable, of writing. ("Illustrate")

The word "fable" could send us on a long detour through the dazzling and dazzled reading of the poem "Fable" by Francis Ponge, which furnishes, in "Psyche: Invention of the Other," the principal example of a fabulous fiction. This reading relies especially on the first line of the poem, "By the word *by* begins then this text," an incipit that unfolds by quoting and rolling up on itself. One should quote this whole analysis, or even the whole text of "Psyche," which is pertinent through and through to the question of beginnings. Just once, I am going to break the rule adopted here, which is to cite only first lines, so as to quote a passage in which a sentence of Valéry's gets added to the series of those that begin "in the beginning":

> ["Fable"] presents itself from the start as a beginning, the inauguration of a discourse or of a textual mechanism. It does what it says, not being content with announcing, as did Valéry, moreover, in "Au sujet d'Eurêka": "In the beginning was the fable." This latter phrase, miming but also translating the first words of John's gospel ("In the beginning was the logos," the word) is perhaps also a performative demonstration of the very thing it is saying. . . . But Ponge's "Fable," while locating itself ironically in this evangelical tradition, reveals and perverts, or rather brings to light by means of a slight perturbation, the strange structure of the foreword [*envoi*] or of the evangelical message, in any case of that incipit which says that in the incipit, at the inception, there is the *logos*, the word. "Fable," owing to a turn of syntax, is a sort of poetic performative that simultaneously *describes* and *carries out*, on the same line, its own generation. ("Psyche," 10–11)

Returning to our rule here and picking up the thread of the beginning, let us cite the incipit of "Psyche," this text that has so much to say on the subject of the fabulous incipit of poetic invention as the invention of the other. At the start, then, a phrase, a question is set off on a single line:

> **What else am I going to be able to invent?**

Right away on reading this, one must wonder: who is speaking, who seems to be talking all alone and wondering thus, asking such a question? Although inflected in the first person, which should refer one right away to the author, the sentence in question resists easy attribution as soon as the next paragraph begins. There it is suggested that the question one has just read is something like a quotation or the reported speech of another:

> Here perhaps we have an inventive incipit for a lecture. Imagine, if you will, a speaker daring to address his hosts in these terms. He thus seems to appear before them without knowing what he is going to say; he declares rather insolently that he is setting out to improvise. Obliged as he is to invent on the spot, he wonders again: "Just what am I going to have to invent?"

Notice how, with this reprise of the question referred back to an imagined other, the "I" of the incipit becomes detached from any certain place of enunciation.

Similar effects of detachment or substitution around the place and person of enunciation frequently mark these beginnings, even when they do not adopt the form of a polylogue. It happens more than once that this movement is kicked off by the imperative: "Let us imagine," or as we have just heard, "Imagine." Here are some more examples:

> Let us imagine a scholar. A specialist in ritual analysis, he seizes upon this work, assuming that someone has not presented him with it (something we will never know). ("Passions")

> Imagine him, picture someone who supposedly cultivates French.
>   What is called French.
>   And who supposedly is cultivated by French.
>   And who, as a French citizen moreover, would thus be a subject, as we say, of French culture.
>   Well, suppose that one day this subject of French culture comes to you and says, for example, in good French:
>   *"Je n'ai qu'une langue, ce n'est pas la mienne,"* "I have only one language, it is not mine." (*Monolingualism*)

One would of course be perfectly within one's rights, and especially within the laws of copyright, to attribute such moments to the sole signatory. But one would also thereby bypass what is coming to pass here in fact and which has been called, for almost forty years, the scene—or the stage—of writing, "la scène d'écriture" (see "Freud"). It is a scene that, despite so many appearances, cannot be played unless the other is allowed to come and, therefore, unless there is more than one speaking. Indeed, as one may read at the beginning of the polylogue titled "Restitutions," it cannot be played or acted unless there are more than two: there must be "more than two in order to begin."

> And yet. Who was saying, I no longer remember, "there are no ghosts in Van Gogh's paintings"? Well, what we have here is a ghost story. But we must wait until we are more than two in order to begin. ("Restitutions")

More than two, *plus de deux*. In an incomplete sentence or without determining syntax, this piece of language also allows or appeals to more than one sense. It says a number 2+n (which will thus always give rise to a polylogue) and, at the same time or in turn, it demands, it orders, by means of a verbless imperative, *plus de deux*, that one be done with the number two, with the dual, the couple or, in general, with binarity: no more two.

Having to be more than one in order to speak, one is already more than two, 2+n. So we should no longer speak of dialogue, still less of monologue. (A quick detour here by way of "Ulysses Gramophone," which remarks on Molly Bloom's famous closing "monologue": "Molly says to herself [apparently speaking to herself alone], she reminds herself, that she says *yes* in asking the other to ask her to say *yes*, and she starts or finishes by saying *yes* to the other in herself, but she does so in order to say to the other that she will say *yes* if the other asks her, yes, to say *yes*" ["Ulysses," 303]. As for its incipit, "Ulysses Gramophone" begins almost off the page, the first sentence rolling up in its very first words—"Yes, yes"—use and mention, as speech acts theorists would say, but also response to an implicit question or demand from another: **"Yes, yes, you are receiving me, these are French words."**) Saying "I" to begin, the subject never accedes to speech without being divided as soon as it opens its mouth—or inscribes the very first word:

I—mark(s) first of all a division in what will have been able to appear at the beginning. ("Qual quelle")

Always take note of the punctuation, no less than the font of the characters. Dashes, hyphens, quotation marks, parentheses, capital letters, and so forth: these are so many conventional marks that keep the trace of the articulation of the passage of and by the other. For example, the dash plays at dashing off the portrait of the "I" at the beginning: "I—mark(s) first of all a division in what will have been able to appear at the beginning." Or else, when they are doubled, dashes draw "me" toward a place apart in a sentence that introduces the other in translation—unless they introduce "me" into the very middle of the writing.

I introduce here—me—a translation. ("Me")

This is as good a place as any to remark that, although I have been citing these opening lines in translation, not one of them submits docilely to that operation without leaving behind a residue of the original idiom. That this writing always calls attention to untranslatability will be obvious to any reader. But an inventory like this allows one also to notice that the opening lines are almost always stamped out in a particularly untranslatable idiom. And these effects are often achieved with the help of punctuation and other syntactic markers.

But to return to these punctuated or punctured openings: there is another incipit that consists simply of an ellipsis between brackets. Signaling perhaps toward that "blank voice" of apophasis that will be in question right away in this polylogued text, "Sauf le nom," the ellipsis also figures that offstage voice or *voix-off* that must approach the stage in order for speech/writing to get started:

> —[. . .]
> —Sorry, but more than one, it is always necessary to be more than one in order to speak, several voices are necessary for that . . . ("Sauf")

Elsewhere, a word, a noun must be hammered out in capitals and set aside either in order to abandon it to its shameful ignominy:

> **APARTHEID—let that remain the name from now on, the unique appellation for the ultimate racism in the world, the last of many. ("Racism")**

or else in order to salute, praise, and call again to the name:

> **FRANCIS PONGE—from here I call him, for greeting and praise, for renown, I should say, or renaming.** (*Signéponge*)

As already noted, it happens, and often, that what comes at the beginning is a name or words spoken sometimes in well-formed sentences, or sometimes merely little shards of speech, in any case, what could in principle be pronounced, proferred in speech. And yet, these shards and slivers (sometimes simply phonemes, aggregates of consonants without voice or vowel—*gl*, *str*, *tr*, *cl*) arrive from no specific provenance or else their provenance is buried somewhere outside memory. When this happens, we are no longer asked to imagine *someone*, even indeterminate, someone who would come forward to say, for example, "I would like to learn to live finally," or "What else am I going to be able to invent," or yet again "I have but one language, it is not mine." However unusual, unexpected, or enigmatic, such sentences or phrases appear still to stand on this side, so to speak, of the relation to language, that is, on the side where it is a matter of saying and hearing/understanding something in common and between us. But there is also the side of this relation that is—almost—without relation to any linguistic community or commonality, where a language, perhaps, begins that is not yet one, or where it comes into contact with its external edge. This edge resembles a threshold drawn right on the ground of the text. Every writing, every incipit must set off from such a threshold, which, as is almost always forgotten, does not give access only to the other *in* language, the fellow speaker of a language, this one or any one, but also to the other, without face or name, who could come, who will come, perhaps, from outside it. This is what I am calling the other edge or border of the threshold and it is also remarked by these texts when they seize in flight some scrap fallen from the explosion that results when language touches its outside.

All the beginnings inventoried so far could be reread from this perspective, from the other side of the threshold. Let us, however, close this catalog (which is a truly laughable term here) with three or four more examples that are among the most explosive:

> More than 15 years ago a phrase came to me, as though in spite of me; to be more precise, it returned, singular, singularly succinct, almost mute. (*Cinders*)

> One day, yes, one day, once upon a time, a terrific time, terrifically addressed, with as much violence as tact at its fingertips, a certain question took hold of me—as if it, or "she" [*la question*], came of me, to me. (*Touching*)

> The crude word . . . that morning, a November 29, 1988, a sentence came, from further away than I could ever say, but only one sentence, scarcely a sentence, the plural word of a desire toward which all the others since always seemed, confluence itself, to hurry, an order suspended on three words, *find the vein* . . . (*Circumfession*)

One word, a verb, comes back here and we have already seen it inscribed in almost every opening already cited: to come, *venir*. But what does it mean, "to come," when it is inscribed in an incipit or, even more enigmatically, in a title?

> A question of "good sense," first of all, and of sense: what "to come" means in "The Book to Come" does not go without saying. ("Book")

To call "come" a verb or a word does not do justice to its place at the edge of these writings, the place it holds precisely on the border between, on the one side, a fully made, spoken, and understood language, and, on the other, what can come about, come down on it, befall it. Like an event. The event made phrase: "a phrase came to me," "a certain question took hold of me," "a sentence came." One has to let it come and inscribe the event whose phrase or words form only its graspable face, like the name *Khōra* that "reaches us, and as the name. And when a name comes, it immediately says more than the name: the other of the name and quite simply the other, whose irruption the name announces." Thus, to let names, nouns, words come, but also not to take them for what or who comes about. To remember that, before making itself into word and language, the "to come" would have let an appeal be heard, a demand, a command, a desire, a prayer, an opening:

> —Come.
> Come: how to call what I have just—what I have just what? What I have just said? Come, is that a word? (*Pas*)

Let us imagine him, I said at the beginning. But beyond any power to imagine, one calls him, Jacques Derrida, by the name that announces an irruption always to come.

Note

1. See Marian Hobson, *Opening Lines* (New York and London: Routledge, 1998). The occasion on which the English version of this essay was presented, at Queen Mary and Westfield College, University of London in July 2004, was a colloquium to mark the award of an honorary doctorate to Jacques Derrida, which was convened by Professor Hobson.

Chapter 5

To Follow

It is impossible that we should each survive the other. That's the duel, the axiomatic of every duel, the scene which is the most common and the least spoken of—or the most prohibited—concerning our relation to the other. Yet the impossible happens—not in "objective reality," which has no say here, but in the experience of Romeo and Juliet. And under the law of the pledge, which commands every given word. ("Aphorism," 422)

So *wrote* Jacques Derrida in 1986.

So he *writes* in "Aphorism Countertime."

These two assertions attempt to say something about the legacy of one who was an unflinching thinker of inheritance and legacy. Between them, the first in a dated past tense and the second with its descriptive present tense, they conjugate the times of a survival into a present without limit, which is also and *at the same time* the limitless future of a promise. This "at the same time" points, at the same time, to the contretemps of a survival, a living on, that was already given by the law commanding "every given word" in every duel. Already, which means not just in the wake of a dreaded, lamented event that can be dated and that happens only once. Already before that date there will have been living on, before and therefore also beyond the event. The impossible happens, the impossible event happens every day, and not merely on that day when "The sun for sorrow will not show its face," which is recorded and dated as the beginning of mourning in "objective reality." Mourning dawns with the given word, with the promise that is friendship, that it is, was, will be, and will have been. "It is impossible that we should each survive the other," and yet no relation to the other begins except with this impossible double, at least double survival, destining and promising the relation to infinite repetition. And it is not only lovers or friends who destine each other to this experience. To every stranger as well is extended, even before one begins to speak, the promise of the word's repetition. The given word binding one to another does not even have to be given "in person," as we say. It binds me as well to all those I never encounter except by responding to an address tendered in mediation, through what is called a text, that is, through any kind of trace left by one to be repeated by another.

So wrote Jacques Derrida.

And so he writes, in this text or in any other on which his signature remains like a pledge of fidelity to all the words given to the other, to all the others, without number. To all the friends who cannot be counted. Friendship, he writes, is not a matter of numbers; each time singular, it is infinitely repeatable.[1]

What need is there to speak or write in such close proximity to a death that has plunged millions—and I do not employ that number as a figure of speech—into grief whether or not they knew or loved Jacques Derrida, and even if they hated him, as many have wanted to claim they did? I first posed this question aloud on 29 October 2004, to those who had gathered at a colloquium titled "The Legacies of Theory."[2] I then added that even before we fell into this infinite sadness, the prior invitation to ponder theory's legacies would doubtless have led us to turn first and foremost to the thought of one who constantly recalled the testamentary structure of writing just as he never ceased interrogating the possibility of "theory" in the domains of the humanities, or in any other domain. There was no question, therefore, about the central and pervasive pertinence of Jacques Derrida's immense work for the subject of such a gathering. Rather, I was then and I am still asking about the need to speak or write in the aftermath of the death of one who was my dearest friend, to write, to speak of him while battered by waves of grief, and to do so not just with a few of the hundreds of his other dearest friends—for the superlative of friendship with him was never an exclusive privilege—but in public and to unknown readers.

To question this need does not mean to resist it, but on the contrary to give into it even while trying to learn from it, to let oneself be guided by this impulse, but one hopes not too blindly. It is to go on learning from and following Jacques Derrida, who, in 1981, following the sudden and shocking death of Roland Barthes, allowed himself for the first time to write, as he put it, "*following the death*, not after, not long after the death *by returning* to it, but just following the death, *upon or on the occasion of the death*, at the commemorative gatherings and tributes 'in memory' of those who while living would have been my friends . . ." ("Barthes," 49–50). Thanks to the incomparable vision and devotion of Pascale-Anne Brault and Michael Naas, who collected fourteen texts Derrida wrote, as he writes, "following the death" of a friend, we, his friends, are now able, if indeed we are able, to *follow* him in too many senses of that word, including the most painful one: just following the death of the friend.[3] But we may also follow the thread of this public, published meditation on what he is doing right then, in 1981, and for the first time, he says. It is the first time he allowed himself to break a more or less secret promise never to do what he has just begun to do: "But what I thought impossible, indecent, and unjustifiable, what long ago and more or less secretly and resolutely I had promised myself never to do (out of a concern for rigor or fidelity, if you will, and because it is in this case *too* serious) was to write *following the death* . . . of those who while living would have been my friends" ("Barthes," 51).

Titled "The Deaths of Roland Barthes," Derrida's meditation follows the lead of this broken promise, of the need to yield to the impulse even as he highlights the treacherous terrain under the feet of anyone who crosses into it. The most irresponsible way to advance there would be to yield to one's impulse blindly, without interrogating it, without acknowledging at every step what is occurring at that moment of writing or speaking immediately following the death of the friend, of the one who can now be addressed only within oneself and who can respond only as the interiorized other who is no longer limited by the other him or herself, the external, "real," or absolute other. Derrida is thus tracing the outline of this sudden and terrible experience of being brought face-to-face so to speak with an interiorization at the moment it is wrested out of its correspondence—which may have been very close but just as likely, even more likely, very tenuous or even utterly at odds—with the other him or herself. He thus looks into himself at the very sore spot, the wound named Roland Barthes, at the place within him gathered under and by that name, which is now a bare name without bearer. It remains the name of someone who is now only within him and within all the others whom Barthes touched, from near and afar, his friends, first of all, but also through his oeuvre, all those readers for whom Roland Barthes will have always been a name detached from a bearer. Derrida does not here follow common sense or opinion insofar as it might suppose a sharp distinction between the interiorization that, on the one hand, a reader carries out from afar on coming into contact with only this writer's signature, name, and work, from the one that, on the other hand, Barthes's friends, lovers, or family might have nourished over a lifetime of contact with the man himself. This break with the common measure of proximity is one of the keys to following out the implications of Derrida's unfailing lucidity in describing and interrogating the experience of the other's death for *all* who survive, the nearest ones—*les proches*, as he would say in French—as well as those held at the furthest remove by all the mediations and media that can carry a name and an image around the world. And it is not just because, following a death, there is no longer any difference to be measured in distance from or nearness to the now-absent other, given that the distance is now equally infinite, if one can say that. As was pointed out a moment ago following the remarks on the impossible experience of Romeo and Juliet, *already* before the event of the other's disappearance, and whether he or she is the lover or only the signatory encountered through a text's mediation, there will have been an interiorization that prepares the survival of each one by the other.

The surviving structure of names, indeed of all language or all marks as traces of iterability, has been one of the most consistent, indeed obsessive currents running from one end to the other of Derrida's work. It is set out starkly in his earliest writings, for example in *Speech and Phenomema* (1967) where the assertion "I am dead" is analyzed as the condition of possibility of the functioning of language as such and becomes one of the wedges driven into Husserl's theory of the indexical sign, and above all of the sign "I." One realizes, therefore, regarding Derrida's claim in 1981 to have broken for the first time his promise to himself never to write *following* the death of a friend, that this is both true, in the most poignant sense, but also not strictly the case, if one follows up the other senses of "following" that lead back to all the myriad ways he approached and solicited the structure of the name itself as, from the moment it is given, at birth, that which begins to survive and to function without the bearer.

But it is also risky to follow him as he follows others after the event of their death. Unlike Derrida, who can follow Barthes into the latter's texts only so far and then must mark, however discreetly and generously, intervals of difference from him (for example, as regards precisely their sharply divergent analyses of the assertion "I am dead," which Barthes wants to understand as being "literally, according to the letter, foreclosed" ["Barthes," 64]), unlike Derrida, then, who, in this meditation at least, is able to catch a foothold on certain disagreements that jut out from those texts by Barthes he cites and to which he returns here, my own return to *The Work of Mourning* risks finding no such footing with which to brace against the fall that following can also become. For if I follow him here, if I am a follower of Derrida, that is because he is still teaching me everything needed to confront the experience into which we are plunged following his death. Jacques Derrida *was* and *is* my teacher, and I am still learning every day from what he wrote and what he writes.

To break the fall, then, I will tell a brief story about Derrida the teacher.

When I returned from Paris after Jacques's funeral, the most pressing task was the preparation of a weekly seminar two days later. Not only was it hard to concentrate on the texts assigned for the week's discussion, these became, as Barthes might say, *literally* unreadable: sentences and paragraphs failed to make patterns of sense, or else they would stay but an instant in memory and then plunge into a strange oblivion that was accompanied by a quasi-physical sensation of vertigo. Several hours before the seminar was due to convene, I gave up the effort and turned to Jacques for help. I began to reread passages from *The Work of Mourning*, but now for the first time following Derrida's death. Then, not only did my dyslexic vertigo immediately dissipate, but I experienced the sharpest clarity surrounding every word on the page, as if these were backlit and their outlined contour unmistakably defined against a dark ground. I resolved (but, truth to tell, there was little choice) that the seminar would read a few passages from this book. Thus it was that, a few hours later, teaching happened and at a level that I will forever envy from now on. I say I envied it since I less conducted the experience than submitted to it and received it from the one who one day wrote, in the opening sentence of *Spectres de Marx*, using the most spectral voice or rather voices, at least two: "Quelqu'un, vous ou moi, s'avance et dit: *Je voudrais apprendre à vivre enfin*" (*Specters*, xvii).

The wish here formulated, by someone, you or me, is forever untranslatable and indeed undecidable, between teaching and learning to live. The voice(s) say(s) at once, at the same time: "I would like to teach how to live/ I would like to learn how to live" (and, after all, what else is there to teach or to learn?). The two wishes or desires indissolubly spoken together give a figure of what teaching/learning to live will have to have been if indeed the experience, the one and the other experience, has ever happened. It will have happened, if it ever did, to one and to the other, undecidably and at once, as teaching to/learning from, in an asymmetrical relation that is never simply reversible without remainder.

At some point in this experience, I could never say exactly when, the decision was made, not by me but somewhere in me, that for the upcoming "Legacies of Theory" colloquium, I had to try to write a different paper than the one already announced, the one that was half finished when, at almost exactly midnight in California between 8 and 9 October, I received the phone call bearing the news of Jacques's death. This decision precipitated out as the question of how to honor, now, following Jacques Derrida, my commitment.

I was surely not the only one visited by such a question. Nevertheless, I will add just a little more about my own experience, as we say so blithely, as if "my own" experience were mine alone, without reliance on all manner of interiorized others who, all along, in his or her own way, will have been teaching me how to live. Which is not to claim, not at all, that I have ever yet learned what that means.

The paper I had projected to present on that occasion had the title "Experienced Theory" and would have set out (and here I cite an abandoned draft)

> from the observation that the idea or concept of experience has been subjected to a great deal of pressure in the last few decades, a pressure brought to bear from a number of directions. Above all, however, it has been exerted by philosophers and thinkers who have also given us a lot of grist for that mill called "theory," the legacies of which we are here to interrogate and to measure. (That the term "theory" and its common uses often functions as a machine for grinding up ideas, or even for making a mush of them, has to complicate our present task, which is already quite complicated as it is.) I say that the idea of experience has undergone pressure so as to give an image of what I will be attempting to describe or demonstrate in what follows, which is that experience has experienced a transformation, more precisely, a deconstruction that has given this notion an altogether different shape from either its familiar and common-sense one or the shape it had assumed over the last 350 years or so in a systematic philosophical tradition, there being finally perhaps only a negligible difference on this score between philosophy and so-called common sense.[4] To stay with this pressurized image for just a moment longer, what I convey with it is the sense in which the concept of experience has been bent out of shape, emptied, under pressure, of both its familiar and philosophical "contents." This emptied concept-container, however, has neither been refilled nor discarded; rather it has been pressed into use in a wholly different shape that defies any simple outlining of its edges or borders, thus any resemblance whatsoever to a container. . . . All of the work fed into the theory mill over the last thirty years or so can, I believe, be read as revising significantly, from one angle or another, the notion of experience and not just the notion or the idea of it, but the very experience of experience.

This unfinished paper then went on to announce the plan to pass a thread through different places in the writings of Benjamin, Levinas, and Derrida. Essentially, what remained unwritten at midnight on 8/9 October was the final section on Derrida. The passages lined up from his works were all moments at which the term "experience" was claimed and assumed despite or beyond its heavy philosophical legacy from the empiricists on, but especially as freighted and burdened by its passage through the hands of Kant, Hegel, and Husserl. I argued that Levinas, for his part, had more or less renounced the term rather than risk provoking a relapse of understanding into the subject-centered concept of experience inherited from phenomenology. And then I wanted to show how Derrida, by contrast, worked no less at displacing this inheritance, which is well known, but also how he was quite manifestly unwilling to give up the word "experience" itself. *Il y tenait*, I would have said in French, an expression that can mean at once he was fond of it, he insisted on it, and he held onto it. But in his hands and through his work of displacement, "experience" would now name first of all experience of the impossible, a phrase that he often reverts to when reaching for a gloss on deconstruction: deconstruction, in other words, the experience of the impossible.

I will cite just one such glossing moment, which is also particularly relevant to the topic of legacy since it asks how one inherits what in any case must always be inherited, but necessarily not just any which way. As Derrida often affirmed, most insistently perhaps in *Specters of Marx*, a legacy is also a decision, a selection, an election, a choice, a responsibility taken. In the later text where the following passage occurs, Derrida has just laid out, very succinctly, the new "logic" of forgiveness that depends on thinking the conditions of its unconditionality. And then he asks:

> What would it mean to "inherit" a tradition under these conditions, from the moment one thinks on the basis of this tradition, in its name, certainly, but precisely *against it in its name*, against the very thing that tradition believed had to be saved to survive while losing itself? Again the possibility of the impossible: a legacy would only be possible where it becomes impossible. This is one of the possible definitions of deconstruction—precisely as legacy. I once suggested as much: deconstruction might perhaps be "the experience of the impossible." ("As If," 352)[5]

The last phrase in quotation marks is followed by a footnote that sends us to a passage from another text, "Psyche: Invention of the Other," which concludes: "If the force and the desire of deconstruction have a significance, it is a certain experience of the impossible . . . the experience of the other as the invention of the impossible, or in other words, the only possible invention" ("Psyche," 36).

So I would have wanted to show how Derrida holds onto the vessel-term experience in order to fill it with what he calls the impossible, or else the "perhaps" ("this experience of the 'perhaps' . . . the experience of what arrives [*happens*] . . .)" ("As If," 344) or else the "as if" ("As If," 353) or else cinders ("this experience of incineration which is experience itself" [*Points*, 209]), and the list could be extended. The constant is the word itself, which is retained but in order to let be heard the unheard-of in its legacy, Derrida thereby doing what he points to above as thinking "on the basis of this tradition, in its name, certainly, but precisely *against it in its name*." He inherits the term and the thinking of experience just as he says one must always inherit anything: by selecting and accepting the risk of active interpretation.

I select just one more of the notes I had taken in preparation for the unfinished paper. It is a passage that affirms Derrida's affection for the word itself. In response to an interviewer's proposal of several different words with which to designate his "route, path, adventure, experience, trajectory," and after some hesitation, Derrida responds: "I rather like the word experience whose origin evokes traversal, but a traversal with the body, it evokes a space that is not given in advance but that opens as one advances. The word experience, once dusted off and reactivated a little, so to speak, is perhaps the one I would choose" (*Points*, 207).

This, then, was some of the raw material I had thought to stitch together under the title "Experienced Theory." Little did anyone know that the experience awaiting us would be the one called mourning, in its most wounding aspect. Especially painful and vertiginous because we now mourn the one who taught/learned how to live in the mourning that dawns with every relation to the other. And how to love life and living not despite but because of the fact that it mourns itself in us from the first given word.

Epilogue I

Although it would have been preferable to stop there, "events dictated otherwise." I yield to this cliché out of weakness, even as my whole being protests against the notion that these epilogic "events" are worthy of the name. No, rather, this epilogue or aftermath is dictated by those mediatic practices whereby the recording of events cannot be distinguished from the forming, fashioning, and shaping of them as the events that they then "are," at least for the moment, for the day of the daily journal.

With their reaction to the event of the sudden death of Jacques Derrida, many public media displayed even less than their customary circumspection in this regard. If distaste did not prevent it, many examples could be cited especially from US and British print media. It was dispiriting, to say the least, that so few journalistic publications hesitated even a whit to repeat someone or other's "interpretation" in the guise of recording this event. And then there were, there still are, all the pages of signed commentaries gladly and generously turned over by these publications to just about anyone willing to rush into print with an opinion or even with mere trivia. There is one noticeable and all but total exception to this welcome extended to all sorts of articles and op eds in the days, weeks, and months following Derrida's death: almost no one of those whom the newspapers would probably call "experts," that is, those who have long accompanied with interest Derrida's work and given it resonance in their own writing or teaching—and they are legion throughout the world, easily thousands just in the English-speaking world alone—virtually none of whom was solicited to write or even to comment for these daily publications upon the event. One may well ask why.

(Because this might sound like a complaint flavored by sour grapes, I must hasten to correct it. First of all, I do not underestimate what would have been for me and for many others an insuperable difficulty, indeed a torture, had we been pressed into writing on this infinitely sad event, which is why I admire all the more those few who found the serenity necessary to write for the mainstream English-language media and speak out quickly with warmth and understanding of Derrida's work. One must admire no less their generous will to communicate this understanding to those "non-specialist" readers or listeners that our public media imagine to be their only audience. Second, I too was solicited by a journalist from the *Chronicle of Higher Education* for an "interview," to which I submitted although not without regret once I saw the selection and reframing of my remarks in print.)

I will cite no further examples. Instead, I want merely to extend the question with which I more or less began, by posing it now *to, or at least about* this aftermath.

When it was asked "what need is there to write or speak following the death" of someone, it was perhaps understood that the question was addressed only to those nearby, *les proches*, near and far, in their need, if it is one, to bring words to bear on an irremediable disappearance and silencing. The point in asking the question, I said, would not be to resist or refuse such speech, but to examine the impulse so as not to yield to it too blindly. For the risks are, as Derrida warned and feared, very grave. Nothing less than the friend and other within oneself is at stake, his or her habitation as companion and witness of the life remaining, from then on, under his or her purview. All distance abolished, there remains only this: the life remaining under the other's purview, within me, within you, at whatever distance, now forever immeasurable.

But still, given that the risks are so serious, why take them? It is not just, as Derrida also suggests in his meditation following the death of Barthes, because silence "would be another wound, another insult" ("Barthes," 50). Another sentence, or rather a grammatically incomplete and thus ambiguous phrase from the same text appears to come closer to an answer: "To write—to him, to present to the dead friend the gift of his innocence" ("Barthes," 44). Everything trembles in this phrase in the infinitive mode without subject, suspended as an act of address never to be confirmed at arrival, a pure address "to the dead friend within oneself." To the question: what need is there to write following the death of the friend, it answers with what can also be heard as an imperative, a command. It is the command to write to the other, that is, to present to him within oneself, to the companion who is not accompanying me, the gift of his innocence. (And here, no less than anywhere else in his writings, one goes far astray if one understands the verb "to write" solely in a restricted, "literal," linguistic sense—in the sense of what I appear to be doing here, for example.)

Is this command "to write" one that can be heard and followed only within a circle of friends, whether near or far? What about all that gets written and said from neither near nor far, neither close nor distant, in other words, from the place that passes or stands in for the self-styled neutral, factual, or objective discourse that takes daily or weekly shape as the public record of journalism? Should not the same questioning admonition also be addressed *to, or at least about* it, that is, to or about this very public form of writing? But, one may well wonder, to what end, to what purpose? For, as the aftermath at issue illustrates all too clearly and unambiguously (but the full dossier of evidence would be massive and would not date from just yesterday): daily journalism, especially but not only in English-speaking countries, actively forecloses any channel that could open it to precisely this kind of inquiry.

As regards Derrida, his work, and the work he inspired, this foreclosure institutes itself on the "ground" of a few unchallenged articles of faith, relentlessly repeated: deconstructive thought is impossibly, deliberately, infuriatingly obscure, and/or simply frivolous, without pertinence for the urgent concerns of the day, and/or responsible for countless ills besetting us today . . . and so forth and so on. Newspapers, of course, have no trouble at all finding academic "experts" willing to intone these articles of faith and thereby renew the expiration date on the alibi or excuse that maintains the foreclosure in place. It little matters to these newspapers' editors that such self-designated experts openly and even proudly declare their ignorance of more than just a few sentences of the offending bodies of work. Such flagrant disregard for basic journalistic deontology apparently raises no alarm in the closed rooms where it is regularly given a pass, where eyes are collectively closed, so that yet another blessing may be conferred on the impacted pact blocking news from elsewhere.

No one was more lucid, incisive, and tireless in analyzing all of this willful blindness to the practices of journalistic foreclosure than Jacques Derrida.[6] His vigorous engagement with such questions never flagged, despite the almost constant onslaught the media waged against his own work and that of others who associated themselves with it, a level of unremitting and unjustifiable hostility that would have discouraged long ago any less courageous thinker. Throughout this engagement, he never abandoned an ethics of writing, an inviolable respect for the work of others, including those with whom he disagreed profoundly.[7] This elementary respect was extended even on the rare occasions when he felt he had to respond in print to enemies who openly declared themselves as such by attaching his name or his work to something they wished to attack. His responses on such occasions could be withering, devastating, but they did not leave any doubt that what was in dispute was a signed piece of writing, rather than the person of the one who signed it and whose signature engaged every reader of it in a relation to the signatory's future death that it already declares. The structure of the name and of the signature, as we were recalling a moment ago, dictates, should dictate respect for the grave act of writing about another, whether or not it is upon and immediately following his or her death.

It is, then, this entire reflection on any writer's responsibilities that is foreclosed, blocked from all possible interaction or interference with journalism's own reflection on its ordinary practices. Clearly the key deontological principle of "objectivity" or "neutrality" is a hopelessly compromised tool, indeed a useless one unless it is an alibi, since it cannot prevent invidious abuse of public discourse even on that grave occasion when newspapers and other media take it as their responsibility to write following the death of persons of note and importance. Called obituaries, such writing might seem to be a very limited and specific genre, unless, by thinking about it with Jacques Derrida's help, one unblocks understanding of how all writing, discourse, speech, and in general, all work, all forms of oeuvre of whatever sort that carry a signature, or even what is called a byline, are testamentary. All are legacies that also inherit, and they never take a graver risk of violent appropriation than when they dare to countersign the legacy of another. Quite clearly, then, this form of writing is not in the least confined to our daily newspapers, and for that we can only be grateful. We should be grateful, that is, that public writing or speaking is not confined under the premises and promises of putative principles of "objectivity" or "neutrality," which finally open journalistic discourse to abuse even more than they underwrite its validity.

Perhaps, then, alongside the risk, there is also a chance to reaffirm the responsibility that falls to all those who, unlike most journalists, can refuse the foreclosures and still hold open the texts that call upon one to inherit a thinking of inheritance. If so, then it is a chance to be taken without complacency before the magnitude of what is engaged whenever one writes or speaks following another, in another's wake. Which is to say and whether one acknowledges it or not, the responsibility that is always and everywhere engaged, for—this is the specter Derrida conjured up so as to learn to teach how to live—there is *literally* no other place but in the wake of others from which to write, speak, and sign. The specter teaches that this inescapable, irremediable condition does not dawn with the sunless day of mourning, even if one may be forgiven for thinking so when a sudden, unexpected eclipse wrenches thought into this dark light, out of the slumber that seals spirit.

Epilogue II

I have never felt less sheltered from the purview of the true friend who tells you your own truth, from that place to which, *from now on more than ever*, is granted the last word, within me as within every friend, near and far, within all who now harbor the genial spirit who brings the future:

> He looks at us. *In us.* He looks in us. The witness sees in us. And from now on more than ever. ("Barthes," 161)

Notes

1. See *Politics*, esp. Chapter 1.
2. Organized by Karyn Ball, Kir Kuiken, Michael O'Driscoll, and Massimo Verdicchio at the University of Alberta.
3. Among the twenty or so identified conventional uses of the verb "follow," the *OED* singles out a funereal sense: "To attend (the body of a deceased person) to the grave; (*colloq.*) to attend a person's funeral. Also *absol.*"
4. "Experience in the classical, philosophical, and usual senses (all the same) . . ." ("Speculate," 290).
5. On legacy, inheritance, and so forth, see Elizabeth Rottenberg's very fine introduction to *Negotiations*, "Inheriting the Future," where she cites this passage from another chapter in the volume: "whoever inherits chooses one spirit rather than another. One makes selections, one filters, one sifts through the ghosts or through the injunctions of each spirit. There is legacy only where assignations are multiple and contradictory, secret enough to defy interpretation, to carry the unlimited risk of active interpretation. It is here that a decision and a responsibility can be taken ('The Deconstruction of Actuality')" (*Negotiations*, 6).
6. The references here would be very numerous and would include: "Call It a Day for Democracy" in *Heading*; "*Le Monde*—on the Telephone," in *Points*, and "Journalists." See also above Chapter 1 "Tape-Recorded

Surprise" for an analysis of some aspects of Derrida's critical engagement with the journalistic interview.

7. In this regard, see Derrida's postface to his debate with John Searle, "Afterword."

Chapter 6

La Morsure

It is very hard to select what to say here, in a few minutes, that could be worthy of this occasion, in this place, which means above all worthy of the one we remember today with such sadness in our souls—with, as one says in French, *la mort dans l'âme*.[1] My memory of Jacques Derrida is so vast and so deep that I can hardly recall the flavor of my life before I first met him, in January 1974, in Paris.

I was then a graduate student starting a dissertation on Rousseau, which had been set in motion, a few years earlier, when I read *De la grammatologie*. That January in 1974, I began to attend Jacques's seminar at the École Normale—on Kant's Third Critique—as well as a special seminar for students from Johns Hopkins, Cornell, and SUNY Buffalo on Nietzsche's *Zarathustra*. I felt especially lost in the latter context, disoriented and uncertain at every moment. It remains, therefore, a great mystery to me how it happened that, one day in the *Zarathustra* seminar—it must have been in March or so—after Jacques proposed the theme of "la morsure" as a good subject for an oral presentation, I responded, before twenty or more witnesses, that I would do it the following week. *La morsure,* in other words: the bite. Jacques floated this suggestion for anyone to bite at. He knew, he must have known, that the word could lead one very far indeed into Nietzsche's text, but also that the paths in and out again were infinitely singular, each time, each path following some desire and according to the shape of a particular wound, to a reality bite that had drawn blood.

This was my first and most determining experience of Derrida's enormous power as a teacher, the power to elicit another's response, without the least appeal to the authority of knowledge, in absolute freedom, therefore, relying only on the unspoken, unavowable strictures of whatever makes anyone want to speak and to respond. It is a teaching that finally renounces all foreknowledge, that consigns and entrusts itself to a future, and thus to the other. A teaching of the future, from the future, of the unknown, and for an untold time yet to come.

La morsure: if thirty years ago Jacques's word had the power to sting me, to awaken the wounded desire to live and to respond, today it is the homophonic echo within that word of a two-word phrase, *la mort sûre*, certain death, that leaves the most evident teeth marks on memory. But these were already and always sunk deep into his word and his thought. His teaching of the future, from the future, never flinched from *affirming*—yes, affirming—that to certain death we are all consigned; it is thus what signs and binds together, as precisely the most wounding event of singularity and of singular friendship. His teaching has always offered the chance to respond with life, for life, for the life of *la mort sûre*, of certain death. And to learn why that is not a contradiction.

My friendship with Jacques Derrida was sealed on that day in March 1974 and, for my part at least, it has never wavered. I cannot, of course, speak for Jacques, now less than ever, but by telling you that my friendship for him never thereafter looked back, I confess as well my belief that neither did his for me. For that was the very nature of what was sealed and consigned: a belief in the friend, which was and remains the belief that thereafter, henceforth, *désormais*, he would always believe me, believe in me.

And yet, I also remember, on one of the few occasions, years later, when we evoked together our separate memories of the event I have just recounted, Jacques gave me some pause about my own reliability as the friend whom he began to address on that day in 1974. On one of these occasions, I told him I recalled that after my presentation, in the course of his generous response to it, he had referred to me as "la mordue," that is, she who has been bitten. His reaction when I reminded him of this remark was strenuous, almost indignant denial: "I never said that, I would never have said that," he protested. This reaction made me not only doubt my own recollection, but also wonder at whatever phantasm of mine could have inserted retrospectively such an erroneous word in his mouth. Impossible to doubt, however, was the evidence of yet another homophonic phrase buried in *la mordue*, that ill-remembered epithet, which Jacques was certain, with the certainty of friendship, he could not have pronounced on that day or any other. *La mort dûe*: death owed, death deserved, death paid back. No doubt, this is what he never could or would have said, not just to a friend, but never to or concerning any mortal. *La mort sûre*, certain death, yes, but *la mort dûe*, no, never: no death, ever, is due, deserved, owed.

That was, I must think, his certainty, the certain conviction of his life and the life he taught so many others to embrace. I expect that here, at UC Irvine, many will recognize this conviction as that of the first philosopher in the Western tradition to make a philosophical, and not just personal, argument against the sovereign right to impose the death penalty, in other words: *la mort dûe*.[2] We were many who had the privilege of being in attendance right here at that event in Jacques's seminar on "Death Penalties."

One more word and I will conclude. Although we are here, in principle, among Jacques's friends, even as many of these are missing, and although we have all listened long and hard—and with great gratitude—to Jacques's seminars, lectures, and conversations as they were conducted here, in this very room, I still fear somewhat that I have risked leaving a wrong impression. Have not my recollections just confirmed caricatures of the man elsewhere described, so prevalently, as a mere word-player, one who was so wrapped up in language he could no longer touch the very stuff of life or of reality? My testimony—for that is what each of us is putting forward here—would bear witness to just the opposite, that is, to the fact that none more than Jacques Derrida remained awake and attuned to life's reality as it is consigned to the ordinary and common language stigmatizing every experience, however banal. I learned from Jacques that I was indeed bitten by life, by death, and that whoever opens her mouth to speak and to respond spreads the lips of the shared, but still so singular wound.

Notes

1. This is the text of remarks read at the memorial for Jacques Derrida at University of California, Irvine, on 3 December 2004.
2. See below, Chapter 16, The Philosopher, As Such, and the Death Penalty.

Chapter 7

"One day someone . . ."

One day someone may make an inventory of the conferences, symposia, and colloquia, throughout the world, that were concerned with Derrida's work and at which he was present as an interlocutor. These would probably number in the hundreds. Countless, then, would be all those who had the chance to receive the generosity of his thought when, as so frequently happened, he was called upon to engage others in public discourse. I heard many such exchanges in the last twenty-five years, beginning in the summer of 1980 with a ten-day colloquium at Cerisy-la-Salle in Normandy, France. There were three more "décades Derrida" at Cerisy—in 1992, 1997, and 2002—which remains an unprecedented series in the history of this legendary conference center. I also attended or participated in numerous other events, and can now reflect on some of the reasons for which Derrrida was repeatedly sought out in a public forum.

I have mentioned his generosity, an attribute invariably cited to characterize his response to interlocutors. But I believe this recognition arises from the experience of something altogether unlike ordinary ideas of generosity. It was certainly not the experience in the vicinity of the "great man" whose greatness is such he can bestow tokens on lesser mortals without diminishing his own store, indeed while adding to his reputation for generosity. As the greatest thinker today, or in any age, of the paradoxes of the gift, and as pitilessly lucid as he was about his own or anyone else's "greatness," one may be sure Derrida was not easily deluded about the endless ruses of narcissistic calculation. He showed why a gift, if it is possible, must be impossible as the experience of any subject, giver or givee. This is an impossibility, however, that he thought affirmatively—generously—for, as he wrote, "if the gift is another name of the impossible, we still think it, we name it, we desire it. We intend it. . . . Perhaps there is nomination, language, thought, desire, or intention only where there is this movement still for thinking, desiring, naming that which gives itself to be neither known, experienced, nor lived" (*Time*, 29). His generosity, I would say, expanded the room for this movement of thought, desire, and naming; it happened time and again in all of those hundreds of conference rooms when he was there listening, responding, "thinking, desiring, naming." His presence, in other words, was expansive.

Another quality of the man which may have led many to repeat their encounters with him was his gaze. To look him in the eyes was to see someone seeing you see, which sounds a bit dizzying, and perhaps it was, but I would say rather that one had then the physical sensation of trembling in the awareness of being more-than-one to see. His gaze held yours, did not let it disappear into the merely seen or looked at of an object of perception. Wordlessly his eyes said: you are another, altogether other, looking now at me. This quality of the gaze was neither transfixing nor piercing, but once again expansive and moving. It moved one into the open space where one's own look does not return to itself and can never see itself. In the extraordinary text Derrida wrote for the Louvre in 1990, *Memoirs of the Blind: The Self-portrait and Other Ruins*, his analysis, which is also a self-portrait, pursues the hypothesis that the central trait of every self-portrait is blindness. The blind man or woman would thus be the supreme figure of the artist. Derrida, whose gaze seemed to see without end, also saw the blind man in or as himself. And that is perhaps what made his gaze so touching, a quality that remains visible or sensible even in many photographs of him. I do not mean touching in the weak sentimental sense, but in the sense of the sense of touch, a gaze or eyes that touched one as if they were fingers. His great text on the sense of touch at the heart of the work of his friend Jean-Luc Nancy begins with just such an image, in the form of a phrase that, he writes, invaded and touched him before he saw it coming: "When our eyes touch, is it day or is it night?" (*Touching*, 2). This astonishingly beautiful book, which is an immense deconstructive retouching of the tradition of discourse on the five senses, sets out from the question that this image-phrase provokes in the one it has invaded. He asks: "let's see, can eyes manage to touch, first of all, to press together like lips?" (ibid.). He who pretends to ask that question would surely have known that, yes, they could—and they did.

I will mention one last trait about the immeasurable radius of Derrida's radiance at the gatherings his work made happen and will doubtless continue to make happen for a long time to come, although—and this is our enormous loss—without his voice or his gaze, and without his laughter. His taste for laughter never seemed to fail him, except when he addressed those who gathered upon the death of a friend. On all other occasions, and indeed in all his writings, laughter punctuates even the most serious discussions. Laughter was rarely a subject or theme of analysis for him; it was more like a sustaining tone always running in the background. All of the public events with Jacques that I recall, including all the weekly seminars I attended in Paris or at UC Irvine, were visited by bursts of laughter, usually provoked by his own exuberant sense of wonderful absurdities and ironies or by his incomparable attention to the surprises of language. With each outburst, one sensed his immense joy in being alive to and with others.

How fortunate are all those with whom he shared that joy. How much we will miss him from now on.

Chapter 8

The Affect of America

My remarks are going to be somewhat personal.[1] I do not mean I am preparing to talk about myself, at least not much. Rather, I want to say something about Jacques Derrida's personal America. Many attempts have been made to characterize the intense relations that, forty years ago, began evolving between Derrida's work and his readers (or non-readers) in the US, relations mediated in very complex ways by the body of his writing, by its reception and translation, by the different institutions or traditions that welcomed or resisted it, and so forth. Instead of another attempt in that general direction, I thought I would try to address the topic of "Derrida's America" in a less, or rather differently mediated sense by saying something about his affective relation to the US. Certainly this is hardly less complex, if only because affect can rarely be assigned to a positive or negative pole without admixture. But there is also the complication—if indeed one can call it that—introduced when someone presumes to be able to talk about another's affective experience in order to say what this other feels or felt, the quality of his affect, what has affected him, and how. This ought to be not just complicated but impossible, practically and morally, or rather ethically. To think it is not impossible is to yield too complacently to the biographer's temptation and to the belief that whatever obstacles there may be in the way of putting oneself in the other's place can be swept aside by dint of good will. Derrida is especially vigilant about the risk of this complacency; he never lets one forget that the others he writes about are constituted by that writing as *texts*, that is, as folded layers of sign-traces offered up to interpretation. To say that the other is encountered as text not only makes all ethics an ethics of reading, but also thereby recalls that the other person is not, first of all or above all, a potential site of knowledge that I can appropriate, at least not without leveling all that makes that other other. Even with those who have been or seemed the closest companions of his life's intellectual adventures, Derrida never relaxes his vigilance in this regard and especially with those friends whom one might presume he knows well; he never ceases, for example, to wonder how they experience what affects them.[2]

And yet, it is also true that, as regards so many of his own experiences, Derrida speaks freely and, in his writings, even appears to seek a kind of absorption by language of the excesses of experience that overflow the ordinary vessels of words, compelling him to reinvent the shared medium of meaning. Some such image has often described the gift of the poet, but in Derrida the poet cannot be distinguished from the philosopher, and likewise the gift or task of inventing a language cannot be distinguished from the work of formalizing, generalizing, conceptualizing that invention and its conditions. One could cite countless examples, indeed every text bearing Derrida's signature, for this is one of its principal characteristics. I will mention just *Circumfession* or "A Silkworm of One's Own" to index what I mean by an excess of experience, its unplumbable singularity or idiomaticity, that drives this writing constantly to reinvent itself or to let itself be reinvented within a general language.

With texts like those just mentioned, Derrida has seemingly given a certain philosophical establishment ample provocation to dismiss what he is doing on the grounds that it is clearly not philosophy but either autobiography or poetry or some unstable mixture of the two. For does not the singular experience of the philosopher himself or herself name the category of everything that the project of philosophy demands be set aside, bracketed, studiously ignored? And if it appears that someone writing as a philosopher has not ignored all this, well then, whatever he or she puts forward may be considered of little worth for the rest of those laboring in the fields of general, philosophical truth because it will have been corrupted or contaminated by the merely empirical, contingent, finite, or particular. Derrida, however, does not simply fly in the face of this prohibition but advances, in conceptual or quasi-conceptual terms, a thinking of contamination in general. He thus raises the stakes considerably for the profession of philosophy, which, even as he displaces what we can profess to hear and understand by "profession," he never renounces, vigorously defends, and tirelessly renews through his teaching.[3] At stake from now on, for all those who have learned it from and with Derrida, is not only the possibility of distinguishing philosophy from all it professes to exclude (literature, poetry, autobiography, individual experience, the singular idiom, and so on), but also the possibility of "personal," that is, singular experience uncontaminated by repetition and generalization, by substitution and metonymy. For this is perhaps the greater scandal of Derrida's thought insofar as it flaunts the exclusion of singular experience or affect from the realm of general truth: his work shows us how to read that distinction as a barrier that has protected not just the idea of truth's generality but also—and perhaps above all, for each and every philosopher no less than everyone else—that of the propriety or property of one's own experience, of experience as, in the ordinary expression, irreducibly "personal," and thus inaccessible to another. With his thinking of differance and general contamination, substitution, and metonymy, Derrida makes or rather lets the distinction between self/not-self, ownness/otherness, as well as generality/singularity tremble and blur, a trembling and blurring that, he would argue, is the irremediable condition of what one wants to call, so as to appropriate it, one's "own" experience.

But I seem to have been led off the track, and what is worse, to have backed into a blatant contradiction. For did I not just say that another's experience and affect have to remain unknowable in their singular unrepeatability? Yes, certainly, as such and by itself, by definition, the singular does not repeat; its time is "one time only," without possibility of coming back, starting over, and over. And yet, by the same token, singular unrepeatabilty would always be lost, utterly and irretrievably lost, unless its trait *at the same time* can also be repeated, reiterated, remembered. This is true not only "for the record," for example, the biographer's record of another's life experience, but already and ineluctably for the "one" (in quotation marks because it is indeed "oneness" along with "ownness" that is thrown into question by the necessary repetition of singularity) whose experience it supposedly *is*, but that it *is*, in the present, only on the condition of coming back, returning, and repeating as the experience it never was in any past present. Readers of Freud's *Beyond the Pleasure Principle* and the studies of trauma spawned by that text (written in the immediate aftermath of the killing fields of World War I) may recognize in the description of this temporal torsion or distortion, as well as in a certain compulsion to repeat, an essential affinity between what is identified and singled out as trauma and what is here being summarized about Derrida's thinking of experience in general. Experience is traumatic or has the structure of what can be analyzed as trauma, as Derrida has said somewhere pretty much in those terms. And this is true no less of a "happy" experience—e.g., falling in love—than of a devastatingly "unhappy" one.[4]

The figure of singularity is thus what bids, appeals, or calls for a repetition in order to "be" the singularity that, therefore, it is—not. Close to the heart of Derrida's thought and work is the affirmation of this very contradiction, an inheritance in part from Nietzsche's affirmative thinking of the eternal recurrence of the same. Within Nietzsche's affirmation, Derrida hears and amplifies the call to repeat as having necessarily to be *addressed* to another, to others, and thereby dispatched into differance, dissemination, deferral, *without* guarantee of arrival at destination. It is this "without" that Derrida affirms, not or at least not simply in its privative sense, but as the very condition of repetition. "My" experience returns to me, recurs to me, if it does, as the experience of another, at once another "me" and absolutely other, uncanny therefore. After Derrida, the category of the uncanny, no less than that of trauma, spreads and thus dissolves into the general structure of experience as extra-ordinary, where "extra-" marks an irreducible extra-dition or extra-diction outside the self, an extra-vagance, if you will, but one that would not so much exceed a pre-existing self's balanced economy as instigate and re-instigate what is called self.

These remarks are far too compact and elliptical. But they are meant merely as prologue. For I set out in what follows from the fact that, with his friends or even with strangers, many of whom would soon become friends, Derrida often confides details about his "own" experience. But one will not find in his writings extended accounts of his complex and long (almost 50-year) experience of or in "America,"[5] a fact that contrasts sharply with his frequent, painstaking, and often painful evocations (especially in *Circumfession*, but also *The Monolingualism of the Other* or "A Silkworm of One's Own") of childhood, adolescent, and family experiences in his birthplace, Algiers, which he left for the first time at age 19 in 1949. One might well say that this is natural or normal, given that infancy, childhood, and youth leave a deeper (more traumatic) mark than adult experiences.

I should make clear that it is not some American trauma, however one chooses to understand this term, that I am trying to reconstruct. Having accepted the assignment "Derrida's America," however, I could not help hearing a very wide range of the title's or topic's possible meanings, and thereby the mandate to choose from among them. In the circumstance, it is Derrida's own not-so-private America that came to the fore of my recollection, but at the same time, unavoidably, a hesitation, a scruple. For how can one justify repeating another's account of his experience, especially once he can no longer correct as need be any misunderstandings, exaggerations, *malentendus*, not to mention deliberate distortions or even wholesale inventions? Hence this prologue. Which, however, provides no guarantee that my recollections are not somewhere mistaken. Everything that follows should therefore be read under the sign of "perhaps."[6]

* * *

I have the good fortune of following my friend Michael Naas, who has just recalled a great many of the most pertinent facts about Jacques

Derrida's career in America as a teacher, lecturer, and colleague.[7] There seems little left to add. One could ask, however, if it is indeed possible to set a limit on facts of a relation-to-America that someone would likely have had or been subjected to had he been born in 1930, especially anywhere within the sphere of "old Europe" and its old colonial powers. Like everyone, which is also to say unlike anyone else, Jacques Derrida begins to have a relation-to-America long before he happened to set foot there, in 1956, in Cambridge, Massachusetts, not far from the landfall of some earlier European pilgrims.

In 1943, when he was 13, Americans arrived in Algeria, part of the Allied forces that liberated Algiers, his native city. When Derrida speaks of witnessing these events, he seems a little bemused by the image of himself in this very-soon-to-be cliché-picture of the Yanks bringing baseball and chewing gum to the populations under their occupying authority. He recalls that his family became friendly with one GI, who came to their home a number of times and with whom letters were exchanged after the war, but then they stopped. I think he even still remembers the GI's name, but I cannot recall it.

His bemusement at these recollections is not easy to read. In 1942, right before the Allies landed and began to retake North Africa, he had been excluded from his *lycée* as a Jew, the result of an application of the so-called "Jewish laws" by the Vichy loyalists in Algeria. The Allied liberators, along with the new Free French regime they installed in Algeria, took their time canceling and reversing the effects of these laws. So perhaps he saw the liberators rather quickly, at age 13 (I now realize that these events would have coincided with the year of his bar mitzvah) as somewhat compromised heroes, at least in their—witting or unwitting—complicity with injustice. He has talked about the experience of his expulsion from school in so many different texts that there is little doubt about how deeply it affected him. And it would have been from the place of this wound that he witnessed and judged the promise of a new world.

But, of course, well before these events the New World had already sent some spectacular proxies to represent it and not only to Algiers or to Europe: I mean of course American movies. When he talks about going to the movies in his youth, however, his memory seems to evoke less the films he might have seen, than the places, the "movie palaces" that, like so many Western cities, Algiers saw sprout up between the wars. He especially remembers the names of the movie theaters, which I cannot recall but they were not unlike the names one would have found in other cities and that were so many exotic clichés: Rialto, Rex, or El Dorado. He likes to recollect the names but, it seems to me, they come back with bitter taste of a city divided by its colonial history and reality, where those "palaces" were located in a "European quarter" more or less officially off limits to the majority of the city's inhabitants.

Yet, if one were to try to reach all the way back to some first "fact" of Derrida's relation-to-America, then it would be necessary to back up even before the beginning of his own experience of America, whether through proxies or not. Indeed, one would have to reach back even before his birth. And it would be necessary to put a name to this fact, and even to locate it in a name, his name, not Jacques but Jackie, spelled like that, despite several rules of French onomastics. As he explains in *Circumfession*, in the milieu of his family between the wars, there was a vogue for giving children English (not particularly American) names, which were often nicknames in the culture they came from. Hence, Jackie Derrida. As with the names of the movie palaces, this given name would have been mixed up with the marks of social division, which is not to say he ever complains about it, not to me at least, even when we have conversations about the fact that I too was given a dimunitive for a first name which, unlike Jackie-Jacques, I did not have the good sense to set aside once I began signing things for publication. But I also notice that he seems unready to admit that his name has any link to the American child actor Jackie Coogan, although this reluctance may be just as well his caution at the idea that anyone's name ever comes from an identifiable donor or model. But of course one's parents have their own ideas about such things and act on their own impulses, perhaps never more so, as parents, than when they give their child a name.

Thanks to a brief sequence in the film *D'ailleurs Derrida,* which was first shown in 2000, it may be that one has now something like an image of the impulsive desire that accompanied this strange and fateful naming gesture, which would have taken place some time around 15 July 1930. The sequence is shot in the house in El Biar (a suburb of Algiers) where Derrida spent most of his childhood and youth. It is the same house his family had to abandon, with almost all its contents, in 1962 after the declaration of Algeria's independence. When it enters the house in 1999, the camera uncovers a few remnants of this abandonment that surprisingly have survived intact: above all, the mother's piano and hanging above it, most improbably, the framed movie poster of Charlie Chaplin's 1921 silent film *The Kid,* showing the little tramp towering protectively over the boy actor Jackie Coogan, who played the eponymous kid. The framed, enshrined poster clings to the wall like some miraculous castaway of a shipwreck, as if the house itself had kept safe the memory of a possible namesake, Jackie Derrida, and had issued to all who subsequently found shelter there an obscure command to preserve this image artifact.[8]

In signaling toward this mark of a certain relation-to-America that he must inherit or accept as one accepts a given name, I am suggesting that one has perhaps to retrace the "facts" to unconscious drives of prior generations. Derrida would doubtless be the first to encourage such a procedure. If so, then it becomes hard to think that there was not put in place in his very own name a kind of *draw* to America, if only unconsciously. I do not know why I say "only unconsciously," as if there were any more powerful force drawing one toward or away from the choices of a life.

To come or come back to 1956, which is where Michael Naas began his account with "just the facts": Jacques (who at the time, I suppose, was still called Jackie by everyone and not just by close family) recounts some traveling he did that year, when he and Marguerite rented or borrowed a car and drove through the American South towards I forget which destination. The Southern United States in the mid-1950s was still a very segregated place, although the US Supreme Court had begun to rule against the constitutionality of Jim Crow laws. Nevertheless, below the Mason-Dixon Line, public space remained very clearly and obviously segregated. Certainly anyone traveling there, but especially Europeans unused to these primitive customs and most especially those whose sensibilities had been sharpened by Algerian apartheid, would have remarked it. He remembers that they picked up an African-American hitchhiker, a sailor or soldier I think, in North or South Carolina I believe it was. The man they stopped for must have been quite astonished to be offered a ride by a white couple. Their hitchhiker seemed nervous, ill-at-ease in ways that Jacques and Marguerite were not sure they knew how to read. As I recall the story at least, no misfortune befell them, but doubtless their passenger was quite aware that the trip could have turned out very badly if they had had a run-in with local police. When Jacques returned to Cambridge and told his American friends about the experience, they let him know he had taken a considerable risk.

Following a kind of unconscious thread, I connect this story about the hitchhiker to a remark he says Paul de Man made to him at some point during their friendship, which began well after the driving trip through the South in 1956 or 1957. To judge by his laughter, he likes to repeat this remark, as if it flatters some idea he has of himself, in addition no doubt to the pleasure he takes in reviving the speech of his friend. Paul de Man told him that he, Jacques, spoke English "like a black sailor." I ask and he does not deny that what he especially likes is to be told he does not have a typical or caricatural French accent when he speaks

English as he so often must. Speaking English in public remains clearly a special kind of torture for him. There is above all the irreparable loss of his idiom, but also, despite his remarkable fluency and ease in the acquired language, a sense that his non-native accent exposes him, denudes him. It is very difficult, impossible in fact, to reassure him on this score. (Whenever he hears a fellow Frenchman speaking English with a typical, Maurice-Chevalier accent, he turns to whoever he is with and says "I don't sound like that, do I?") But finally perhaps it is not reassurance he seeks so much as an understanding of the generalized condition that he has called "the monolingualism of the other" and that he pins down in one of those incomparable aphorisms or watchwords for which he has always had a special genius: "I have only one language, it is not mine" (*Monolingualism*, 1).[9]

Even though it is not the language in which he prefers to communicate by any means, he has a keen ear for American English, for the idiomatic in our language that, as habitual speakers, we cease remarking. I think of two expressions in particular that he often isolates from the most humdrum conversations and reflects back to his interlocutors, as if he has a particular fondness for them and wants to restore the force of what they, what we are saying. First, to "look forward to" something. This expression often makes him smile. It is true that in French there is no equivalent idiom for marking one's eager anticipation of something promised, something to come. To be turned thus by a turn of speech toward the future is doubtless what he savors and wants to save for the unthinking native users of the language. Another turn of phrase that he frequently fishes out of our current of everyday exchange is the expression "take care," the phrase one often says upon leaving someone, as a sign-off in a letter, or at the end of telephone conversation: "Take care." Derrida remarks it, repeats it, and reflects it back, prompting each time a reflection on what exactly one is saying thereby: Take my care with you? Take it away from me?

To his fondness for these commonplaces of language, I would add a few words about Derrida's love of places in the US. Not just in the US of course, but his relation to America stands apart from the relation to other locales by virtue of the regular, annual repetition of his migration to the same places. Through long-standing associations with several universities, which cause him each year (and after a certain point, more than once a year) to return to the same cities or campuses, his relation to America is rhythmed by a movement of return, of revisiting that which he has already found to be to his taste, of re-tasting, re-finding what was once found: *des retrouvailles*, as he might say. This taste for return, for *retrouvailles*, is such that it cannot be satisfied in the abstract, in the mere knowledge that one is once more in a place called Baltimore, New Haven, New York, Irvine, Laguna Beach, Los Angeles, or Santa Monica. Instead, it requires a movement towards concrete landmarks, although these are only rarely marked in any tourist's guidebook. Rather, they are the same restaurants, the same corners in Central Park, the same cafés, the same streets or even the same shops in the same shopping malls.

Most frequently, I meet him in Irvine, California, where he began giving his annual seminar in 1987. Jacques often invites friends to dinner after the seminar, but there are not many restaurants to his liking in the vicinity of the university. There is one, however, to which he gladly returns and brings his friends: a Japanese restaurant called Koto not far from the campus. Few indeed are his visitors who are not brought to this pleasant place, to its interior courtyard with a koi pond and waterfall. Calm and inviting, quiet enough for conversation.

On 3 December 2004, a memorial took place in the same auditorium at UC Irvine where Jacques returned to give his seminar every Spring since 1987. Afterwards, Elisabeth Weber and I have the same impulse: to go back to Koto. We drive the short distance there . . . and find it closed. Out of business, by the looks of it. We cannot help thinking there is a certain justice in that.

Derrida is, in general, a very keen observer of the American public scene, of its politics, university, legal system, judicial system—one of his last seminars is on the death penalty and makes constant reference to capital punishment in the US—of religion in America, but also its eating habits (which he mostly deplores), child-raising customs, television, movies, violence, journalism, and so forth.

He is fascinated—I do not think the word is too strong—with the practice in the US of televising congressional hearings, with this particular form of public testimony. He watched hours of the so-called Iran/Contra hearings, broadcast I believe in 1987, thus at the end of the second Reagan administration. The hearings concerned the very shady financing of the Nicaraguan "Contras" and their rag-tag rebellion, propped up by CIA-filtered American money, against the legitimately elected Sandinista government. The scheme involved illegal US arm sales to Iran in exchange for the release of American hostages in Teheran, with the proceeds going to the Contras for the purchase of weapons. In short, a remarkably sordid affair, on which the televised hearings shed a certain amount of light. And from the way Jacques talks about the experience, it would seem he watched these broadcasts both with admiration for this very open democratic process, which exposes for all to see a government's crimes and deceptions ("Such hearings could never happen in France," I recall him saying), but also with a sense of the naïveté of American faith in legal procedure as a guardrail against the corruption of power.

These observations of a pervasive legalistic culture in America no doubt are fed into his own increasing reflection on concepts that straddle the domains of law, ethics, philosophy, and literature, such as truth-telling and testimony (and thus perjury or lying), pardon and forgiveness, as well as capital punishment. These concepts or practices not only set the program of his later seminars, but also numerous texts written in their vicinity. A few years ago I realized that I had translated in a fairly short interval several essays by Derrida that dealt with lying, perjury, forgiveness, excuses, cruelty, and the death penalty. I edited them in a volume that was eventually titled *Without Alibi*. The title comes from the volume's final essay, "Psychoanalysis Searches the States of Its Soul," which is scanned by a repetition of that phrase. All the essays make significant reference to the US: for example, "History of the Lie" devotes a long analysis to Hannah Arendt's writing on lying in politics and her famous article on the Pentagon Papers, while the essay titled "*Le parjure*"—perjury or the perjurer—deals principally with a novel by the French writer Henri Thomas that is set in America and models its principal character on the young Paul de Man in the first years after his arrival in the US. For these reasons, I had originally considered as a title for this collection: *What Lies in America*. My editor at the press was adamantly opposed, and no doubt rightly so, to my too-clever-by-half equivocation. Perhaps, however, it is not inappropriate to let that abandoned phrase come to rest (or lie) here, in these reflections on "Derrida's America."

Michael Naas has already underscored the important place Derrida allowed for religion in any understanding of "America," above all in its difference from the pervasive secularism of Europe. What always impresses itself upon him is that this importance has regularly to be marked and reaffirmed by its elected officials, who have been elected at least in part to perform this gesture in public and for the public. Long before a second President Bush began to play "the religion card" even more baldly than Jimmy Carter had dared to do, Derrida is heard to remark to American audiences or to friends in conversation that it is simply unimaginable for anyone to be elected President of the United States who is an *avowed* non-believer.

I emphasize the avowal, confession, or profession of faith—that is, the performance of a certain speech act—because I believe that this remark points above all to the pertinence he grants to categories of speech act theory for the analysis of politics, in America or elsewhere. Concepts from speech act theory become a nearly constant reference in his writings after 1971, the date of his famous essay on J. L. Austin, "Signature Event Context," whose seriously comic aftermath, *Limited Inc, abc . . .*, is provoked by a dyspeptic reply from the American philosopher John Searle. (Now that I think of it, *Limited Inc* offers one of Derrida's most sustained responses to "America," at least as impersonated by Searle in his earnest misprision of what is at stake in the deconstruction of certain of Austin's categories and assumptions.) Another American philosopher, Richard Rorty, will have been one of the few to acknowledge the proximity of Derrida's thought to that of American pragmatists.[10] And yet it is with reference more to Nietzsche than to Peirce, James, or Dewey that Derrida accepted on several occasions to call his thinking *pragmatics*, leaving the "ism" of pragmatism to whoever finds it indispensable to adjudicate between schools of philosophy, which is a gesture that never interests him very much.

He is fascinated as well by the phenomenon of Christian evangelists on American television. He watches these programs whenever he can, a habit that seems often to puzzle some of his American interlocutors. In 1995, in an important essay on religion, "Faith and Knowledge: The Two Sources of 'Religion' at the Limits of Reason Alone," Derrida advances a complex argument regarding an essential non-contradiction between religious faith and scientific technology or knowledge (see "Faith"). I do not recall his making any reference there to televised evangelism, in America or elsewhere, but his argument in this essay, concerning religion's positive and productive relation to technology, can easily be connected to his interest in that phenomenon. This argument, which obviously I am pointing to in a merely minimal fashion, engages with a certain interpretation of Enlightenment and counters the presumed historical antagonism between "faith and knowledge," to repeat the terms of Derrida's title or, to put it another way, the axiom according to which wherever enlightenment advances, religious belief retreats, and so forth. Certainly the American everyday and political culture Derrida observes closely, but with the benefit of a certain abstraction from its ordinary preoccupations, gives the lie to this axiom by mobilizing every technological advance also to spread religious belief.

This is not at all to say that he ever gives up his own faith in enlightenment and reason, although he insists that the understanding of "reason" is severely impoverished whenever it is restricted to pure logical calculation.[11] He is even above all, I would say, a thinker of the irreducible tie between faith and reason or enlightenment. There is, he insists, no reason, no relation in language, no understanding that does not rely on faith or belief, on the faith, for example, that the other is speaking the truth and not dissembling, lying, perjuring. It is this irreducible belief that is on display in practices of testimony, whether in a judicial legal context, in that televised testimony I referred to earlier, or in the most intimate confessions between lovers. Derrida's profound reflection on testimony is always guided by and brought back to a line from a poem by Paul Celan: "No one bears witness for the witness," which states the inviolable secrecy of the witness's act and thus its irreducible appeal to belief.

I also believe he sees America's religious traditions as forestalling for a long time yet the new enlightenment of a faith placed not in some all-knowing God or in His providence but in the conditions of the relation to singular others, who are each one absolutely other. Indeed, I would say that he foresees not only a continuation but a further extension of American belief in its own sovereign right to know, its own right, that is, to enforce "truth" as revealed to it by God. Hence the unshakable American belief in the necessity of capital punishment; hence a current US government that disregards international conventions prohibiting torture; hence the retreat of hospitality for non-citizens and the abrogation of civil rights for citizens in America today.

Derrida's America. Just as the US responded strongly to Derrida's work, he has responded to "it"—or rather to many things marked by or as American. It has been a selective response and also a non-totalizing one. (Unlike some other prominent European intellectuals one can think of, Derrida has always been careful to avoid monolithic judgments of "America.") His critique of US policy, especially post-9/11, is thorough-going and severe.[12] I would thus tend to agree with Michael Naas that in the last decade or so Derrida's thinking has been drawn increasingly to Europe as the more promising place of the future, where both new forms of shared or limited sovereignty and new possibilities for hospitality seem, for the time being, to have a better chance of being invented than, for example, in the present-day US.

Nevertheless, despite all the obstacles he sees to enlightenment in America, I do not believe Jacques Derrida has ever been seriously tempted to abandon his ties to that place, and certainly not to all his friends there, anymore than to the places and friends who love him throughout the world. Derrida has kept his promise to go on criticizing and deconstructing America from wherever he might be, whether within America or elsewhere. Indeed, he has kept asking how one could even know today where America begins and ends. He might even say the same thing of himself, whose relation to America did not start the day he first set foot there and has not ended because he will never return there. A Frenchman, a European, a North African, an Algerian, Derrida is also none of the above, except formally. Not essentially. He is not even of this world, but has always belonged to what is coming not simply from but *as* the future.

Before Jacques died so suddenly and unexpectedly in 2004, I had several conversations with him about the then-upcoming US presidential elections. He asked me more than once what I thought was going to happen. And I told him without hesitating and with conviction that President Bush's bid for re-election would be defeated. I believed it then, even if my belief bespoke sheer hope. But it was a hope that I thought reasonable and grounded. He never argued against this prediction and this hope, but only reiterated it by saying "I hope you are right." On one occasion he added with emphasis "*Il faut*," "It must be," "It has to be," "It is necessary," "It is needed." I do not know of course if he really shared my hope, or if he thought it was as naïve as it proved to be several weeks later. But I do believe that had we been able to speak again after the hope was dashed he would still have insisted that it remains necessary.

Notes

1. This essay began as improvised remarks presented in the series "For Derrida" at the Tate Modern, London, organized by Simon Glendinning, to whom I am greatly indebted for his transcription. The topic for the evening to which I was invited to contribute was "Derrida's America."

2. See, most pertinently, "Justices," an essay in honor of J. Hillis Miller: "How does J. Hillis Miller *himself* feel when he says 'je', 'I' or when he has the feeling of 'himself'? These borders of the I are vertiginous, but inevitable. We all rub up against them, make contact without contact, in particular as concerns our dearest friends. This is even what is astonishing about friendship, when it is somewhat alert. It is also vigilant friendship that startles us awake to this strange question: what does it mean, for an I *to feel itself*? 'How does he *himself* feel, J. Hillis Miller? J. Hillis Miller *himself*, the other, the wholly other that he remains for me?'" ("Justices," 690). In *For Derrida* (New York: Fordham University Press, 2009), Miller is particularly concerned to elucidate this figure of the "wholly other" in Derrida's thought. It is no doubt out of modesty that he does not attempt to do so with a reading of this text on himself as wholly other for the other who is Derrida.

3. See, in particular, "University," as well as the two-part translation of *Right to Philosophy* (*Philosophy* and *Eyes*), which collects a number of Derrida's writings on the philosophical institution.

4. "What is a traumatic event? First of all, any event worthy of this name, even if it is a 'happy' event, has within it something that is traumatizing. An event always inflicts a wound in the everyday course of history, in the ordinary repetition and anticipation of all experience" ("Autoimmunity," 96).

5. An important exception, one could argue, is "Envois" in *Post Card*, where

the author frequently depicts his—fictive, we should recall—letter-writer sending post cards from the US, namely, from New Haven, Connecticut, where indeed Derrida himself spent several weeks every year teaching at Yale University between 1975 and 1987. But the condition of fiction has to forestall any simple assimilation of this character's "experiences" to that of its author, even if the resemblance between them is unmistakable. Another exception would have to be made for *Counterpath*. This time, Derrida himself signs the post cards he sends to Catherine Malabou from his travel destinations, four of which are in the US (New York, Villanova, Baltimore, Laguna Beach).

6. After shaking out, with an admirable analysis, the assumptions that structure and accompany the specific genre of the biography-of-the-philosopher, Geoffrey Bennington writes, in 1996: "It is of course to be expected that Derrida will some day be the subject of biographical writing, and there is nothing to prevent this being of the most traditional kind. . . . I imagine that there are anecdotes to be told (probably mostly to do with cars and driving) and remarks to be reported (probably to do with other philosophers). But this type of complacent and recuperative writing would at some point have to encounter the fact that Derrida's work should at least have disturbed its presuppositions" ("A Life in Philosophy," in Bennington, *Other Analyses: Reading Philosophy* [CreateSpace (Web publisher), 2008], p. 425). Complacency and recuperation are indeed what I would avoid, if possible, even though I do recount one anecdote having to do with cars and driving.

7. This is a reference to the talk that had preceded mine at the Tate Modern event. See Michael Naas, "Derrida's America," in *Derrida's Legacies: Literature and Philosophy*, Simon Glendinning and Robert Eaglestone, eds (New York and London: Routledge, 2008), 118–37; reprinted in Naas, *Derrida From Now On* (New York: Fordham University Press, 2008).

8. See below, Chapter 10, "Stunned: Derrida on Film," for an extended presentation of this film.

9. This paradoxical double assertion has a particular status among Derrida's watchwords. What is remarkable about the refrain, which forms something like a swinging hinge in the text where it recurs numerous times, is that its provocation depends not on the syntax or semantics of a French idiom, but purely, if that is possible, on the logical relations it installs between the two clauses, which are moreover, at least in the initial occurrence, separated only by a comma without coordinating or subordinating conjunction ("Je n'ai qu'une langue, ce n'est pas la mienne"). Unlike, therefore, many other aphoristic formulations that Derrida has put forward, which will torment and incite translation from now on (e.g., "Tout autre est tout autre"), this gem, this pearl, passes into translation seemingly without resistance, for example: "I have only one language [or tongue], it is not mine," where the loss between the one tongue and the other seems almost negligible. Its action is thus counter-Babelian, inasmuch as it points to the condition of a universal tongue, which is universally translatable because it cannot be appropriated by any "mineness."

10. See Rorty, *Consequences of Pragmatism* (Minneapolis: University of Minnesota Press, 1982), p. xx.

11. See especially "The 'World' of the Enlightenment to Come (Exception, Calculation, and Sovereignty)," in *Rogues*.
12. See in particular Derrida, "The Reason of the Strongest," in *Rogues*, and "Autoimmunity."

Chapter 9

From Now On

> ... voilà ce qu'on n'aura pu désormais penser sans lui.[1]
>
> (Jacques Derrida, *Glas*)

> The survivor, then, remains alone. Beyond the world of the other, he is also in some fashion beyond or before the world itself. In the world outside the world and deprived of the world. At the least, he feels solely responsible, assigned to carry both the other and *his* world, the other and *the* world that have disappeared, responsible without world (*weltlos*), without the ground of any world, thenceforth, in a world without world, as without earth beyond the end of the world. ("Rams," 140)

Had these lines been written before 2003, they might have found a place in the volume Pascale-Anne Brault and Michael Naas first edited in English translation before collecting the same writings in their original language under the title: *Chaque fois unique, la fin du monde*. Indeed, for this French edition of his texts written upon the death of many friends over the years, Jacques Derrida concludes a brief foreword by signaling its close connection to the work from which I have just quoted. He writes: "If I dared to offer a true introduction to this book, it would be the essay I am publishing simultaneously with Éditions Galilée, *Béliers. Le dialogue ininterrompu: entre deux infinis, le poème*. It prowls around a line by Celan that has not left me for some years: *Die Welt ist fort, ich muss dich tragen*" (*Chaque fois*, 11; my trans.).[2] The world is gone, I must carry you. The essay *Béliers* ("Rams"), which takes its title from the poem by Celan in which this line occurs, was a lecture given at a memorial for Hans-Georg Gadamer in Heidelberg. Before it cites the poem for the first time come the lines with which I began and that speak of the surviving friend who remains alone, alone responsible for "bearing both the other and *his* world, the vanished other and *the* vanished world . . . from now on." Italics underscore the definite article: *the* world, and it is indeed with this thought of *the* world vanishing and ending with every singular death that Derrida defies commonplace arithmetic and sentiment according to which only a part of *the* world disappears when someone dies, or else, as is often said, *a* world comes to an end. But, as he writes in "Rams":

> Death does not put a term to someone in the world or to *a* world among others; it marks each time, each time in defiance of arithmetic, the absolute end of one and the same world, of what each one opens as a one and same world, the end of the unique world, the end of the totality of what is or can present itself as the origin of the world for some unique being, whether it is human or not. ("Rams," 23)

This thought of "each time the end of the world" does not submit easily to understanding. Moreover, Derrida sets aside any probing demonstration of these assertions, and speaks rather of "what I feel, upon the death of anyone and in a more intensely irrefutable fashion upon the death of someone near to me or a friend" (*Chaque fois*, 9). What is intensely irrefutable is the feeling of "the world after the end of the world," of being "in the world outside the world and deprived of the world." No doubt it was this intensity of feeling that prompted Derrida's indignant reaction, as I well recall, when the book review supplement of *Le Monde* published an exceedingly brief mention of the collection it referred to as *Chaque fois unique, la fin d'*un *monde*, thereby confirming what one has often suspected: that book reviewers do not always feel obliged to read the books they write about, although they rarely invent new titles for them. In this case, however, the journalist would have had to read only a little beyond the very first lines of the foreword to hear Derrida insisting on the paradox of that definite article. As if, he writes,

> the *repetition* of the end of an infinite totality were still possible: the end of the world *itself*, of the only world that there is, each time. Singularly. Irreversibly. For the other and in a strange way for the provisional survivor who endures the impossible experience. That is what "the world" would mean. This meaning is conferred on it only by what is called "death." (*Chaque fois*, 9)

"That is what 'the world' would mean." The world means, comes to mean, that which is gone, *fort*, and in departing confers the task of carrying the other, the world of the other.

To reread today these texts, among the last Derrida saw into print, for whoever counted Jacques Derrida as a friend, from whatever distance near or far, is to assent beyond all understanding to the irrefutable experience of the impossible world-outside-the-world, of being in the world and yet *weltlos*. The world of Jacques Derrida is gone and that is unbearable, therefore, it is what must be borne, carried, carried on in the world that is no more. Rather than the burden of bereavement and grief, however, I would try to understand this burdensome task in terms of the feeling of responsibility that Derrida twice mentions in the lines I began by citing. The world, the vanished world of the other, is that for which one must also feel alone responsible. How is one, anyone, me for example, to take responsibility now for the world?

That question sounds unbearably presumptuous. And yet, it was some such question that posed or imposed itself, with urgency and quite loudly, in the shock wave of Derrida's death. Three weeks later, an election in the United States delivered a sharp rebuke to all the world's citizens who had dared to hope for a different outcome. Hope in an alternative future not just for one nation but for the whole world of nations fell into an abyss already hollowed out by the end of the world that was Jacques Derrida. I am talking about myself, but the feeling seemed to be largely shared among friends with whom I spoke in those early days of November 2004, a feeling of grief compounded and all-engulfing, a grief for the whole world. At the same time, I had the acute sense and even certainty that, had it been possible still to speak with Derrida about the disappointment of that election, he would have shown little patience with the dark mood of lament and the depressive reaction that it took me so long to shake off. This certainty, of course, was no comfort since it only deepened, if possible, the sense of loss. All the same, it took up shelter somewhere in that darkness and emitted faint but steady signals from the vanished world to this one that is too much with us. I could even hear ghostly, gentle laughter at the naïve improvidence of my credulous belief in what was, after all, the more unlikely and improbable outcome of that election. This laughter wastes no words but leaves me to supply them, as if talking to myself and saying something like: "It is fine to hope against the odds, but quite foolish to lose sight of them. What happened was entirely foreseeable, a non-event, therefore, and it's childish to regret for more than a moment what might have been if only a miracle had occurred."

These remonstrations, however, are the matter of an instant and instantly they are to be forgotten. What remains is something else, which I strain now to hear more distinctly. Not just Derrida's clear-sighted realism, but whatever it is that allies his realist incredulity with faith in the promise of another world to come. Not only in my heart and my head does this alliance bespeak itself; it is voiced for anyone to hear in the writings of a lifetime and especially those in which Derrida, over the last decade or so, directs his thought toward the coming of another world, other than that one world claimed by the promoters of so-called *globalization*, an English word whose dominant use he always supplements with the French term, *mondialisation*, because the latter, although its use may be no less fantasmatic, at least retains reference to, precisely, the *monde*, the world, rather than the globe. Not the globalized, rounded-off, and totalized world, but a *coming* world of unforeseeable events and therefore *coming* as or from another than this same world: it is to thinking this event of the world's future that Derrida devotes so many of his last major works, to a few of which I will now turn.

There is perhaps no more consistent preoccupation across these writings than with *event* as unforeseeable interruption of any program, the eruption of an impossibility without horizon of expectation, the arrival of the incalculably other. An essay from 1984, "Psyche: Invention of the Other," itself marks something like an event in Derrida's thought in this regard, not only because it sends deep probes into all the concepts that derive their names from the Latin family of *venire* (invention, event, advent, convention, as well as the French *venir* and *avenir*), but especially because it puts in place a logic that will continue to be refined and extended in everything Derrida writes thereafter. It is a logic of impossibility and, as such, it wreaks a certain havoc on the logic of ordinary language and goes something like this: an invention that invents what is already possible is not an invention, but a calculable extension of the known. The only possible invention, therefore, is the invention of the impossible, which is not possible. And yet it is necessary to think the impossible invention as the only possible invention (see "Psyche," 44). With the necessity of this self-deconstructing syntax, Derrida strikes a vein that his thought will proceed to mine from then on, although it is just as surely true that the vein has already been worked in everything that came before.[3] But what now becomes possible, so to speak, is an explicit rethinking of the whole legacy of the concept of possibility, of what ever since Plato and Aristotle has been thought under the name, for example, of *dynamis*, meaning at once the ability to do a thing, but also strength, power, might, or authority.[4] Especially after 1984, Derrida challenges this powerful legacy more and more directly to give up its hold over thinking in general, over what is possible always for "me," for some me, or as he prefers to say especially in later texts, for some ipseity, that is, for whatever poses sameness to itself, returns to itself, and claims sovereignty over its selfsame self as over its own homogeneous, undifferentiated domain—not only, therefore, individual subjects, as we say, but also those abstract entities called sovereign states, nations, or simply sovereigns. Sovereignty, ipseity, and possibility: this is the powerful triumvirate brought increasingly into focus—I hesitate to say into the crosshairs—as Derrida advances his work along the path of this im-possible necessity.

Unless I am mistaken, another term, which will later assume great importance as we will see, does not yet figure prominently in the earlier *mise en place* of this necessary im-possibility of the event, invention, or simply the coming of the other. Its place, however, seems already prepared there. It would appear that the term and notion of *unconditional-ity* moves into the foreground of his thinking only once Derrida begins to follow out the pattern first traced in *Given Time* (1991) as concerns the concept of the gift. It is, I believe, in the seminar and published texts on hospitality (1995–1997) that Derrida first advances his thinking under the name of the unconditional. Although the latter term figures as well a certain impossibility, Derrida will reserve its use for deconstruc-tive analyses of ethical and political concepts. By unconditional hospital-ity, for example, it is necessary to understand a welcome without any limits or conditions on what the guest may expropriate of the host's, a pure hospitality, if you will, without admixture of its contrary, without any keeping to oneself and for oneself, without any of the boundaries that a guest is expected to observe in ordinary, practical, and therefore conditional hospitality. Unconditional hospitality (or gift or forgive-ness) is therefore impossible in practice and yet there is the necessity to think it, because it alone "can give meaning and practical rationality to a concept of hospitality" (*Rogues*, 149). To think the unconditionality of such concepts is not at all to remove thought from the practical expe-riences we wish to call hospitality, gift, forgiveness, or justice. On the contrary, this thinking registers the very desire to go on calling to these names for that which remains impossible as present experience.

(In a somewhat pedestrian manner, I realize, I have begun to recon-struct the emergence of a few key articulations that Derrida starts to flex more and more insistently after 1984. I also realize that the necessity of such a reconstruction is not readily apparent. Stepping back to ques-tion it, I am tempted to understand that the impetus in this direction was given by the need to gather enough momentum before attempting a leap from the point at which Derrida's writing will break off, the point that is now, alas, no longer in an indefinite future and whose certainty is no less definite than irrevocable. If so, then it is something like the momentum of Derrida's own thought discovering or uncovering itself in writing that I would be hoping not to revive but to play back from a certain arbitrarily designated beginning: 1984. The illusion of such a playback risks masking, however, the most vital axis of this written thought: the fact that it does not often or perhaps ever claim to foresee where it is going. Hence one has in its vicinity the often vertiginous sensation of falling into the unknowable future, a condition which these writings never simply mime but as which they arrive, I am convinced, in the experience of their signatory. If this experience has been one of the most prodigiously inventive in modern thought, if it has so thoroughly unsettled the rules of philosophical discourse, if it is the experience of Derrida's thought that will divide our age from what came before—and I do not doubt that it has and it will—then, I submit, it is because of this headlong welcome given to an unknowable future. In everything he writes, beginning long before 1984, it is the certainty of uncertainty and incalculability in which, paradoxical though it sounds, Derrida placed his faith. With unequaled acuteness and vigilance, he listens for what might be coming, to the yet-unknown who or what he dubbed the *arrivant*. What strikes me now above all when I reread almost any text of Derrida's, but especially texts of his last twenty years, is how consistently and constantly the energy of his thought is bent toward seeing or hearing the shape of things to come without, oddly enough, suspending the sensation I just described as one of falling headlong into the future's unknowability. It is as if with one hand he could appear to point to the coming of a future while the other hand were all the same compelled to go on writing in the dark. If such ambidexterity does not produce a simple contradiction, that is because, rather than a matter of one hand not knowing what the other is doing, it is a question of the future *arrivant* who or which remains always to come in relation to knowable possibilities. To put it another way: Derrida's thinking makes its way by not losing sight of what it cannot see coming. But also, and this is what I hope to connect with, by affirming a certain faith in the future that the other, the *arrivant*, is bringing.)

Let us return to what I just called the triumvirate of sovereignty, ipseity, and possibility. First of all, is sovereignty a viable concept, or one defined merely through or as an imposition of force? A moment ago, we heard Derrida explain that he had recourse to the figure of unconditionality—e.g., unconditional hospitality, gift, forgiveness, or justice—as the sole manner in which to give meaning to these ethical, political, or juridical concepts. But the essay titled "The University Without Condition" from 1999 also begins to work out a distinction between unconditionality and sovereignty, a distinction that will remain important from then on and especially in *Rogues* (2003).[5] It is significant that this line of thought first fully emerges in a reflection on the university, that is, on an institution that, in principle, can claim something like sovereignty over its own affairs and that, once again in principle, poses its independence from other sovereign entities, in particular, so-called sovereign states. If one must say each time "in principle" it is because, as Derrida begins by acknowledging in this essay, the sovereign, independent, or rather unconditional university "does not, *in fact*, exist, as we know only too well" ("University," 204). There is thus an obvious relation between the concept of the unconditional university and all those other unconditional concepts, like hospitality, that Derrida elaborates. But as the unconditionality of the university also resembles the concept of sovereignty—as Derrida puts it in *Rogues* both "escape absolutely, like the absolute itself, all relativism. That is their affinity" (*Rogues*, xiv)—its elaboration proceeds in good measure by way of a distinction from the other, nearby concept. Derrida insists several times on the difficulty involved in dissociating sovereignty from unconditionality. The distinction is, he writes, "difficult or fragile . . . I consider it scarcely possible yet essential, indispensable even—as an ultimate lever" (*Rogues*, xiii). "An immense problem: . . . How can one dissociate sovereignty and unconditionality, the power of an indivisible sovereignty and the powerlessness of unconditionality?" ("The University," 232). By the very terms of this latter question, one understands that the difficulty is not a terminological or definitional one. Rather, if the dissociation is said to be "scarcely possible," then it is perhaps because the very dynamic or power of possibility would have to be put in question by such a dissociation.

But is that even possible? The lever of the dissociation would have to be inserted somewhere between whatever figure it is that can say or signify "I can," "I may," and the unfigurable im-possibility of that which arrives or happens without first posing or opposing itself as one autonomy faced with another. A heteronomous event, therefore, or the event of heteronomy. The concept of sovereignty, assuming that it is a viable concept rather than a phantasm that forces itself upon reason, thus a forcing of reason or reasons, seems to subsume or repeat the concept of a self-governing, autonomous ipseity of any "itself" as power and master over its own domain. Beginning once again with his writings on hospitality, Derrida grants increasing importance to the analysis of the term *ipseity*, the roots of which Émile Benveniste, in *Le Vocabulaire des institutions indo-européennes*, uncovered in its entanglement with the roots of *hospitality*.

Rather than attempt a paraphrase of the multiple ways in which Derrida comes to rely on the branching roots of ipseity's concept, especially in his late work on sovereignty, I cite a long passage from *Rogues* where this reliance is declared and explained. At this point, Derrida has also begun to make explicit the reason for which the first essay in this volume, "The Reason of the Strongest (Are There Rogue States?)," from the outset so prominently pursues the figure of the wheel, the turn (that is, *le tour*, whose homonym is also by turns mobilized: *la tour*, the tower, and more than one tower, the two towers and the *deux tours*), the rotation, all that which turns on itself or turns back to itself.[6] The very desire for democracy, he suggests, is difficult to imagine without "some automobilic and autonomic turn or, rather, return to self," that is, of the *ipse*, "of the one-self that gives itself its own law," of all that which Derrida proposes to call from now on "*ipseity* in general."

> By "ipseity" I thus wish to suggest some "I can" or at the very least the power that *gives itself* its own law, its force of law, its self-representation, the sovereign and reappropriating gathering [*rassemblement*] of self in the simultaneity of an assemblage or assembly, being together [*être-ensemble*], or "living together," as we say. . . . [E]ach time I say *ipse, metipse* or *ipseity* . . . I also wish to suggest the self [*le soi*], the one-self, being properly oneself. . . . I thus wish to suggest the oneself [*le soi-même*], the "self-same" [*même*] of the "self" [*soi*] (that is, "le même," *meisme*, which comes from *metipse*) as well as the power, potency, sovereignty, or possibility implied in every "I can/I may" [*"je peux"*], the *pse* of *ipse* (*ipsissimus*) referring always, through a complicated set of relations, as Benveniste shows quite well, to possession, property, and power, to the authority of the lord or seignior, of the sovereign, and most often the host (*hospites*), the master of the house or the husband. . . . But do we really need etymology when simple analysis would show the possibility of power and possession in the mere positioning of the self as *oneself* [*soi-même*], in the mere self-positioning of the self, as properly oneself? The first turn or first go-round of circularity or sphericity comes back round or links back up, so to speak, with itself, with the same, the self, and with the proper of oneself proper. The first turn does it; the first turn is all there is to it [*Le premier tour, c'est tout*]. The turn, the turn around the self—and the turn is always the possibility of turning round the self, of returning to the self or turning back on the self, the possibility of turning on itself around itself—the turn turns out to be it [*le tour, c'est tout*]. The turn makes up the whole and makes a whole with itself; it consists in totalizing, in totalizing itself, thus in gathering itself by tending toward simultaneity; and it is thus that the turn, as a whole, is one with itself, together with itself. We are here at the same time around and at the center of the circle or the sphere where the values of ipseity are gathered together [*se rassemblent*], the values of the together, of the ensemble and the semblable, of simultaneity and gathering together, but also of the simulacrum, simulation, and assimilation. (*Rogues*, 10–12)

I have underscored the emphasis being placed here on the figure of sameness, on the *même* in the term *soi-même* (translated as "itself" or "oneself"), but also the stress on the family of terms *semblable, ensemble, assemblée, rassemblement*, which generally tend to get broken up in English by "fellow man," "together," "assembly," or "gathering." The "semblable" is the similar, the like, and "être-ensemble" also says the being-together of the like, just as "rassemblement" gathers up the similar. In this emphasis on the vocabulary of the similar and the same,

Derrida is himself gathering evidence for the necessity of the question that, he confesses at the beginning of this essay, did not cease haunting, indeed torturing him throughout the preparation of this keynote lecture for a ten-day colloquium titled "Democracy To Come." It is the question of the incompatibility of an axiomatics of democracy as autonomous ipseity that assembles the like and the same, on the one hand, with, on the other, another truth of the democratic space as heterogeneous, heteronomous, asymmetrical, the space of "disseminal multiplicity, the anonymous 'anyone,' the 'no matter who,' the indeterminate 'each one'" (*Rogues*, 14–15). Does not democracy also, indeed first of all, have to be thought in a manner that does not return the like to itself, in other words, non-ipsocentrically? But that exigency would come down to having to dissociate democracy from autonomy, a task which Derrida compares to the "more than difficult, indeed im-possible" dissociation of sovereignty from unconditionality, or law from justice (*Rogues*, 84).

I underscore the stress on this language of the same and the *semblable/ensemble* for another reason: by circumscribing these ipsocentric turns or by highlighting this ipsocratic force, Derrida's analysis shows up the considerable failing at the core of any rethinking or critique of traditional doctrines of sovereignty that would treat these as essentially political constructs subject to historical transformation. In political philosophy and the discourse of international affairs or international law, it is commonplace today to understand the all-too-evident woes currently besetting sovereignty's doctrine as merely signs that the ground of its legitimacy has continued to shift over time: from the sovereign ruler of a territorial state to the people inhabiting that territory (the American and French revolutionary doctrine of popular sovereignty) to the individuals who make up that people. There is even a marked tendency of late to speak of sovereignty as regularly undergoing revolutions and to account for today's stresses on the coherence of its concept as marks of the latest revolution that is still in progress.[7] This discourse, of course, does not intend the trope of revolution in the sense of a wheel turning around a fixed axis, but rather in the sense of an upheaval of the ground, an overthrow or upset of what came before. At stake for these discourses is often enough a re-legitimation of sovereignty on what are taken to be new grounds or else in the name of what are supposed to be new figures who or which can make ever more legitimate claims to sovereignty.

The problem is not that such historical characterizations are entirely without pertinence. Rather, the problem is that they offer little or no purchase on what keeps these "revolutions" turning on the same axis, the axis of the same, the like, the *autos* or the *ipse*, whether one thinks of this wheel as rotating in the circumference of a same kingdom, a same state, a same people, a same individual (who can join in assemblies of other like individuals to adopt laws protecting each one's property and proper interests, through the democratic exercise of liberty), or finally perhaps even a same world of a same humanity. For these discourses of political philosophy and international affairs, the essential synonymy of sovereignty and ipseity can be heard whirring on unsuspected in the background, its wheels turning the very machinery that is producing it as discourse.

This is to imply, then, that Derrida's thinking does let us gain purchase somewhere on ipsocratic, ipsocentric sovereignty, not by discerning its new revolutionary or more democratic face—it has no other face, which is also the sense, as I understand it, of asserting that "le tour, c'est tout"—but, for example, and as I have already noted, through that difficult dissociation of sovereignty and unconditionality. A moment ago, we heard Derrida acknowledge this to be "scarcely possible, but essential, indispensable even—as an ultimate lever." To seek leverage or purchase on sovereignty's ipsocratic machine seems to me one way to describe what it could mean to take responsibility for the world Derrida has left. To conclude, therefore, I am going to outline just three kinds of levers that have been left within reach.

The first lever I would describe as that of deconstructive critique in its most constant, even classic, features. The analysis of sovereignty as ipseity, or vice versa, can clearly be situated along a direct line that leads from Derrida's earliest writings on Husserl's, Rousseau's, Saussure's, or Plato's semiotic theory. The dream of full self-presence, of an auto-affection without difference, delay, or disruption, and of an unalloyed properness will have always been the sovereign dream or phantasm, whether the dreamer dreams in the name of a state or of another ipseity, for example, an individual or indeed in the name of God. Dream or phantasm because, as Derrida observes in the reading of Rousseau's "dangerous supplement" in *Of Grammatology* (1967), "that which would accord us (to) pure presence itself, if such a thing were possible, would be only another name for death" (*Grammatology*, 155). In a like manner and even with a similar syntax, Derrida will follow out the logic of indivisible, fully self-present sovereignty or ipseity to the point of its necessary death, its vanishing from any imaginably present, past, or future world, that is, from time, space, and language:

> sovereignty itself (if there is one and if it is pure) always keeps silent in the very ipseity of the moment proper to it, a moment that is but the stigmatic point of an indivisible instant. A sovereignty is indivisible or it is not at all. . . . This indivisibility excludes it in principle from any partition [*partage*], from being shared, from time and from language. From time, from the temporalization

that it infinitely contracts, and thus, paradoxically, from history. In a certain way, then, sovereignty is a-historical. . . . As a result, sovereignty withdraws from language, which always introduces a sharing [*partage*] that universalizes. As soon as I speak to the other, I submit to the law of giving reason(s), I share a virtually universalizable medium, I divide my authority. . . .

Now, if sovereign force is silent, it is not for lack of speaking—it might go on speaking endlessly—but for lack of meaning. (*Rogues*, 100–1)

For lack of meaning, sovereignty's concept self-deconstructs, which does not mean, obviously, that it is without force. On the contrary, this non-meaning means that its only meaning is force, the reason of the strongest that imposes itself as sovereign reason. The self-deconstruction of sovereignty's concept also does not mean that it goes without saying. Once again, on the contrary, as suggested by the brief characterization above of current discourses on the subject in political philosophy or international law, the non-concept's inertia is clearly sufficient to go on for quite some time, perhaps endlessly, driving the effort to shore up its theory in the face of a general disintegration of the doctrine of indivisible authority. Which means that a counter-effort of deconstructive critique will also continue to be required. And because such critique has never been tolerated by the rules constraining discourse in the public media, it will continue to demand and therefore to challenge to exist the discursive space of a "university without condition," which would

treat . . . the history of democracy and the idea of sovereignty, that is to say as well, of course, the conditions or rather the unconditionality on which the university and within it the Humanities are *supposed* . . . to live. The deconstruction of this concept of sovereignty would touch not only on international law, the limits of the nation-state, and of its supposed sovereignty, but also on the use made of them in juridico-political discourses concerning the *subject* or the *citizen* in general—always presumed to be 'sovereign' as such (free, deciding, responsible, etc.). ("University," 231–2)

The appeal to a space of unlimited questioning, to a university without condition that poses its powerless unconditionality in resistance to the force of another sovereign entity, situates the stakes of critical, deconstructive discourse otherwise than in a purely academic arena. It thus appeals not only to keep open a space in which to elaborate the difficult, "scarcely possible," dissociation of unconditionality and sovereignty; the very idea of such a place independent of every other sovereign instance can also only arise through and as a dissociation of the absolute or supreme authority of sovereignty from another instance that, without force or arms, will always be powerless to defend its borders, which moreover do not exist other than as a pure abstraction.

The second lever I would mention can even less easily be thought in the mechanistic terms of some control point to be activated or not by a machine's operator, or rather by its would-be saboteurs. (Not only today, in the post-Patriot Act US, is it particularly dangerous to evoke sabotage of the machine of sovereignty.) In adopting this mechanical metaphor, I was pursuing Derrida's figure of the turning wheel, but this figure, we recall, also corresponds more to the dream or phantasm than to the reality of sovereign states in a world where nothing ever turns quite so neatly or as it is supposed to: *ça ne tourne pas rond*, one might say in French. Although sovereign entities have to dream of efficient machines of totalization, and although such dreamed-of figures are certainly not without very real effects, in order to account for the way things actually unfold and happen, one must have recourse, Derrida advises, not to a mechanistic comparison but to a biologistic one. The notion of auto-immunity is first highlighted by Derrida and its worth tested in the essay "Faith and Knowledge: The Two Sources of 'Religion' at the Limits of Reason Alone" (1996). It inserts itself there and prises apart (once more, like a lever) what Derrida calls at one point "the very thing of religion": the *indemne*, which is to say, the unharmed, untouched, unscathed, intact, the holy, the sacred, the saintly, the saved, and so forth. At the point at which he refers to the "terrifying but fatal logic of the *auto-immunity of the unscathed*," Derrida appends a long note that reviews a few historical uses of the notion of immunity or the immune (*immunis*), before connecting the pre-modern legal sense (to be immune was to be exempt from taxation and other obligations to the state) to the modern biological or, more precisely, immunological sense. This note concludes with a kind of announcement: "we will take as a pretext this enlargement [of the sense] and will speak of a sort of general logic of *auto-immunization*" ("Faith," 80).

It is as if this notion of the auto-immune had just been waiting for Derrida to come upon it and work out a general logic going beyond both its legal and biological extensions. Or rather, to take up that name for a general logic of deconstruction as a "contamination" of the proper at the origin. Doubtless the explosion of the AIDS epidemic, in the 1980s and then beyond, brought to everyone's attention the potential for organisms to fight their own immune systems, that is, to protect themselves from their systems of protection.[8] What is interesting now when one looks back to the text of "Faith and Knowledge" is that its "announcement" of a general logic of auto-immunization did not yet anticipate explicitly the momentum or traction it would gain by being extended to the analysis of sovereignty. This might not be worth noting were it not for the fact that among the still very current uses of immunity in the legal, rather than biological, sense is the principle or doctrine of sovereign immunity. This doctrine essentially precludes and proscribes the institution of suits against sovereign governments. In American jurisprudence, where this antique doctrine is still frequently invoked by both federal and state governments, its justification is supposedly no longer the one presumed under English law, for example, according to which the "sovereign can do no wrong," which doctrine was, one may easily surmise, promulgated by the sovereign him- or herself. Rather the present-day justification is supposed to be found in the principle that the "sovereign is exempt from suit [on the] practical ground that there can be no legal right against the authority that makes the law on which the right depends" (205 US, 349, 353).[9] This legal sidelight, which Derrida leaves in the wings, makes apparent the originality of the conceptual graft he has carried out between an organic pathology and legal, institutional, political, religious, and ethical "normalities." Moreover, the graft allows one to question the settled idea that the legal grounds justifying the doctrine of sovereign immunity or simply of sovereignty have progressed beyond the ipsocratic assertion of the right of the strongest. When the sovereign government with the most military might on the planet, which it is demonstrably not shy about using, can refuse to cooperate with any international initiative that it deems, quite correctly, as constituting a limitation of national sovereignty—for example, the International Criminal Court, the Law of the Seas Convention, the Kyoto Protocol on Global Warming, even the Geneva Conventions and the Universal Declaration of Human Rights, and, in general, any agreement that would be enforceable by an international agency—then there is manifestly a huge flaw within narratives of the progressive enlightenment of sovereignty's doctrine.

And yet, if might makes right it still cannot make things right in the sense of correcting what is wrong. It cannot, that is, protect itself from the auto-immunization of indivisible sovereignty in whose name its might is deployed. This flaw is not a contingent one but, as Derrida will put it at the end of "The Reason of the Strongest," a failing or a falling short, even a falling down or collapse of the ipsocentric return upon itself of time when it is given only to the self or to the same, without other. Insofar as the indivisible sovereign can know no other, then that is its irreducible flaw, failure, fault.

> Sovereignty neither gives nor gives itself the time; it does not take time. Here is where the cruel autoimmunity with which sovereignty is affected begins, the autoimmunity with which sovereignty at once sovereignly affects and cruelly infects itself. Autoimmunity is always, in the same time without duration, cruelty itself, the autoinfection of all autoaffection. It is not some

particular thing that is affected in autoimmunity but the self, the *ipse*, the *autos* that finds itself infected. As soon as it needs heteronomy, the event, time, and the other. (*Rogues*, 109)

Finally, the third lever will have already made itself known: it is simply the idea and the fact of more than one sovereignty and therefore of its division. Discussions of sovereignty today among political theorists and international law experts invariably point out all the ways in which national sovereignty has had to cease enforcing itself as everywhere indivisible, unsharable, or inviolable, presuming that it ever could. Practices installing a shared, partial, or limited sovereignty are today so common as to belie the very unity of the concept. In the almost sixty years since the adoption by the UN General Assembly of the Universal Declaration of Human Rights, the principle of a sovereign right above and beyond that of states has, to be sure very unevenly and with far more failures than successes, staked out grounds justifying forceful intervention in the internal affairs of sovereign nations, thereby overriding the promise of mutual non-intervention that long stood as the linchpin or touchstone of the post-Westphalian respect of borders. The European Union is most often held up as evidence that the era of Westphalian state sovereignty has come to a close. Yet, these same analyses just as invariably concede that, whether the model is the European Union or the United Nations or some other entity, the practice of inter- or extra-nationally shared responsibility for economic, social, political, ecological, physical, and cultural welfare of all those living on earth remains severely hampered so long as force cannot be brought to bear in defense of the principle. And therefore, that these supposedly new extra- or non-national instances of sovereign right are finally powerless to contain or restrain its oldest form, which may be also its only true form: the right and the reason of the strongest.

Certainly the signatories to the 1997 "Statement of Principles" of the Project for the New American Century had no difficulty recognizing that the military might of the United States would remain key to that nation's ability to refuse with impunity any other authority not only over its own affairs, but over those of an entire world. But this Statement and, above all, the practices of the State it inspired also provoke the question as to whether there can ever be impunity from the auto-immunity that such a super-sovereignty imagines for itself. Here are the key passages from this brief document (some of whose signatories were Elliott Abrams, William J. Bennett, Jeb Bush, Dick Cheney, Midge Decter, Francis Fukuyama, I. Lewis Libby, Norman Podhoretz, Dan Quayle, Donald Rumsfeld, and Paul Wolfowitz):

We aim to make the case and rally support for American global leadership.

As the 20th century draws to a close, the United States stands as the world's preeminent power. Having led the West to victory in the Cold War, America faces an opportunity and a challenge: Does the United States have the vision to build upon the achievements of past decades? Does the United States have the resolve to shape a new century favorable to American principles and interests? ... We seem to have forgotten the essential elements of the Reagan Administration's success: a military that is strong and ready to meet both present and future challenges; a foreign policy that boldly and purposefully promotes American principles abroad; and national leadership that accepts the United States' global responsibilities. ... [W]e cannot safely avoid the responsibilities of global leadership or the costs that are associated with its exercise. America has a vital role in maintaining peace and security in Europe, Asia, and the Middle East. If we shirk our responsibilities, we invite challenges to our fundamental interests. ... The history of this century should have taught us to embrace the cause of American leadership. ... [W]e need to accept responsibility for America's unique role in preserving and extending an international order friendly to our security, our prosperity, and our principles.[10]

Our security, *our* prosperity, *our* principles, *our* interests: the insistent possessive "our" imprints sovereignty's mark as ipsocentric turn and return toward the self's property over and against some not- or non-self, some other with other interests, which are its own or their own and therefore not "ours." Yet this mark insists and is remarked, paradoxically, in the protocol and project of a one world gathered under one leader. Who, then, is the "we" whose interests, prosperity, and security can be advanced over those of all others? Do not interests that are "ours," distinctively and sovereignly, suppose the interests of some others, some "not-us," thus a multiplicity of worlds (at least two), a world shared out among more than one and therefore, immediately, dividing and redividing? The properly possessive "our," in its very insistence, *at the same time* insists on the time of another, and therefore at the same time another time. The hour of the properly "our" can never strike without tolling auto-immunity's tax on itself, without fighting off its own defenses.

The language I have just cited speaks four times of responsibility in as many lines: the "United States' global responsibilities," the "responsibilities of global leadership" that "we cannot safely avoid," the "responsibilities" that cannot be shirked without inviting "challenges to our fundamental interests," and finally and most incoherently, the responsibility "we need to accept ... for America's unique role in preserving and extending an international order friendly to our security, our prosperity, and our principles."[11] Unabashedly, this repetition attempts to say that a responsibility is involved in acting to preserve and extend an order friendly to oneself alone. There is, it says, a responsibility to *oneself*, to preserve oneself, to extend one's influence, and to increase one's prosperity. This document calls (but to whom?) for the responsibility of saving oneself.

It is difficult even to think of a more irresponsible use of the term responsibility than the one being hammered into place here in the sense of a responsibility to oneself *alone* and to one's own sole interests. This is bare-handed ipsocracy slipping on the glove of moral resolution, even of sacrifice. But what is also thereby engaged is the auto-immunity of an auto-affection that, so long as it can say "we," "our," ours," indeed so long as it can speak at all, has already acknowledged, responded to, and been shared out among more than just one. It is sheer force, might, and the power of ipsocentric possibility ("I can, therefore I will") into which is lost, buried without regretted trace, the idea of responsibility as the burden of responding in a world with others. The latter idea is of responsibility, therefore, toward a future that, we know and from now on, can only arrive by shattering the program or the project of a new American century.

* * *

"Only a god can save us": Derrida closes the essay "The Reason of the Strongest" with a meditation on this phrase that Heidegger dropped so enigmatically into his famous posthumously published interview with *Der Spiegel*. Warning his listeners and readers that he is quite aware of how provocative such a reference will appear in the context of this lecture and essay, Derrida proceeds patiently to take Heidegger's sentence apart, in each of its German words ("Nur noch ein Gott kann uns retten").[12] But finally it is the French word *salut*, precipitated out from the saving force of "sauver" ("Seul un dieu peut nous sauver"), that absorbs his attention here, as it has done elsewhere.[13] What is so absorbing is that two uses of *salut*—as noun meaning salvation ("in the sense of the safe, the immune, health, and security" [*Rogues*, 114]) and as exclamatory greeting or salutation of the other, something said to greet an arrival and upon departure, as a send-off—these two uses are *at once* irreconcilable and indissociable. They are irreconcilable inasmuch as *salut*/salvation would redeem ipsocentric "selfness" (whether of an "I" or a "we"), saving it, preserving it from the endless contamination that auto-immunizes without end. The *salut* of salvation promises an end; it promises to put paid to all the debts that *otherwise* would keep the books open forever. Whereas *salut*/salutation places any and every one, performatively, exclamatively, in the other's wake, calling to what comes or goes, goes and comes *without the self*, heteronomously, heterogeneously.

Irreconcilable, therefore, *salut* and *salut*, but they are no less indissociably identified in the same tongue. Nevertheless, Derrida says he will attempt to dissociate them, to wedge apart what cannot be divorced given that these are not merely homophones in his language but very strictly the same word. The Dictionnaire Littré entry notes, parenthetically, that as an "external and common demonstration of civility, friendship, respect made in the direction of persons one encounters, approaches, visits," *salut* is said "because to salute [*saluer*] is to wish salvation [*le salut*]." And yet, to save the salutation by dissociating it from the figure of wished-for salvation is what Derrida says he is tempted, again, to attempt.

It is a gesture "without hope" that was anticipated in the foreword to *Rogues*:

> . . . the call for a thinking *to come*, of the democracy *to come*, of the reason *to come*. This call bears every hope, to be sure, although it remains, in itself, without hope. Not hopeless, in despair, but foreign to teleology, the hopefulness, and the *salut* of salvation. Not foreign to the *salut* as the greeting or salutation of the other, not foreign to the *adieu* ("come" or "go" in peace), not foreign to justice, but nonetheless heterogeneous and rebellious, irreducible, to law, to power, and to the economy of redemption. (*Rogues*, xv)

These are the last lines of the "Avant-propos," the foreword or preface, which, exceptionally, bears a title: "Veni." The Latin imperative ("Come") of this four-letter title may give a clue as to the confounding hope-without-hope of dissociating *salut* and *salut*. For, like every title, it trembles on a threshold, but here the threshold is at least double and therefore doubly divided since, as the title of an "Avant-propos" (literally: "before-the-topic), it introduces into what is itself an introduction or foreword. This foreword on the threshold issues one into a volume collecting the corresponding essays of *Rogues: Two Essays on Reason*. That there are two essays, more than one, and that they (cor)respond one to the other leads Derrida to evoke the call and response of Narcissus and Echo, in Ovid's precise language: "'*Veni!*' says Narcissus: 'Come!' 'Come' answers Echo. Of herself and on her own" (xii). Then, in a note that cites the passage from the *Metamorphoses* at greater length, Derrida, even as he appends an English and two different French translations of the Latin, observes that here "translation is more or less impossible" (*Rogues*, 162, n4).

The impossible dissociation of *salut* and *salut*, which is not attempted hopelessly but yet without hope, is *consigned* to something like this trembling of "Veni" between Narcissus and Echo as well as between languages or idioms. It is consigned, that is, turned over, surrendered, exposed to the other for response. Only there, on the forever uncertain border of the call to come—"come!"—can the *salut* of the one's redemptive economy be dissociated from the *salut* that greets the other or bids farewell. It can, it might, perhaps, which is not to say that it is possible, that it is a possibility for some ipseity, or that it lies in any one's power so to save *salut* from *salut*. Rather, as a consigning or consignment to the other's understanding, it will remain always for another to say, to repeat, as does Echo, the last words of the speech she hears.

Like her, one is called to respond. "Democracy to come, *salut!*": these are the last echoing words of "The Reason of the Strongest" and they consign democracy's future to all who will greet them from now on.

Notes

1. As Michael Naas has noted, Derrida professed a particular fondness for the French adverb *desormais* (from then on, from now on); see Naas, *Derrida From Now On* (New York: Fordham University Press, 2008), p. 236, n11, where he also explains the coincidence between the title of this chapter and that of his own book.
2. This foreword does not appear in the English edition, *The Work of Mourning*.
3. In his famous address to the 1966 Johns Hopkins colloquium "Critical Languages and the Sciences of Man," Derrida announces at the outset that his preoccupation is with the "structure" of an event: "Perhaps something has occurred in the history of the concept of structure that could be called an 'event,' if this loaded word did not entail a meaning which it is precisely the function of structural—and structuralist—thought to reduce or to suspect. Let us speak of an 'event,' nevertheless, and let us use quotation marks to serve as a precaution. What would this event be then?" ("Structure", 278). See my "Event of Resistance," in *Alibi*, 1–3, for a reading of these lines and what follows from them, in that essay and beyond.
4. See, for just one example, *Rogues*, 137.
5. In that same year the brief lecture titled "Unconditionality or Sovereignty" ("Unconditionality") interrogates the alternative posed in the title. (For a discussion of this lecture, see also my essay "Names of War" [*Oxford Literary Review* 31, 2 (2009)].) Since the initial publication of this chapter in 2006, the publication of the two volumes of Derrida's last seminar on sovereignty, *The Beast and the Sovereign*, have considerably augmented the corpus of his writings on the subject.
6. For a stunning reading of the figure of the wheel in Derrida's writings, see Michael Naas, "Derrida at the Wheel," in Naas, *Derrida From Now On* (New York: Fordham University Press, 2008).
7. See, for example, Dan Philpott, *Revolutions in Sovereignty: How Ideas Shaped Modern International Relations* (Princeton: Princeton University Press, 2001), and Alan Cranston et al., *The Sovereignty Revolution* (Stanford: Stanford University Press, 2004).
8. I am not suggesting, however, that Derrida is merely essaying a metaphorical extension of biological, immunological, or histological terms.

In the 1989 interview "The Rhetoric of Drugs," he is attentive to the "metaphoric" uses of terms like virus, parasite, infection, contagion, and so forth, but he also doubts that what is going on is simply an extension of their literal or proper meanings: "The *prerequisite* to this sort of problematic would have to concern rhetoric itself, as a parasitic or viral structure: originarily and in general. Whether viewed from up close or from far away, does not everything that comes to affect the proper or the literal have the form of a virus? . . . And doesn't rhetoric always obey a logic of parasitism? Or rather, doesn't the parasite logically and normally disrupt logic?" ("Rhetoric," 472, n9).

 9. See "The Lectric Law Library Lexicon" entry at http://www.lectlaw.com/def2/s103.htm.
10. For the full text of this statement, see http://www.newamericancentury.org/statementofprinciples.htm.
11. There are two further uses of "responsibility," "responsibilities" in parts of the statement that have been elided in the quotation.
12. In "The Indefinite Article, or the Love of a Phrase," Samuel Weber works out a detailed reading of this sentence, which bears down especially on the seemingly pleonastic "noch" and finds concentrated there the untranslatability of the singular idiom on which Heidegger draws (in *Reading Ronell*, ed. Diane Davis [Champaign: University of Illinois Press, 2009]).
13. See in particular "Salut."

Chapter 10

Stunned: Derrida on Film

First, let me list a few facts about the film we are going to watch.[1] *D'ailleurs, Derrida* had its premier showing in Spring 2000 on the Franco-German public television station, Arte, which co-produced it. It was written and directed by Safaa Fathy, an Egyptian filmmaker, playwright, and poet who has long lived in Paris where she also studied for her doctorate in English. It has since been screened many times at film festivals, in commercial theaters, and at numerous conferences such as this one, very often in the presence of the film's director and/or its subject, Jacques Derrida. The film was shot in 1999 at various locations, very few of which are identified in the film itself.

These settings are often used as evocative visual backdrops for the forgrounded figure of Derrida, who is heard and often shown speaking throughout the film's sixty-eight minutes. The only other figure who speaks on camera is Derrida's friend, the philosopher Jean-Luc Nancy. Occasionally one hears Fathy's faint voice off-camera posing a question, making a comment, or reading a passage, and once Marguerite Derrida is heard to speak, but otherwise it is Derrida's voice that fills the sound-track, sharing it only with haunting airs of Arabo-Andalusian music or sounds of wind, birds, ocean, and sea.

The Mediterranean sea, along the coast of Algeria, at the port of Algiers, and on the southern coast of Spain, the Pacific ocean, seen from Laguna Beach in Southern California, are the most insistent visual presences alongside Derrida's. The film's editing tends to blend these coasts into a same shoreline along which advance and recede repeating crests of waves. Of these three coastal locations, two are strongly tied to Derrida's individual biography: on the one hand, his native city of Algiers, many images of which flash by intercut throughout the film, including sequences shot in and around Derrida's family home in El Biar, a suburb of Algiers; and, on the other hand or the other coast, the shore of Southern California near the campus of UC Irvine and not far from the ruined Spanish mission at San Juan Capistrano, where like a migrating bird or a soaring pelican Derrida returned every spring for seventeen years to continue in English the seminar begun each year in Paris, in French. (The film records him teaching in both places, in both languages.) From all of the sequences shot in Algeria, Derrida is absent, the camera going from one site of memory to another accompanied only by his dislocated voice, which almost never identifies synchronically the images as they accumulate and are rapidly intercut: the waterfront in Algiers, with its arcades beneath which his father, René Derrida, worked, the Great Synagogue, which formerly had been a mosque and after Algeria's independence in 1962 was again converted back into a mosque, the Jardin d'Essai, Algiers' large botanical park, the cemetery in which small above-ground tombs recall the deaths of Derrida's two infant brothers, the narrow alleys of the Casbah, the Arab quarter of Algiers that Derrida knew well before it became virtually off-limits to the European inhabitants of the city, the courtyards of several schools that he attended in Paris and before that in his native city, one of which expelled him under the cover of Vichy's imitation of the Nazi regime's policy of "racial purification," and above all the house and the garden in El Biar, where Derrida grew up and to which he returned often until 1962, when it and almost everything in it had to be abandoned in the family's forced flight north across the Mediterranean. When it enters the same house in 1999, the camera uncovers improbable remnants of this abandonment: the mother's piano and above it the framed movie poster from Charlie Chaplin's 1921 silent film *The Kid*, showing Chaplin's character with a protective arm around the American boy actor Jackie Coogan, who played the eponymous kid.

Less improbable but no less moving is the glimpse we are given of the flaw in the geometric pattern of the villa's tile floor. As an interruption or accident befalling the floor's regular, repeating pattern, this single misplaced tile is something like the house's own signature or fingerprint, the mark of its undeniable identity as the house of Derrida's memory. In *Tourner les mots*, the book that Fathy and Derrida co-wrote to accompany the film's debut, Derrida lingers at greater length over this detail than any of the countless others he evokes in his recollection of the filming. The thought or image of the disadjusted tile plunges him deep into recollection of the years during which he daily trod upon it. At the same time, however, and under the same provocation, he takes up a meditation on the law that immediately metonymizes every irreplaceable singularity, for example, a particular flaw in the floor pattern of someone's childhood home, into a general structure of wounded memory, the infinitely repeatable event of a circumcision that Derrida here captures in the idiomatic phrase, in French, of *une fois pour toutes*, once and for all. You have to watch for the single, very brief apparition on the screen of this detail, which, no more than most of the other images, is not explained or situated.

I have mentioned both the Algerian coast on the Mediterranean and the Southern California coast on the Pacific, both of which are prominently featured in the film. But there is also a third coastal location, which the film never explicitly situates or identifies. These sequences were shot on the southern coast of Spain, in the province of Almeria that lies to the east of Andalucia. The film opens and closes with shots filmed at this location, which I am able to name only because Safaa Fathy betrays their secret in *Tourner les mots*. As far as I know, it will have been the first and only time that Derrida ever set foot on this deserted terrain, which lies more or less due north from Algeria across the Mediterranean. In the film, however, he is frequently shown there traversing its empty landscape, utterly isolated by the camera's frame from all contact with a living thing except the oversized cacti that often fill the screen.

Another location in Spain is very important to the film's visuals and themes: the city of Toledo. Derrida is filmed walking its streets and through medieval courtyards as he evokes the significance for him of figures of the marrano, that is, those who remained behind, after the expulsion of Jews from Spain and Portugal in 1492, to continue in secret the practice of Jewish rites and observances. But it is also the Toledo of El Greco that the film features very centrally, with a long sequence shot before "The Burial of Count Orgaz," a painting that Derrida had evoked at length in *Circumfession*.

By omitting nearly all toponyms and other nominal or verbal devices for captioning the images, the film bids to place them in an unsettled and often unsettling relation to language. As a consequence, the images almost never illustrate a verbal picture (there are a few notable exceptions), nor does language ever supply an ekphrastic description of the image, even when the camera plays at length over the surface of El Greco's famous painting. At many points, the image track and the sound track seem to be parallel lines that do not touch, at least not in the conventional ways of the caption, the illustration, the commentary, ekphrasis, or even just the name. Through this *mise en parallèle*, word and image are both held in relation and divorced from each other; they are, in other words, articulated, held together/apart. In this and other ways, the listener/viewer is kept constantly alert not only to the texture and dimension of film, but also to its artifacture as Derrida might have called it. Or simply, to its writing.

It is not, however, only the film's editing that maintains this alertness. The subject who is "captured" here, as we say, is repeatedly heard underscoring the film's operation and his role there. In an early sequence, shot on a balcony overlooking the Pacific, Derrida emphatically points off camera in the direction of the film's operators as he evokes the "text that *you* are going to write and sign. I am here," he continues, "like some raw material for your writing." This sequence functions something like an establishing shot for the entire film because it goes outside the frame and remarks it. Throughout this sequence, Derrida has been speaking about the finitude of writing, by which he means that

> as soon as there is inscription, there is necessarily selection, and consequently, erasure, censoring, exclusion; whatever I may say now about writing . . . will be selective, finite, as marked by exclusion, silence, and the unsaid as by what I will say.[2]

Having thus called attention to the necessary selection limiting whatever he might say about anything, he points to the film's framing operation as an obvious example of writing as selection and effacement. The camera records whatever falls within its frame, but the film is written by cutting and splicing, deleting and selecting. Thus, the gesture toward the film's author or writer points in the direction of the highly compounded effect of effacement and censorship. It also gives clear warning to the viewer that, despite his appearing here himself or as himself, the one named "Derrida" is not this work's signatory or author; he is raw material deposited in the hands of others, his image and his speech turned over to them to make with it what they will.[3]

Even though this exchange of viewpoints takes place in the most pacific manner, there is a readable tension on its surface. By remarking his passivity as raw material, Derrida also, and with the same gesture, attempts to slip beyond it, to overturn it by verbally shooting the film's own writing. Indeed, intercut into the image of Derrida speaking are two spliced clips, very dark and grainy, in which we see members of the film crew on the same balcony, but as shot by Derrida with a little handheld camera. The film seems thereby to translate into images what its subject refers to, in the very next segment, as his impatient patience or patient impatience as he waits for the film crew to set up, test the sound equipment, determine the camera angles, and so forth. In this subsequent segment, a large aquarium fills the screen; numerous blue-colored fish slowly pass back and forth behind the head of the subject, who after turning to look at them, looks back toward the camera and says:

> The impatience of fish; what I'm thinking about is the patience, the impatience of fish. These fish have been catalogued, imprisoned, put under glass

> . . . I feel like a fish here, obligated to stand in front of the window, behind
> the window before a gaze. I am made to wait, the time, the time, the time it
> takes, the time it takes. . . . It's the image of hell. . . . Moreover, they are like
> me subjected, patiently, impatiently, to the wishes of the masters.

Throughout this sequence, one hears a drip, drip, drip of water, which in the prism of Derrida's commentary is slyly converted into an "image of hell," a prisoner's recollection of water torture. He compares himself to the imprisoned fish and when he elaborates this association by describing how he is "obligated to stand in [*figurer*] in front of the window, behind the window, before a gaze," his outspread hand is advanced palm first toward the camera and held there a moment as if pressed up against a glass division. We know from Fathy's descriptions in *Tourner les mots* that this sequence was shot on the first day of filming with Derrida on location, in the Musée des arts d'Afrique et d'Océanie in Paris, and that, nothing having gone according to plan, the film's subject quickly became exasperated by the whole process. She writes that "when the camera stopped to change the film cartridge, or for any other reason, Derrida felt threatened, dispossessed, as if he had been abducted" (*Tourner*, 135).[4] Impatient patience, patiently impatient: the subject is a patient who goes under the knife of the film's operators, an imprisoned animal patiently, impatiently turning round his cage while his movements are recorded by the turning camera.

The tension I am pointing to, however, is less between the subject Derrida and those who, by cutting and splicing, selecting and deleting, are writing the film that will bear his name in its title. It is rather a tension already between Derrida and himself, between someone who submits to the operation and someone who cannot bear to be patient or a patient. Derrida has a word for this implacable contrariness in *Circumfession*: he is or he gives, as he says several times, the *counterexample* of himself. Long passages of *Circumfession* are read aloud in the film. It is indeed, if I am not mistaken, the only work of Derrida's that the film quotes and excerpts. The last of these excerpts, which also supplies the last words spoken in the film, names the counterexample:

> what I would have liked to announce . . . what you have to know before
> dying, i.e. that not only I do not know anyone, I have not met anyone, I
> have had in the history of humanity no idea of anyone, wait, wait, anyone
> who has been happier than I, and luckier, euphoric . . . drunk with uninter-
> rupted enjoyment . . . but that if, beyond any comparison, I have remained,
> me *the counterexample of myself*, as constantly sad, deprived, destitute,
> disappointed, impatient, jealous, desperate, negative and neurotic, and that
> if in the end the two certainties do not exclude one another for I am sure
> they are as true as each other, simultaneously and from every angle . . .
> (*Circumfession*, 269–70)

This counterexemplarity is what any film titled "Derrida" has to try to bring within its frame, and not only through sequential juxtaposition, but as I just read, "simultaneously and from every angle." In *Tourner les mots*, Fathy refers to the film's extensive use of what she calls a *contre-champ*, a counter-field, whereby, for example, Derrida is shown slowly walking through a ruined house in a deserted location while on the soundtrack we hear him speaking about hospitality from the balcony in Laguna Beach, recognizable by the background sounds of waves crashing and seabirds calling. In the initial sequence, immediately following the opening titles, this technique of the counter-field is ushered in with a jump cut to the first shots in Algiers as we hear Derrida gloss his sense of the term "ailleurs." The sequence begins once again with the ruined landscape, Derrida traversing it from screen right to screen left and looking broodingly toward the camera, while his voiceover speaks of crossing the limit toward an *ailleurs*, an elsewhere:

> It is a matter of thinking from this limit-crossing. The *ailleurs*, even when it is very nearby, is always the beyond of some limit but [pause] in oneself, one has the limit in one's heart [*and on this phrase the image track jumps to a shot taken from a moving vehicle of a street scene with several women in white chadors and half-veiled faces in a crowd of passers-by*], in one's body, that is what the *ailleurs* means, the elsewhere is here. If the elsewhere were elsewhere, it would not be an elsewhere. [*And with this last sentence, the image track jumps again to a vista out toward the sea as seen through a large public garden, which is not identified as the Jardin d'Essai in Algiers; in the foreground a man is leading a small boy down the steps into the garden. This segues to the next shot of Derrida emerging at the top of a long staircase at the bottom of which one sees a rocky beach and breaking waves.*]

This principle of the counter-field, whereby a limit is traced and crossed between an elsewhere and a here, guides the editing of the film throughout, but it is not yet such a deliberate and well-known cinematic technique that captures (and I use the word advisedly) Derrida as counterexample of himself. To return for a moment to *Circumfession*, which provides something like the subtext or superscript of the film's scenario, I will recall that the first of this text's fifty-nine periods speaks of "a desire toward which all others since always seemed, confluence itself, to rush," a confluent desire, therefore, that would gather into itself all conflicting or contrary ones, a single main artery of desire without counterexample. This arterial desire announces itself first with a phrase, which immediately suggests a sequence of images that come to the surface from a reserve of memory bathed in affect and sensation, fear and a wave of appeasement. The opening sequence of *Circumfession* thus reads like a film script, with image track and sound track on which a three-word phrase would be spoken first in a ghostly, unidentified voiceover and then repeated by one of the actors in the scene who plays a nurse and who manipulates a complicated apparatus that draws his lifeblood from the child, now adult, remembering the scene:

> a sentence came, from further away than I could ever say . . . the plural word of a desire toward which all the others since always seemed, confluence itself, to rush, an order suspended on three words, *find the vein* [trouver la veine], what a nurse might murmur, syringe in hand, needle upward, before *taking blood* [la prise de sang], when for example in my childhood, and I remember that laboratory in the rue d'Alger, the fear and vagueness of a glorious appeasement that both took hold of me, took me blind in their arms at the precise moment at which by the point of the syringe there was established an invisible passage, always invisible, for the continuous flowing of blood, absolute, absolved in the sense that nothing seemed to come between the source and the mouth, the quite complicated apparatus of the syringe being introduced in that place only to allow the passage and to disappear as instrument, but continuous in that other sense that, without the now brutal intervention of the other who, deciding to interrupt the flow once the syringe, still upright, was withdrawn from the body . . . the blood could still have flooded, not indefinitely but continuously to the point of exhausting me, thus aspirating toward it what I called: the glorious appeasement (*Circumfession*, 6–8)

Almost every detail of this flowing, flickering passage could pertain to the description of any film titled *Derrida*, or *D'ailleurs, Derrida*, more precisely to the making or taking of such a film. Its subject is held, blind, between the two arms of fear, which makes him impatient, and its appeasing dissolution, the promise awaiting his passivity and patience. A surrender, then, into the hands of others who wield a complicated apparatus for *prises de vue* and *prises de son*, that is, for camera shots and takes, for sound recording, here imaged as a *prise de sang*, but one that would be absolute and absolved "in the sense that nothing seemed to come between the source and the mouth," the river of confessed, expressed lifeblood flowing without stopping or stoppering in labeled tubes like so many reels of film in their cans. It is desire's own impossible scenario, its life drive as death drive undecidably, but impossible also in the sense that it dissolves the possibility for any subject to say "I can," I can take or make my own self-portrait and be absolved of everything not shown or said there. Impossible because it is the other who must decide to interrupt the flow, it is always the other in me, without me, who decides, and therefore who says me and shows me: "without the now brutal intervention of the other who, deciding to interrupt the flow . . . the blood could still have flooded, not indefinitely but continuously to the point of exhausting me."

At this point, we could cut to another scene or scenario, in other words, another text, the one Derrida titled "Lettres on a Blind Man: *Punctum caecum,*" in *Tourner les mots,* which begins:

Thus, lowering my guard, even before having decided to do so, even before having turned around, I will have let myself be surprised. . . . Never have I consented to that point. Yet never has the consent been as uneasy, as little and as poorly feigned, painfully estranged from complacency, simply power-less to say "no." . . . Never, as if in full knowledge, have I acted so much like a blind man, eyes closed upon a command that dictated: "At this point, to this point, on this date, you must give up keeping back, and keeping yourself, and keeping watch on yourself . . . . Accept hypnosis, yes, hypnosis. . . ." The decision could not have been my own. Assuming that it ever has been.

Never have I been so passive, at bottom, never have I let myself be pushed around, and directed, to that point. How did I let myself be surprised to that point, at that point, so imprudently? (*Tourner,* 73)

À ce point: the repeated phrase both points to the blind point, the *punctum caecum,* that he occupied as the object of the camera's gaze and at the same time, it qualifies an intensity of the experience of having accepted his blindness, as if in full knowledge, to a point much greater than ever before, in a manner so thoroughly against his cus-tomary vigilance. "Whereas I have always been, at least I believe I am very on guard, and I give warning that I am on guard—against this kind of imprudent or improvident situation (photography, improvised interview, the impromptu, camera, microphone, the public space itself, etc.)" (ibid.). Writing after having seen the finished film, on which he will offer absorbing and absorbed commentary, Derrida is surprised by how he was surprised, stunned by how he was stunned, sees then not so much what he did not see, but *that* he did not see. Both Derrida and Fathy, the former more discreetly, the latter more fully, acknowledge that the filming of *D'ailleurs, Derrida* was an ongoing and at times explosive struggle between the two of them, and that the filmmaker had repeatedly to tell her subject that he did not see, he could not see, was unable to see. Although none would have had fuller knowledge of this necessary blind spot than the author of *Memoirs of the Blind: The Self-Portrait and Other Ruins,* none, as well, would have better seen, or rather understood that such knowledge was for nothing in the event as it happened: "No anticipation," writes Derrida a little further in "Letters on a Blind Man," "was able to prevent that all this happened to me, in fact, and happened to me without my seeing anything." (*Tourner,* 76). Concerning the shot of the blind man, filmed on a street corner in Toledo, Derrida confesses his admiration and remarks: "I never saw him, the blind man, while this was being shot, and now, a long time after the shooting, I discover him in a film of which I will remain the stunned Spectator [*le Spectateur ahuri*] . . . in a film in which I was the blind and largely unconscious Actor" (*Tourner*, 82).

But in case one is tempted to take this anonymous blind man as a figure, metaphor, or allegory for the film's subject, that is, himself, Derrida scatters the cards by insisting that (a) the blind man is but one such figure, there are many others, (b) they are each time figures for the film and for every position in relation to the film (Actor, Spectator, Technicians, Author, Editor, etc.) and (c) that the figure in question is neither metaphor nor allegory but rather metonymy. Or as Derrida will prefer to say in common, everyday French, and only in French, these figures are all "une fois pour toutes." I translate this passage but repeat many words in the original:

> And *each time, chaque fois*, it is *at once, à la fois* a figure *among others*, and a figure *once and for all, une fois pour toutes*. A figure that says it all, *qui dit tout*, even as it says only a part of the whole, *tout en ne disant qu'une partie du tout*. What I have just remarked about the blind man (one figure among others but that is valid *une fois pour toutes* . . .) could be referred to other metonymies of the film. For example, *visual images of things*: the ruin, the cat, the ladder or the staircase, the automobile, the floor tile, the mailbox, etc., or to *more discursive figures*, circumcision, excision, hospitality, forgiveness, sexual differences, and so forth. And if a metonymy cuts up a corpus or a body, if it plays between the whole and the part, the latter detaching from the former in order to take its place either by delegation or substitution, well then, circumcision is not just one metonymy among others. It is the metonymy of metonymy, the very play of the film. But there you are, it must be possible to say this about all metonymies—that of the blind man *once and for all, une fois pour toutes* and among others. (*Tourner*, 82)

The blind man, or any of the other figures, whether images of things or discursive figures, *at once* happens only *once*, this blind man on that day reading a certain book in Braille on that street corner in Toledo, and immediately *for all*, immediately detached from the singularity of its event; it stands in for all others, it immediately begins to repeat and replace itself, represent and reproduce itself: *une fois pour toutes*.

Here, at this point, we can rejoin and cut again to Derrida's counterexemplarity, to that which allows him to say of himself that he will have been both the happiest of mortals and the most constantly sad, deprived, and desperate. Read out as Derrida's figure retreats into the background of the blasted Almerian landscape, these final words of the film confess the *une fois pour toutes* as the very principle of the counterexample. As he puts it in *Tourner les mots*, there is no exit from the counterexemplarity of the "once and for all":

this event, the time of what is happening (one time, one time only) is given immediately as *irreversible*, and that is what matters to me: that is what causes me both joy and anguish. . . . this unique event will not happen again, the thing will return no more, it is finished, finite. . . . But, surprise, the "for all" gives one also to understand, right away, without waiting, the contrary: this time stands already for all the others, it replaces them in advance . . . And there, once again, double source of joy and anxiety, double mourning and mourning of mourning: nothing is lost, nothing is irreversible, everything returns ("eternal return"), but inversely, we are already in the midst of substitution, singularity is seen being lost sight of, one loses what one gains. Reversibility procures a joy that is as unbearable as irreversibility. Another way of saying, *une fois pour toutes*, that joy seems as unbearably joyful as non-joy. There is no exit from this. That is what all the metonymies, all the "une fois pour toutes" of Safaa Fathy's film "would mean to say." (*Tourner*, 83–4)

It is time to conclude, and I will do so very briefly, elliptically, for, after all, you are going to watch and hear the film's metonymical operations for yourselves. I will leave you with just two watchwords, the one having to do with the words you will hear and the other with the images you will watch.

First the words. As I have already noted, during one of the sequences shot in Toledo, Derrida is asked to say something about the significance of the figure of the *marrano* for him, and his response, which will move quickly into a discussion of the broader concept of secrecy, begins with a remark on the word *marrane*: "If I have fallen in love with this word," he says, "which has become a kind of obsession in all my recent texts . . ." The remark made in passing reveals Derrida as someone who can say of himself, un-self-consciously and in all seriousness, that he is capable of falling in love with words, not with words in general, but one at a time, particular words. So the first watchword I will leave you with would be to listen for this word-lover and perhaps as well, to ask yourselves as you listen and watch: how can a film film words, the love of words, or the experience of falling in love with a word? How can it, in other words and in the other language, *tourner les mots*, film words? For if Jacques Derrida is a worthy subject for a film, it is because not only has he been capable of that experience but he has communicated it, countless times, in his writings. He did so most directly, perhaps, in an elided part of that passage from *Circumfession* that supplies the already-cited last words of the film. In Geoffrey Bennington's remarkable translation, here are some of the lines that were elided:

this morning it seems to me I am seeing a word, "cascade," for the first time, as happens to me so often, and each time it's the birth of a love affair, the origin of the earth, without counting the fact that the 52+7 and a few times that I have thought I was, like a cascade, falling in love, I began to love each word again, so many words like clean proper names, but the word cascade, you see, itself, I do not see, it falls under my eyes, have you ever seen a word, what's called seen, however long you turn around it, and how to bring off a confession, how to look at yourself right in the eyes and show your face if a word is never seen face on, not even the word *milah*, for "word." (*Circumfession*, 266–7)

The second watchword is an image to watch for. It passes very quickly, in a shadowy background. I do not think I ever saw it the first few times I watched this film. It is the image of a cat, but not the Siamese cat that is alone on screen for several seconds and that Derrida mentions as one of the film's possible metonymies. In *Tourner les mots*, Derrida says that this featured cat reminds him of Lucrèce, one of the cats that long lived with his family, a Siamese whom I met several times and who is buried in the garden of Derrida's home in Ris-Orangis (and the film shows us the burial place). The apparition of this cat in a street of Toledo, observes Derrida, is like a return of the ghost of Lucrèce. The image of this ghostly cat plays over the remarks about the marrano, and secrecy. But in his later commentary on this and his other chosen metonymies in *Tourner les mots*, Derrida never lets on whether or not he noticed how, as this sequence continues, when it cuts back to his own image on screen, another cat, out of focus in the background, climbs out of a window that can be seen over his right shoulder. This other cat pauses a moment on the threshold as if to take in the whole scene, and then jumps down and out of the shot. It all happens behind Derrida's back, silently, so it draws no commentary either in the film or in the commentary later in the book. Unless we may take this chance, unscripted, unpredictable event as a visual metonymy for what Derrida can then be heard saying about secrecy, about a secret that is secret even from its bearer, having been forgotten and become invisible over time: "it's as if I were," Derrida says, "a marrano of the marrano, a centuries-old marrano . . ." Or as if he were the stunned spectator at a film bearing his name, who can no more see what others do than he can see the silent cat leaping down behind his back.

Notes

1. This essay began as introductory remarks to a screening of *D'ailleurs, Derrida* (dir. Safaa Fathy, 2000) at a memorial conference organized at Georgetown University in March 2005 by Roger-Daniel Bensky and Deborah Lesko Baker.

2. Safaa Fathy, *D'Ailleurs, Derrida* © Gloria Films Production/La Sept Arte—France 1999. All translations from the soundtrack are my own.
3. See also *Tourner*, 79.
4. All translations from this work are my own.

Chapter 11

Aller à la ligne[1]

I would venture to say that the French idiom has had no more consistently or ardently inventive practitioners over the last forty years than Jacques Derrida and Hélène Cixous. As my subject, however, is not just the work of the one, the other, or both, but rather the one reading and writing on or about the other, one may begin to imagine how the appeal to the idiom has not merely to be doubled but raised exponentially. The original occasion for these remarks was a gathering of seasoned commentators of Derrida and Cixous who took as their theme precisely this exponentially expanding concentration of the marks of reciprocal reading between the two writers.[2] Although both Cixous and Derrida had signaled in various ways their attention to each other's writing since the early 1960s, it was several decades before they began lifting the seals on these reading relations in published texts. In 1993, Cixous's essay "Quelle heure est-il?" appeared in a collective volume on Derrida;[3] the following year Derrida's essay "Fourmis" staged a dialogue with Cixous on sexual difference; and then in 1995 the joint work titled *Voiles* paired a brief text by Cixous, "Savoir," with a much longer essay by Derrida that wove a reading of "Savoir" into a complex fabric of autobiographical motifs.[4] The next two stages were going to raise the stakes considerably, exponentially: in 2000 appeared *H.C. for Life, That Is to Say . . .*, the magisterial, day-long keynote lecture that Derrida presented at the Cerisy-la-Salle colloquium on Cixous's work (*H.C.*). Almost without delay, in 2001, Cixous published *Portrait of Jacques Derrida as Young Jewish Saint*, her *tour de force* excavation into Derrida's oeuvre beneath the surface of nine sections of his own extraordinary *Circumfession*.[5] I will mention just one other turn in this spiraling, four-handed movement of reading/writing: it was once again a keynote lecture by Derrida, presented this time at the conference celebrating Cixous's gift of her papers to the Bibliothèque Nationale de France. *Geneses, Genealogies, Genres, and Genius: The Secrets of the Archive* was delivered 22 May

2003, mere days following the diagnosis of Derrida's cruel illness (*Geneses*).[6]

Despite what I have just said about the irreducible appeal to the French idiom in this spiraled work, it is nevertheless an English word that comes to mind as I consider how to approach it. This word insists on being pronounced out loud by whoever would seek to enter into the expanses that are the neighboring works of Jacques Derrida and Hélène Cixous, by whoever claims to have, as one says in French, *son mot à dire* in this vicinity. This English word, for which I do not believe there is an adequate French translation, this shibboleth, therefore, that stops me at the border before I have taken a single step, is the word *awe*. At least in its classical use, *awe* mixes terror with respect, or even with veneration, reverence. It describes the condition of one who faces the sublime, or rather who cannot face it without turning away in fear. Going back to the most ancient layers of the Anglo-Saxon tongue, the word named above all the emotion felt before the terrifying divinity the contemplation of which imposed veneration. But even if it is true that the density and immensity of the crossed works of Cixous and Derrida provoke vertigo as in the confrontation with the infinite and thereby inspire respect, it is as much the sound as the sense that urges me to pronounce this word, this syllable, this phoneme: awe. Mouth agape, without articulation, a voiceless voice, the sound of expiring breath, exclamation torn from the throat by what overflows in every direction, onomatopeia, hole in language toward its exterior.

Try to imagine a discourse that would be entirely woven out of such holes or thrusts toward the outside of ready-made language. But it is unimaginable, for nothing can be woven out of holes, *béances*, nothing but the nothing, *rien sauf le rien*. There is no sense in it because it is sense that would seep out of all the holes. And yet, the unimaginable image of such a totally hole-ridden discourse is what I am led to dream of with the arrival of the word, the sound, the syllable or the exclamation *awe*. *Awe* leaves one speechless, awestruck, before the law of these works as each bent over the other has learned and taught to read them. Given to reading by these exemplary readers, the law that must inspire awe is: Halt! Slow down, slow down to the point of seeing the most elementary; every syllable, every phoneme, every letter and character, every punctuation sign, all the blank spaces, all of this is important and gets carried away, all of this combines and is woven otherwise than according to the common sense of language. In her preface to *Portrait of Jacques Derrida*, Cixous announces this law as follows:

> Right away, the first time on the mountain, I realized I had to take him at his word, to the letter, to the summit, literally, to the comma as well, without which the sparks wouldn't fly nor the water gush from his text, meticulously, being attentive to the point of finickiness, to the point as well. (*Portrait*, 7)

From his side, Derrida's *H.C. for Life* insists constantly on the smallest elements of Cixous's writing, the infinite and yet regulated combination of elements, including the elements of punctuation. More than once, he asserts that she has no equal as an artist of punctuation.

It would be tempting to follow these indications and speak of nothing but the punctuation in the one and other's work, by way of presenting here a discourse woven entirely out of holes or punctures. There would certainly be plenty to say. But then, what would be the guiding thread of such a discourse? In order to weave anything together, one must have threads, filaments, links, knots, a warp and a woof, as well as a motif or a pattern. If I was obliged to pass by way of a moment of stunned interjection, by way of *awe*, I cannot stop there, mouth agape, *bouche bée*. Moreover, I have professed speechlessness even as I have carried on saying things without too much difficulty. The moment of awe, then, was but a figure of speech, *une façon de parler*, a way of beginning to speak, or of daring to open my mouth. But it was especially a way of saying first of all the *hors-dire* upon approach to such a thing. Now that speech has begun and the first step taken, another thread must lead us between or over the holes.

I believe I have found such a thread in Derrida's inexhaustible *H.C. for Life*. Even though it is not hidden from anyone else, nevertheless it is only in my copy of the book that I had any chance of being put on its trail and this through the friendly hand of Jacques Derrida. In blue ink, above the words of the inscription, this hand drew a circle or an ellipse around the printed word "lignes" that figures in the title of the collection, "Lignes Fictives," in which the work first appeared. It is in this same collection of the publisher Galilée that were published as well two of the other major stages in this work of reciprocal reading: *Portrait Jacques Derrida* and *Geneses*. But I tell myself the story that it is on the title page (which I prefer to call *la page de garde*) of my copy alone of *H.C. for Life* that the word "lignes"—lines—is singled out by a somewhat elliptical circle. I confess that I do not recall having paid this marking any particular attention until recently, until I had to come up with a title for this essay. I was lost, without hope of being able to respond intelligently, reeling terribly from the blow of the terrible realization that Jacques would not be there to give me the kind of help he had offered on so many similar occasions. With failing courage, I took up the copy of *H.C. for Life* and upon opening it I saw right away the traces of his blue handwriting, and then that circle isolating the plural noun "lignes." I have not yet described how the line circles back on itself and then extends down to the left like a tail hanging just above the first word of the inscription beneath it. What is drawn thereby resembles a little some prosthesis for correcting eyesight, a monocle or a magnifying glass. Or else, it might be a lasso, I think, something I can grab onto so as to pull myself out of the hole of distress. Or yet again, it is a shoe lace like the one that the interlocutors in Derrida's essay "Restitutions" notice in a Van Gogh painting and that they see in the place of the signature Vincent. Derrida also signed sometimes with an elongated, curved line, with his sole initial J., and that is indeed how he signed this inscription. Lasso, lace, but also in French *laisse*, the noun "leash" or else the imperative verb: "leave it," the signature as detached leash, as leftover or remainder.

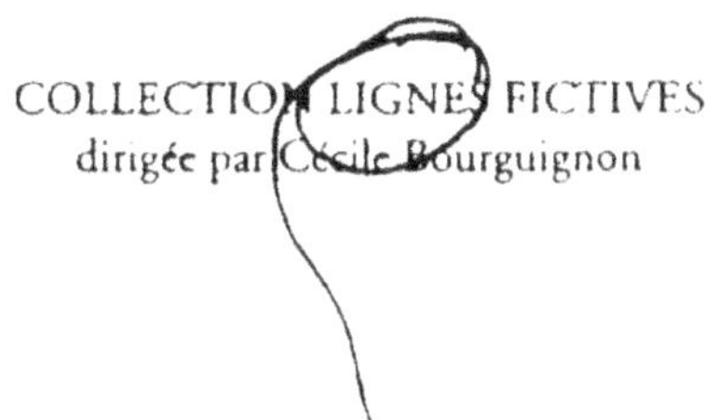

All the same, I was very far from understanding why this word "lignes" was circled like that, why attention was drawn, riven, attached to this word or motif. Unless one was supposed to see, not just the word isolated by the traced line, but also the line that isolated it in its movement of circling back on itself. No doubt in a rather precipitous and superstitious manner (but I could not prevent the impulse), I told myself that Jacques had indicated the thread, the threads to be followed, that with his hand he had made a sign toward the direction to take in my rereading of his very great text on the great oeuvre of Hélène Cixous. So I wrapped this somewhat flattened circle around my waist, and after making sure that the rope was still firmly attached by its tail to the *page de garde* and in the friend's hand, I began to climb the faces of the living mountains that, like two volcanoes, Jacques Derrida and Hélène Cixous have caused to emerge out of the contemporary literary landscape.

For twenty pages I scaled this mountainscape like a tightrope walker crossing between the highest crests. How thin and tenuous the thread seemed! And then at the bottom of a page some lines started to line up very quickly. A long paragraph or *alinéa* in which they accumulate led me to think that perhaps I had not gone completely astray. I quote while skipping a little but landing each time on the word or thing line, "ligne":

> Between the lines of what we have been writing, for decades, that is to say, for people of our generation, throughout a whole lifetime, between so many lines of writing, there will probably have been the unique infinity of a telephone line. . . . So it may no longer be an original situation today for so many of us in this very place. But the shared situation puts us on the wireless line [*ligne sans ligne*] of the telephone, even before being "*on line*" as they say nowadays, and it gives us to think what a line is and what it is not when it describes a certain line between those who, as is the case, are devoted to the line of writing—and even, as is her case, in a writing that is entirely occupied by generation, filiation, the lineage of writing—devoted to the work as lineage. (*H.C.*, 17–18)

Here then the question is asked literally and almost at the beginning of this long lecture: the shared situation of writers who are of the generation of the telephone "gives us to think what a line is and what it is not" when "the unique infinity of a telephone line," a *"ligne sans ligne* of the telephone," can pass "between so many lines of writing." I will not rush to take up the challenge of what Derrida, reading Cixous, gives us to think with these lines, that is, "what a line is and what it is not." I will simply point out two things: (1) that the lines of writing pile up endlessly, beyond calculation, "between so many lines of writing," whereas the telephone line is counted in the singular and as "the unique infinity of a line," and (2) that the question of "what a line is and what it is not" enters right away into a skid that one cannot stop by grabbing onto the mere word "line," whether in the singular or the plural. For a line is also, for example, a filiation, a generation, a lineage, as one says. That "the line of writing" can be everywhere occupied, in and between all its lines, with filiation and the lineage of generations, as is the case, Derrida affirms, with Cixous's writing, causes many threads to cross and scrambles all the clues. This passage, in other words, these lines of Derrida's text, after having initially reassured me that I was following the right path and the right line, begin to slip and slide all down the line, and, consequently, so did I and my reading.

I tried to stop the skid twenty pages further on, in a passage where Derrida speaks of his fatigue with precisely the word "passage," substituting for it several times the word or figure of "lines." Once again, I quote by skipping from line to line, beginning with the opening of a parenthesis:

> . . . a certain passage (I would like to find another word than these hackneyed, tired, and tiring words "passage," "page," or "sequence" to designate

the fragmented units, the "quotes" that I will unfortunately have to cut out in this way. Each of these is a flow or period, a musical movement at once liquid, submarine, aerial, and yet solid, in the ether or in the sea, like a braid of unalterable threads and lines, here a weaving of voices that seek their own style and fortune [*cherchent leur veine*] in a gold mine . . .) The string of lines I am going to cut out would merit centuries of reading. . . . A voice says: "I imagined this letter. One had to be quick. It would say:" (colon, a blank of several lines and a new indented paragraph [*un grand alinéa*] . . . (*H.C.*, 39–40)

Throughout *H.C. for Life*, on almost every line, Derrida apologizes for having "to cut out in this way." This misfortune, to which one should never be resigned, is increased exponentially when someone cuts a passage that already is cutting a passage. Moreover, Derrida denounces this word "passage" as "tired and tiring." But is it not true that this use is exasperating because of its pretense to designate ready-made units, just waiting to lend themselves to quotation, as if all the rest of the "flows" and "periods" could be sacrificed without any loss? As if Cixous's writing could be contained in "passages," "pages," or "sequences"? It is better to assume the commentator's fault and recall that these are lines, among so many lines of writing, "so many lines of writing."

To stay a moment longer with the lines I have just cut out: one hears there something else beside the complaint of their author. He also signals the great envy that the flows and periods signed by Cixous can inspire in him. He even touches on the most profound desire of the one who, beginning with the first period of *Circumfession*, could confess the wish to "find the vein" so as to let flow, without hindrance or censoring, in a single stream or a single line, a writing of confession. Hélène Cixous has not failed to point out the naïveté—the word is hers—of this wish for a writing from which the writer would be absent. In her *Portrait of Jacques Derrida*, she reads this first period under a magnifying glass without cutting off the continuous line in which Derrida confesses his dream to "find the vein." That is the expression he imagines being pronounced by a nurse who is preparing to take a blood-sample from the writer-patient. Derrida repeats the phrase so as to start the flow of writing, without any point of interruption until the end of each period, of which there are fifty-nine. It is all the more striking then that, a few years later, he will write regarding her writing that it is "a weaving of voices that *cherchent leur veine*" and that he remarks his own guilt at cutting the "string of lines." He is guilty of cutting, *coupable de couper*.

Still holding on to the thread of what Derrida gave me to think, that is, "what is a line and what it is not," I began to weave together some reading hypotheses: when one says "a line," when one counts lines out one by one, for example, "so many lines of writing," one pretends to believe in the unity of a thing identifiable as such, delimitable by its two ends, that is, its two extreme points, let's say A and B in the shorthand language of geometry. This ideal object of mathematics, as Derrida showed many years ago now in his introduction to Husserl's *Origin of Geometry* (1963), will always depend, and Husserl can offer no contradiction here, on thoroughly material tracings if it is to preserve its promise of repetition. The origin of geometry can only be "so many lines of writing," in other words, non-finite, non-delimitable, non-unified and therefore non-original lines, if indeed the concept of origin overlaps with that of a unified, undivided point. Just like the point, the line cannot idealize itself in a concept without dividing itself by the iterable trace. And just as Derrida always insisted on the divisibility of the point, he likewise drew all the consequences from the divisibility of the tracing of limits around and between concepts. All of this is at the origin of the most elementary deconstruction. Even as I recalled all this, however, I felt that it was not only some fundamental axiom of deconstruction urging me to follow this line but some other force as well.

Thereupon, I went back to the sixth section of *Portrait of Jacques Derrida*, where Cixous trains her magnifying glass on the point of the divisible point, on that "fundamental axiom of everything he says every-where" (*Portrait*, 63). Her reading is going to excavate beneath this axiom, seek out its links within the language such as he writes it and receives its dictations. While doing so, she maps out points of meeting in the language she shares with him and knows how to put to work or in play. I cut out several lines from this chapter, titled "Point donneur," "Point of Honor/Point Donor":

> Everything he writes, everything he thinks is a protest against the point as indivisible. He writes, divided, in order to divide it, the point. He thinks, he lives, divisibility, he divives [*il divit*]. His sense of urgency on this point exceeds even his own calculations, sometimes he makes a point of attacking the point, sometimes it is his unconscious or the possibilities of the French language that work against the point. He does not admit the indivisible. This refusal is his point of honor. Never does he put a point, a dot, a period, the word, the sign without a shudder. The minute he sights a point he is on the mark, he is off, he is gone. . . .
>
> Everything he writes, he writes from the starting point aiming always for the point that is furthest beyond. (*Portrait*, 63–4)

She then aligns several phrases in "point" that she has snatched here and there from Derrida's work: from "A Silk Worm of One's Own" ("ne point écrire" and "sur le point de"; "to write not at all" and "on the point of") and from *Tourner les mots* ("Jamais je n'ai consenti à ce point"; "Never had I consented to this point"). I cannot reconstruct this aligning of points, the line followed in her reading, but I retained from it something very valuable that I was going to carry with me as I continued to think about what is or is not a line. The force I felt at work there is not so much that of the axiom of divisibility (of the line or the point, it makes little difference), but the living force, the force of the living or simply, if one may say it simply, the force of life. This line, these lines that Derrida has so much trouble cutting or interrupting are lives, the tracings of so many lives.

Hélène Cixous knew this already, her work knew it, but near the beginning of *H.C. for Life*, Derrida says that he does not know "whether, more than her, sooner than her, better than her, anyone will have ever given me to think what *to live* means" (*H.C.*, 16). I had not yet noticed the fact that this sentence, in which one finds the expression "donner à penser," "to give (one) to think" comes just before the remark I had already isolated, and that I quote again: "it [that is, the shared situation of writers in the age of the telephonic line] gives one to think what a line is and what it is not." This repetition is not necessarily deliberate, in any case it is not underscored, but there is nonetheless an alignment of these two "things" that are living and line in the interval of a few lines: to give to think what to live means/to give to think what a line is and what it is not. This alignment is made in thought or thinking but also *for* thought, in the dative sense of what is *given* to thought to be thought. It is Hélène Cixous, he writes, who will no doubt have given him more, earlier, and better to think what "to live" means. Derrida then adds several sentences, several lines that would specify and clarify this declaration, but that effort is interrupted and he apologizes for leaving all this obscure for the moment while promising a better explanation later. There then follows, almost immediately after this interruption, the lines concerning the telephone line between "so many lines of writing."

Now I am really in a quandary. If one must take account of the alignment I have just seen confirmed, and I believe this is indeed necessary, then one should not neglect anything in this text, and quite a few others, but especially in this text that, on the basis of Hélène Cixous's gift, does the work of thinking life in its "puissance," its "might." This term *puissance* is the one that, not without considerable trouble but with Cixous's helping hand, Derrida manages to tear loose from its powerful philosophical filiation with, precisely, power, possibility, potentiality, and so forth. My quandary was that I no longer knew which end of the thread to grab, among all those that now offered to lead further. I therefore decided to back up all way to the *page de garde* so as to interrogate once again the figure drawn at the edge of the inscription.

I am not sure "interrogate" is the best word. I looked at the drawing and it gave itself to be seen and thought. I therefore addressed it as one might a familiar animal, saying something like this: "You roll yourself up around the word 'lignes,' around these lines because you want to protect them, to keep them, is that right? These lines are lives, your lives, but finally any life and all of life that you would like to draw within the protective circle of your writing and your thought. You want to think life as that which one does or makes, *comme ce qui se fait*. Lines of writing, lines of life. That is indeed your gesture throughout the book that you here inscribe with your elliptical line, as well as the gesture of Hélène's almighty writing that gives you so much to think about and that you cause to rebound so far and so high. You have been searching for a long time, since forever, for this *puissante*, mighty thinking of life *for* life, which would be neither that of a life that is each time mine (as Heidegger might have said), mine against yours or theirs, nor that of a response to the ontological question ('What is life?') or the question of being. You've got hold of it here, this thinking, along the thread of an incomparably active reading that is countersigning and that is—I would have said dynamic if you had not demonstrated the necessity of mistrusting the whole inheritance of the Greek *dynamis*, here again in *H.C. for Life*, but with so many other lines of writing as well as in so many other books."

This moment of conversation with my little animal who rolls up in a ball on the *page de garde* (like a hedgehog or an opossum) had the effect of bucking up my courage a little, at least enough to make a final attempt and to venture further in the book. Holding tight onto the rope and the animal's tail, I jumped to a page close to the center of the text. Here, Derrida's commentary follows on some cited lines from Cixous's 1997 fiction titled *OR, Letters from My Father*. I will pick it up from the last few words of the quotation:

> . . . at stake is the **vital bond** that unites two creatures . . .
> [and then Derrida continues]:
>   This vital bond will be metamorphosed as if by an enchantment: from the lock of hair into a telephone wire, into a "telephone cord," into a telegraphic and, therefore, telepathic wire, into a "braid of name" or into the wire of a funambulist or of an acrobatic trapeze artist. The thread of this "vital bond" is the mighty power of life, it is nothing else than life for life, in that it binds to life, which is nothing but this engagement that binds life to itself—and to nothing else: the verb "bind" binds itself tautologically to life, it goes and has meaning only for life, it binds life, which binds itself to itself, at the very point where, in this powerful bond that it weaves with itself and which it

therefore is, it is attached to itself only by a hair—but by a hair of the other, who is none other than a mad trapeze artist, himself hanging above the abyss, without a net, by a thread or by a hair. (*H.C.*, 81–2)

From these lines beautiful enough to make one weep, signed by more than one hand, I retain the analysis of the tautology contained in the phrase "vital bond." Life being what binds and binds to itself, there is no other bond but a vital bond. Life is what rolls up on itself, weaves itself into bonds and links, but from life to life, life for life. Life, then, and not *a* life (and all of this would give one to think what is and is not *a* life, and even whether *a* delimited, discreet life has ever been possible), even if it is also a matter here of the bond from one to the other, from the one who catches the lock of the other's hair to pull him/her out of the abyss. But through this movement of saving or keeping, it is once again life that lends itself a hand or that pulls itself out by its hair.

I am going to go quickly toward a last quotation cut out of *H.C. for Life*, which I insert here without introduction:

> I would have liked to inscribe here the generation of the word *fois* in the lifeline of live words [*dans la ligne de vie de mots en vie*], of the words *vie* [life], *visa* and *visit* . . . as you know, *fois* comes from Latin *vicis*, which is not really a noun but first corresponds to a genitive form—in order to designate the turn, succession, the return, reciprocity, the alternative, therefore a certain replacement, a certain substitutive vicariousness. . . . "For the whole of life," for life, is irreplaceably the time, each time, in all the times. And what is necessary and impossible at the same time, necessary as impossible, in this thought of the "for the whole of life," is the logic of the "whole" as much as this logic of life. . . . [T]his "whole" in the whole of life derives as little from a logic of totality or of totalization as the "mighty power" of the "might" derives from a dynastic logic of power, of the possible or of potentiality, of the "I may" or "it is possible" of this potentate. (*H.C.*, 95)

I do not propose to analyze this braid, which I have shaved moreover of several of its curls. I extract merely the line "ligne de vie de mots en vie" (translated as "lifeline of live words"), an octosyllabic verse that weaves together line/life/words inextricably enough to hold up for a whole life. But I also wanted to remark the link that, four years later, will be made explicit when Derrida once more and for the last time delivers a lecture at Cerisy-la-Salle. This link is, of course, that of life and of "another thought of life," as he puts it in the concluding lines of the prologue to this lecture, "The Reason of the Strongest":

> It is indeed on the side of chance, that is, the side of the incalculable perhaps, and toward the incalculability of another thought of life, of what is living in

life, that I would like to venture here under the old and yet still completely new and perhaps unthought name *democracy*. (*Rogues*, 5)

To conclude very abruptly, I will pose merely a few markers for future work. It seems to me necessary to reread this thinking of the mightiness of life, painstakingly worked out in *H.C. for Life*, in terms not only of its poetic but also its political significance. As we have heard several times, and this is one of the most insistent and consistent arguments throughout this book, indeed its central thesis if there is one, this mightiness does not derive "from a dynastic logic of power, of the possible or of potentiality, of the 'I may' or 'it is possible' of this potentate." Yet, it is precisely as the regime of the "I may" that sovereign power defines ipsocentric sovereignty. The mightiness of the event that Derrida finds at work in the Cixousian text offers itself indissociably and at the same time as poetico-political/politico-poetic. "It is a question here," he writes in "The Reason of the Strongest," "as with the coming of any event worthy of this name, of an unforeseeable coming of the other, of a heteronomy, of a law come from the other, of a responsibility and decision of the other—of the other in me, an other greater and older than I am" (*Rogues*, 84). It is a question, that is, of the life of democracy, unless we should understand the life of democracy as another tautology.

Allez à la ligne voir "la ligne de vie de mots de vie."

Start a new line to see "the lifeline of live words."

Notes

1. Initially written in French, this essay has been translated (more or less) with the exception of this title. "Aller à la ligne" is a typographical term that means to start a new paragraph or *alinéa*. Literally, however, it says to go to or by the line.
2. Organized by Marta Segarra of the University of Barcelona, the conference "L'écriture comme événement: Lire Cixous et Derrida se lisant" took place in June 2005.
3. Cixous, "Quelle heure est-il, ou La porte (celle qu'on ne passe pas)," in *Le Passage des frontières: autour du travail de Jacques Derrida*, ed. Marie-Louise Mallet (Paris: Galilée, 1994).
4. Hélène Cixous, "Savoir" in *Veils*, trans. Geoffrey Bennington (Stanford: Stanford UP, 2001) and Derrida, "Silk Worm."
5. Hélène Cixous, *Portrait de Jacques Derrida en jeune Saint Juif* (Paris: Galilée, 2001); *Portrait of Jacques Derrida as a Young Jewish Saint*, trans. Beverley Bie Brahic (New York: Columbia University Press, 2004).
6. Since this essay was first written, Cixous has added at least three more texts to this series: *Insister à Jacques Derrida* (Paris: Galilée, 2005); *Insister of Jacques Derrida*, trans. Peggy Kamuf (Edinburgh: Edinburgh University

Press/Stanford: Stanford University Press, 2007); "Jacques Derrida as a Proteus Unbound," trans. Peggy Kamuf, *Critical Inquiry* 33, 2 (Winter 2007), which was expanded and reprinted in "The Keys To: Jacques Derrida as a Proteus Unbound," trans. Peggy Kamuf, *Discourse* 30 (Winter–Spring 2008), pp. 1–2.

Chapter 12

Composition Displacement

I ought to begin by confessing my very modest ambitions here.[1] And I would indeed begin on that note if only such confessions were not too often taken to be understatements, according to the rhetoric of false modesty, and thus essentially to be false confessions. And then they are apt to produce the reverse effect of raising rather than lowering expectations. So let me say simply that I plan to interrogate two sets of terms, two notions, or two practices that are deployed across Derrida's great essay "Plato's Pharmacy," the terms/notions/practices of composition and displacement. I will necessarily do this selectively, following out only a small sample of ways one could be led to think about and with these key notions or terms, as much by what the essay says as by what it does—assuming, which I do not, that this distinction can stand up precisely to what the essay is saying and doing, saying about what it is doing or doing with what it is saying. Beyond this proposal to isolate and read a few fragments of "Plato's Pharmacy," I do have one further ambition. It is to gather enough momentum from this selective reading to execute a leap beyond that essay, originally published in 1968, and land, without accident I hope, closer to the other end of Derrida's oeuvre, traversing thereby what is now often referred to as the division between his early and late work. The point of the exercise, however, will not be to ratify or justify the positing of such a divide, which is usually premised on the idea that Derrida's thinking underwent a turn toward a more explicit or simply readable ethico-political version of deconstruction. On this account, such a version would supposedly have lain too implicit in the first-born guise of the deconstruction of the concept of writing and the generalization of the text.[2] Derrida has himself repeatedly repudiated this genealogical narrative, most recently in *Rogues* (39). With my own leap across a twenty-five-year span of the oeuvre, I hope to bring to bear at least one or two more reasons to resist such narratives and to be wary of the figural substitution of chronology or biography for an entirely different "logic" that does not necessarily unfold according to the commonly referenced temporal order. "Plato's Pharmacy" is not yet four decades into the centuries it may take to "undo its web," and this timeline, one suspects, will ruin irreparably any distinction of "early" from "late."

Moreover, in 1968, in "Plato's Pharmacy" already, if one can say that, the matter of the essay's place in an ongoing work is indicated by the signatory himself. And this place is said to be that of an extension of writing's play beyond the limits of a meaning- or wanting-to-say, the animating and organizing principle of someone's living speech. Derrida thus calls up a penumbral space in which writing survives to go on playing beyond the exhaustion of a living intention:

> To a considerable degree [*À très peu près*], we have already said all we *meant to say* [*nous avons déjà tout dit de ce que nous* voulions dire]. Our lexicon at any rate is not far from being exhausted. With the exception of this or that supplement, our questions will have nothing more to name but the texture of the text, reading and writing, mastery and play, the paradoxes of supplementarity, and the graphic relations of the living and dead: within the textual, the textile, and the histological. We will keep within the limits of this *tissue* . . .
>
> Since we have already said everything, the reader must bear with us if we continue on awhile. If we extend ourselves by force of play. If we then *write* a bit . . . ("Pharmacy," 65)

These are the opening lines of the first of the essay's two main sections. They themselves fall in a liminal space, on a threshold between the apparent *entrée en matière* in subsection 1, which follows directly, and two preceding pages, which one might call a prologue if it were precisely not a matter of introducing a writing rather than speech—a prograph, then, or even a program. The lines just cited represent something like a delay, hiatus, or parenthesis between what are plainly marked as a first beginning and then its repetition in the first subsection, which begins, or rather rebegins: "Let us begin again" (65). I underscore these details to hint at the hazards lying in wait for whoever would rush to periodize such a text, as if the mere *date* of its composition were all one had to read, as if the composition of a text coincided with itself in some present that is now past and dated.

In a moment, we will have to return to these lines and take our bearings from them again as we venture to say anything more about Derrida's later work in relation to "Plato's Pharmacy." To get back there, however, I am going to follow a zigzagging path through the essay on the stepping-stones called composition and displacement.

The initial stepping-stone is laid down in the very first sentence, the famous incipit of the essay: "A text is not a text unless it hides from the first comer, from the first glance, the law of its composition and the rules of its game" (63). From such a definitional proposition, there can be no turning back; it cuts loose and strikes a blow (that is, a *coup*, the word whose etymology, set in epigraph to the text, includes a connection to inscription). This cut cuts out a figure of textual composition that has nothing to do with its former appearance, because it has nothing to do with appearance at all, being inapparent, hidden, imperceptible: "A text remains, moreover, forever imperceptible," the next sentence reads, as we say. We can indeed say a "sentence reads" where we would be less likely to say: it writes. But now, right away, we are no longer so sure how to make that distinction and even if it is possible after the first blows of this text. For they leave their mark no less on the idea of reading than on that of writing. The name of text ties or knots them together as the same, in the element of the same, through the repetition: "Un texte n'est un texte . . .".[3] This initial compositional unit, in other words, brings differences into relation through repetition of the same: writing and reading here begin to *compose together* in the same or as the same text. Each obeys, follows, or is constrained by the hidden law of their composition.

(A parenthetical observation here, one which any persistent reader of works signed by Derrida will have had occasion to make: between texts being read, cited, paraphrased, and commented upon, on the one hand, and on the other, assertions, affirmations, propositions, declarations, arguments, and so forth, that are being made in his own name and assumed by the signatory, the seam can often almost disappear, even though when one looks for it, usually it can be retraced with some assurance. There is, in other words, a quasi-seamless incorporation of the read into the written and an injection, a penetration—better yet, an inscription—of the written into the read. This quality is, I have found, one of the principal stumbling blocks for novice readers of Derrida, who are apt to mistake paraphrase or summary of another's argument for his own. A compositional technique that can be especially disconcerting is the use of the singular first person in a general rather than particular sense, which is often a way of testing or extending an argument, trying it out in the grammatical guise of an "I," any "I." Derrida can slip in and out of this non-attributable "I" with the ease of a practiced mimic who delights in the play of masks. To the best of my recollection, the composition of "Plato's Pharmacy" does not call upon this technique and, indeed, avoids altogether the first person singular, either general or particular. This remark is for the attention of those determined to distinguish an earlier from a later "Derrida.")

Reading and writing, I said, *compose together*. The ambiguous syntax can lead us into the storehouse, the *arrière-boutique* of this composition with "composition," as one might say a "still life with flowers." *Composition*, the noun, and *compose*, the verb, in French and to a somewhat less active extent in English, always put in play more than one strand of possible sense. They say, or rather they compose, the *compounding* of sense. From *componere*, to place or put together, these compound words compose, compound the compound, the non-simple. I say "they compose," rather than "they mean," "they say," or "they mean-to-say," to yield not to tautology but, on the contrary, to the only condition of non-tautological sense, which is to say, the relation of differences. As J. L. Austin observed, in a remark that Derrida likes to cite, by themselves words have no meaning; only sentences can have meaning. Which is to say, meaning, sense, is a compound, a composition of differences. But, of course, it is not only the sense of words or of verbal compositions that are put together. In a use that has become obsolete in English but remains active in French, a composition of differences is also an agreement to settle differences, to compromise, to come to terms with another, to decide a dispute. In the language of war, it means capitulation. To arrive at or come to "composition" is to reach a compromise. Hence, someone is said to be *de bonne composition* who is accommodating, good-natured, easy to get along with. And characters who are hard to get on with are said to be *de mauvaise composition* or *de composition difficile*. With these latter expressions, one can begin to hear how modern use has tended to shift the notion away from the composition (or compromise) *with* another and toward an enclosure within the self's own "composition," where the term signifies something closer to make-up, nature, constitution. This is more marked in English where a person's "composition" is glossed by the *OED* as "the combination of personal qualities that make any one what he is," and this sense is further explained as a transfer from the term's use with regard to compound, composite things. In French, this shift has perhaps been slowed somewhat by the still very active uses of both verb and noun to mean compromise and accommodation always *in relation with* some other or some difference. This with-ness is even underscored by a very common use of the verb *composer* with the preposition with, that is, *avec*, a construction often translated as "to come to terms with." Derrida makes frequent use of this construction in "Plato's Pharmacy," which prompts his English translator, Barbara Johnson, more than once to come to terms with it by translating: to compose with.[4]

I will select a first example of this syntax from one of the clearest meta-discursive moments in this text, when it declares the "single theme of this essay" to be a certain "composition." It occurs near the beginning of Part I, Chapter 4, "The Pharmakon," where Derrida picks up again the scene between Thamus and Theuth, having apparently interrupted his reading of it to sketch in the previous chapter a composite portrait of Theuth-Hermes-Thoth-Nabû-Nebo, which is a portrait of the writer as parricidal son who must be preemptively quashed by a father's judgment (one of the epigraphs to the chapter is from *The Portrait of the Artist as a Young Man*). This scene is at the center of Derrida's interest in the *Phaedrus*, or rather one of the centers, both of which he has displaced from the dialogue's margins, the other being the initial exchange with Phaedrus that tempts Socrates to follow him outside the city walls, for perhaps only the second time in his life. As for the myth of Theuth and the invention of writing right before the dialogue's conclusion, its displacement from the margins counters the tradition of interpreting the *Phaedrus* as a "badly composed" dialogue (66), marred in particular by the addition of this "mythological fantasy":

> That entire hearing of the *trial of writing* will one day have to cease to appear as an extraneous mythological fantasy, an appendix the organism could easily, with no loss, have done without. In truth, it is rigorously called for from one end of the *Phaedrus* to the other. (67)

Rigorously called for, that is, commanded by the hidden law of the text's composition. Or as we have begun now to be able to hear this vocabulary of composition, the law, the constraints, the forces *with* which the text composes. In the chapter titled "The Pharmakon," these forces or constraints are going to be organized into opposing camps, or at least into two different moments or gestures that Derrida distinguishes on the one hand and on the other hand. On the one hand, Plato is intent on presenting writing as an occult power, comparable to all the forms of magic whose practitioners he condemns to the worst of fates: expulsion, ostracism, imprisonment, and denial of burial. On the other hand, however, because the king's put-down reply to Theuth turns on the multiple resources of the *same* word, *pharmakon*, which Thamus repeats but in order to say the opposite of what Theuth asserts, something like poison rather than remedy, this reply effectively restores the communication between the opposing values of the writing-*pharmakon* that, "on a different level of the stage," Plato would have sought to block. This reversibility of *pharmakon* is a key instance of what Derrida calls Plato's anagrammatic writing. It is this other writing, commanded by a law of composition hidden in the open of the Greek language, that the tradition of "Platonism" would have contrived to ignore in favor of Plato's "own" intent to prevent the contamination of opposing values by guarding them from repetition in their ideal purity.

I have just summarized quickly two dense pages, but I will now have to slow down and try to follow Derrida's formulations more precisely in order to have a chance to read in what sense "composition" is said to be the "single theme of this essay." For despite the ordering device of "on the one hand," "on the other," when this exposition of force and counter-force begins to wind up, the two forces seem to collapse into, if not one, then the same.

> When a word inscribes itself as the citation of another sense of the same word, when the textual center-stage of the word *pharmakon*, even while it means *remedy*, cites, re-cites, and makes legible [*donne à lire*] that which *in the same word* signifies, in another spot and on a different level of the stage, *poison* . . ., the choice of only one of these renditions by the translator has as its first effect the neutralization of the citational play, of the "anagram," and, in the end, quite simply of the textuality of the translated text. It could no doubt be shown . . . that this blockage of the passage among opposing values is itself already an effect of "Platonism," the consequence of something already at work in the translated text, in the relation between "Plato" and his "language." *There is no contradiction between this proposition and the preceding one* [emphasis added]. Textuality being constituted by differences and by differences from differences, it is by nature absolutely heterogeneous and is constantly *composing with* [emphasis added] the forces that tend to annihilate it. (98)

If I am following correctly, then the two propositions said here to be non-contradictory are advanced in the first two sentences of the passage as cited. The apparent contradiction, an appearance Derrida dismisses unequivocally, would thus be between the play of textuality—citationality, reversibility, anagram, displacement—and the blockage or neutralization of that play no doubt as "the consequence of something already at work" in the same text. But the non-contradiction one is being explicitly challenged to think finds another more economical, idiomatic, and therefore untranslatable expression in the last sentence: "Textuality . . . is constantly composing with the forces that tend to annihilate it," that is, "compose sans cesse avec les forces qui tendent à l'annihiler." When I say this syntax is untranslatable, I do not mean only in its attempt to pass into English, for example. Already in French, at least two senses are pulling at the verb, and it is this traction in different directions that constitutes or composes the non-contradiction, but now within a single verbal locution: on the one hand, textuality *compromises* with the forces of its neutralization, which is without a doubt the sense conveyed by ordinary French usage, and, on the other, it composes with them, that is, it also weaves them into its text, as the text, as the very fabric of its composition, which is in fact what one may more readily understand in the English version. "Composed with," then, as one might say made up of, made out of some materials, just as the sentence begins by affirming that textuality is constituted by differences. This composition, make-up, or constitution would be the form of the compromise and vice versa.

It is this composition of compromise, then, that Derrida singles out, when the passage continues, as "in a certain sense, the single theme of this essay": "One must therefore accept, follow, and analyze the composition of these two forces or these two gestures. That composition is even, in a certain sense, the single theme of this essay." The two gestures just outlined are then reprised and once again with the help of the compositional device of the one hand and the other to keep them apart in their non-contradiction. After reiterating the violent, destructive effects of "Platonism"'s translation on the *pharmakon*, that is, on the original milieu of the decision in which "Plato decides in favor of a logic that does not tolerate such passages between opposing senses of the same word," this recapitulation concludes: "Such an interpretive translation is thus as violent as it is impotent: it destroys the *pharmakon* but at the same time forbids itself access to it, leaving it untouched in its reserve" (99). It forbids itself, in other words, the play of writing as a composition with the forces massed against it that speak in the name of the King, the father, and a certain "Plato," the one who did not write.

Untouched in its reserve, then, is the composition of the Platonic text. But one of the most consistent concerns of "Plato's Pharmacy" is to test the limits of this text, which certainly cannot be understood to coincide with any one signed (or attributed) corpus. This essay, with its single, "unique" theme of composition, is itself composing with the most massive force ever assembled, at least in the West,[5] against the resources, the reserve, that is, the virtual possibilities of compositional play. If I insist on the term play, the reason is not only because it features so significantly in the essay's coming-to-terms with the Platonic legacy.[6] In addition, this insistence seeks to provoke a re-engagement with Derrida's so-called "early" thought at the point where, if you believe his periodizers, it had to date itself—1968, the free play of the signifier, and so forth—and was therefore obliged, at the risk of becoming passé, to turn to more serious matters, by which is usually meant the ethico-political in its most recognizably thematized form but sometimes, more trivially, mere "current events." Such a re-engagement would take up again this thinking of play as compositional, in the senses we have begun to discern, that is, in constant compromise with all the constraints at work limiting and defining the space of its deployment.[7] I want to argue that this thinking and this practice of textual composition, the two indissociably within the uncertain but not unlimited margins of its play, define the deconstructive invention at its most powerful. By that I mean, for a long time yet to come, its resources will remain inexhaustible for the transformative reinvention of institutions and of the inheritance conditioning, governing, and constraining the very experience of "life." Without any question, Derrida's work, from 1968 on, is drawing deeply on these resources, which is what any periodizing notion of a turn, much less of a break, fundamentally misrecognizes.

And yet, we can have no illusions about being able to recognize, today, so soon, the full greatness of this oeuvre; but as its first witnesses, we should also call ourselves to account for it as best and most truthfully as we can. In a moment, by taking up precisely this figure of the witness and the problematic of testimony, to which Derrida devoted several essays in the mid-1990s and three years of his seminar from 1992–1995, I will try to make at least a start at giving one such possible account. For this, however, there are still a few more materials I need to gather from the immense storehouse that is "Plato's Pharmacy."

At least three further occurrences of *composer avec* may be found in the essay. Although there is not enough space to follow up on each of them in sufficient detail, it may be instructive just to string them together with minimal commentary.

Chapter 8, "The Inheritance of the Pharmakon: Family Scene," begins by returning once again to the myth of Theuth's invention of writing, or rather to its immediate aftermath, when Socrates once again speaks in his own name and leaves off repeating fanciful stories:

> After the presentation of the *pharmakon* to the father, after the put-down of Theuth, Socrates takes the spoken word back to his own account [*reprend la parole à son compte*]. He seems to want to substitute *logos* for myth, discourse for theater, demonstration for illustration. And yet, within his very explanations, another scene slowly comes to light, less immediately visible than the preceding one, but, in its muffled latency, just as tense, just as violent as the other, composing with it, within the pharmaceutical enclosure, an artful [*savante*], living, organization of figures, displacements, repetitions. (142)

This other scene is the family scene, which, Derrida observes, "has never been read for what it is" because, unlike the myth, it is composed not narratively but metaphorically, "at once sheltered and exposed in its metaphors" (143). What has also never been read, what "remains untouched in its reserve," then, is how Plato's composition at this point, and against its manifest intent, repeats and displaces *mythos* in *logos*, the two orders that are collaborating in this very theatrical representation of patriarchy's violent dismissal of (the son's) writing. Here *composant avec* has a sense closer to collaboration, although given what is at stake for Plato in maintaining the superiority of *logos* over *mythos*, this collaboration is necessarily as well a compromise, which can only happen backstage, as it were.

The last two occurrences are found in the final chapter and the context of both would deserve careful reading. It is interesting perhaps that Barbara Johnson here chooses each time to translate *composer avec* more idiomatically as "to come to terms with," and not, as we have seen up until now, "to compose with." Given the high level of attentiveness of the translation, I suspect that this was a deliberate choice and for a reason that may become apparent.

As they have done at several points, the analyses of "Plato's Pharmacy" signal clearly their place within a much larger structure and historical context. "Platonism," often in scare quotes, is Derrida's general name for this structure, whereas Rousseau and Saussure lend their proper names to different "epochs" of its history. The last of such reminders that this essay should also be read as the fully developed prequel to *Of Grammatology* is made not just in passing but recapitulates in some detail and with a brief list the constant features across this history:

> what seems to inaugurate itself in Western literature with Plato will not fail to re-edit itself at least in Rousseau, and then in Saussure. In these three cases, in these three "epochs" of the repetition of Platonism, which give us a new thread to follow and other knots to recognize in the history of *philosophia* or the *epistēmē*, the exclusion and the devaluation of writing must somewhere, in their very assertion, come to terms with [*doit quelque part composer, dans leur déclaration même, avec*] . . . (158)

There then follows a three-item list of what Platonism, in whichever of its periods, must "come to terms with": first, a general writing, and within that, second, the "contradiction" of logocentrism's affirmation in writing, and finally, the inclusion in a "literary" work of the logocentric "content," which can then be read anagrammatically, according to the play of the *pharmakon*. What logocentric Platonism, then, must come to terms with is its inclusion within a general space of writing that it does not and cannot command, oversee, regulate, and still less put under ban.

We come now to the last occurrence of *composer avec*, a few pages before the essay breaks off in mid-sentence, having sounded "those knocks from without," those *coups* from the outside.

> But what the parricide in the *Sophist* establishes is not only that any *full, absolute* presence of what *is* . . . is impossible; not only that any full intuition

of truth, any truth-filled intuition, is impossible; but that the very condition of discourse—*true or false*—is the diacritical principle of the *sumplokē*. If truth is the presence of the *eidos*, it must always, on the pain of mortal blinding by the sun's fires, come to terms with [*composer avec*] relation, nonpresence, and thus with nontruth. (166)

Sumplokē, that is, interweaving or *entrelacement* as Derrida most often translates it.[8] But we will also translate again with composition and for the reason that is affirmed here as a necessary coming to terms or composing with relation. "If truth is the presence of the *eidos*," Derrida writes, following a certain Plato: but, precisely, that is an impossible truth, if one follows a certain other Plato, or perhaps simply Plato *as* other. For the only possible truth has to have composed, reconciled with its interwoven implication in nontruth, with its being-in-relation to some difference from itself. Or with what Derrida has designated just a few pages earlier as "the play of the other within being," "le jeu de l'autre dans l'être."[9] Perhaps, then, we can see why the better understanding is conveyed here by the figure of "coming to terms" for it evokes the terms of a negotiation, for example, to end hostilities. Would that we could translate this composition as "truth" *making peace with the play of the other.*[10]

From this last given location in the essay, it would be fairly easy to jump forward in Derrida's oeuvre to his writings on testimony. A well-marked bridge is provided by the assertions just cited to the effect that the full intuition of truth is impossible and "the very condition of discourse—*true or false*—is the diacritical principle of the *sumplokē*." But while this bridge would certainly hold up, it would also be a purely thematic one that, once put in place, gives relatively easy access to whoever comes upon it and thinks to cross to the other side. What would be passed over, however, is how the bridge got there in the first place, before any road signs were in place. For as Derrida writes at a certain point in "Plato's Pharmacy," "ce déplacement . . . il faut le faire."

Without reconstructing its context, I will remark simply that, as used here, this idiom, "il faut le faire," is put in play in several senses and intonations at once: for example, this displacement must be done, you've got to do it, or it's inevitable, but most often "il faut le faire" also poses a challenge to whoever thinks to attempt it in fact, in deed, because it's difficult, not a walk on the beach.[11] Or after the fact, it might be said to correct the idea that just anyone could have done it, as if to say, "that's what you think. Just try it. *Il faut le faire.*" On top of all that, as when he often remotivates or reanimates a so-called dead metaphor (another of his techniques of composition), Derrida invites the reader to hear this expression anew, without all the wear and tear on the very active verb *faire*: the displacement must be *made, done, performed, effected, under-taken, caused to happen, brought about*, and so forth. In other words, it is not just a matter of thinking it, conceiving of it, imagining it, naming it, or talking about it; the displacement has to be brought about in an act of doing or making. One is thus reminded that *déplacement, déplacer* indicate as well, and even first of all, the most basic sense of movement, whether in space, time, or elsewhere. To move or shift something from one place to another or to change an appointment is to *le déplacer*. To be *en déplacement* is to be on a trip, away from home. And *se déplacer* is to put oneself in motion to change places or locations, which one can do in some mode of transport, that is, a *moyen de déplacement*. But as well, a remark that is out of place or inappropriate is said to be *déplacée*, whereas to *déplacer* someone can mean to take his place or his job.

These reminders by way of taking Derrida *literally* when he writes "ce déplacement . . . il faut le faire." Literally, because he then adds: "Il s'écrit. Il faut donc d'abord le lire." "It writes itself. One must therefore begin by reading it" (104). Displacement, then, would be the very movement or gesture of writing, the transfer effected through the space of composing differences, of the play of the other in being. Displacement, movement, but also out-of-placeness, dislocation, without proper place or home, de-placing, the un-doing of place: this is what writes itself, what one must begin by reading, which is to say, by recognizing that one is moving through the space of composing differences. *Il faut le faire!* When reading, then, one is *en déplacement*, but the question would be: when is one not reading, not composing with differences, and therefore also not *en composition*, which is also to say, *in* the composition?[12] In composition-in-displacement, forever unable to reach a *place* of exterior mastery in relation to it, that is, to say, without relation to it, thus always some place that is also dis-placed. Again, "Plato's Pharmacy":

> No absolute privilege allows us absolutely to master [the] textual system [of the *pharmakon*]. This limitation can and should be displaced to a certain extent [that is, *il faut le faire!*]. The possibilities and powers of displacement are extremely diverse in nature, and, rather than enumerating here all their titles, let us attempt to produce some of their effects as we go along, as we continue our march . . . (96)

"As we go along, as we continue our march" renders: "*en-marchant*," a hyphenated invention that is also italicized in the original. Derrida has many times pointed out that, at least according to some etymologists, *marche/marcher* (to walk, step, march, go along, but also to work or function) would be related to both *marge* (margin, border, frontier) and *marque/marquer* (mark). Perhaps, then, if the question is how one got from the displacements of "Plato's Pharmacy" to, for example, the deconstruction of the concept of testimony, the answer would simply (or not so simply) be: *en-marchant*, step by step, marking the margins all along the way. And if that sounds too easy, then just remember: *il faut le faire.*[13]

* * *

If I am not mistaken, the witness and testimony are never named as such in "Plato's Pharmacy" (at least not in the French original).[14] And yet, the essay is suffused with a juridical vocabulary and especially with the lexicon of the courtroom. In a very pertinent and explicitly thematized manner, the mythic scene between Thamus and Theuth is read and analyzed as a courtroom scene, whereas the whole Platonic discourse is described as a trial and condemnation of writing, "un procès de l'écriture." Thamus, the "king of all Egypt," sits in judgment on writing, whose inventor sits in the witness box. The king pronounces sentence (76). When the king falls silent, Socrates takes over the prosecution: his discourse is called a "réquisitoire," that is, an indictment, an arraignment, a formal set of charges (75, 106 [translated as "diatribe"]). Writing is on trial (67), it is the accused (75, 77, 148), and its case is grave, serious (103); it is cited to appear (135), hands tied, before the tribunal of *logos*, there to be interrogated (136) and summoned to respond. I cite this latter fully dramatized courtroom scene:

> If writing and painting are convoked together, summoned to appear with their hands tied, before the tribunal of *logos*, and to respond to it, this is quite simply because they both are being *interrogated*: as the presumed representatives of a spoken word, as agents capable of speech, as depositaries or even fences [*receleurs*] for the words the court is trying to force out of them. If they should turn out not to be up to testifying in this hearing [*Qu'elles ne se montrent pas à la hauteur de ce procès-verbal*; a *procès-verbal* is a ticket for a minor infraction, e.g., a parking ticket, but literally it says a "verbal trial." The translation by "testifying at a hearing" bears on the assumption that testimony is verbal and that the witness speaks for him/herself], if they turn out to be impotent to represent a live word properly, to act as its interpreter or spokesman, to sustain the conversation, to respond to oral questions, then bam! [*et du coup*], they are good for nothing. (136)

Writing, the accused, is helpless to testify in its own defense. And this is, of course, the principal indictment that Plato lodges against it: it cannot testify, bear witness, respond to questions put to it. More precisely, unlike the testimony of speech, there is no father who can present himself to testify on its behalf. As for Theuth, whom Thamus refers to as the father of writing, his testimony in favor of his own invention, his own child, is summarily dismissed by the court as, at the very least, in error, mistaken, overly indulgent for his offspring, but it may just as well be a false witness, a perjury. Commenting on this testimony or testimonial, Derrida says "by ruse and/or naïveté," [Theuth] has exhibited the reverse of the true effects of writing" (97). From the point of view of the king, that is.

Given that the scene of trial and testimony is never brought center-stage as such to be examined or interrogated, one could be tempted to read it as mere accessory. Thus, for example, when upon initiating his reading of the dialogue, Derrida refers to the last section of the *Phaedrus* as "cette instruction du *procès de l'écriture*,"[15] we might understand something like the operation of metaphor, where the figure of investigating and interrogating "writing," as accused party before the law, would be the chosen vehicle to convey the tenor of Plato's discourse. Instead, however, I suggest this figure has to be apprehended along the lines of the reversal that Derrida performs in order to read the "metaphor" of the father, a reversal that is key to all the analyses of "Plato's Pharmacy." The necessity of this overturning is laid out in Chapter 2, "The Father of Logos," a moment I cite, to save space, only in a few of its most essential articulations:

> Only a power of speech can have a father. The father is always father to a speaking/living being. In other words, it is precisely *logos* that gives us to think something like paternity. If there were a simple metaphor in the expression "father of logos," the first word, which seemed the more *familiar*, would nevertheless receive more meaning *from* the second than it would transmit *to* it. . . . Even though this *hearth* is the heart of all metaphoricity, "father of logos" is not a simple metaphor. . . . One must thus proceed to undertake a general reversal of all metaphorical directions, no longer asking whether *logos* can have a father but understanding that what the father claims to be the father of cannot go without the essential possibility of *logos*. (80–1)

As Derrida does reading Plato's "metaphor" by standing it on its head, with the effect that "it is *logos* that gives us to think something like paternity," so, in the general space of writing now opened up by "Plato's Pharmacy" (and its contemporaries, especially *Of Grammatology*), are we able to read the "trial of writing" in the opposite metaphorical direction: it is "writing" that gives us to think something like trial and testimony, in other words, the process of truth that can take place only *in the absence of the father*. Every witness, and not just in the formal setting of the courtroom, testifies in this absence, which is to say, *as* writing: without a father "who speaks *for* him and answers *for* him" (77). For there is indeed no witness *for* the witness: "Niemand/zeugt für den/Zeugen," in the words of Celan that Derrida takes as the focus of his densest interest and concentration in "Poetics and Politics of Witnessing." To testify, to bear witness is to *write* in the absence of the father witness-for-the-witness: without, therefore, the full presence of the truth itself to the intuition of one's hearers and judges. In the absence of the father of *logos*—the condition of writing—there can be no certainty, no proof as to the truthfulness of the testimony.

Rather, there is only belief. Every witness says, in effect, "You must believe me," "It is necessary to believe me," "Il faut me croire":

> It is necessary [*Il faut*] to hear and understand this "you have to believe me" ["*vous devez me croire*"]. "You have to believe me" does not have the meaning of theoretico-epistemological necessity. It is not presented as a *probative* demonstration to which one has no choice but to subscribe to the conclusion of a syllogism, in the course of an argumentation, or indeed to the display of a thing present. Here, "you have to believe me" means "believe me because I tell you to, because I ask you to" or as well "I promise you that I will tell the truth and be faithful to my promise, and I undertake to be faithful." In this "it is necessary to believe me," the "it is necessary," which is not theoretical but performative-pragmatic, is as determining as the "believe." At bottom, it is perhaps the only rigorous introduction to the thinking of what "believe" can mean to say. . . .
>
> "What is believing," what are we doing when we *believe* (which is to say all the time, and as soon as we enter into relation with the other): this is one of the questions that cannot be avoided when trying to think testimony. ("Witnessing," 76–7)

To think testimony is to think an order of necessity that is not the necessity of a theoretical or epistemological proof.[16] Rather, it is that of the necessary *condition* under which and in which testimony is given and received. In "Plato's Pharmacy," as we have seen, this condition is called, for example, *sumplokē*, the interweaving composition *with*, in relation to the other: in the terms we cited above, "the very condition of discourse—*true or false*—is the diacritical principle of the *sumplokē*. If truth is the presence of the *eidos*, it must always . . . come to terms with relation, nonpresence, and thus with nontruth." When, two pages later, Derrida restates this condition, the displacement toward an explicitation of the condition of testimony is all but manifestly accomplished, already in place, held in reserve in parentheses:

> The disappearance of truth as presence, the withdrawal of the present origin of presence, is the condition of all (manifestation of) truth. Nontruth is the truth. Nonpresence is presence. Differance, the disappearance of any originary presence, is *at once* the condition of possibility *and* the condition of impossibility of truth. At once. "At once" means that the being-present (*on*)

> in its truth, in the presence of its identity and the identity of its presence, *is doubled* as soon as it appears, as soon as it presents itself. *It appears, in its essence*, as the possibility of its own most proper non-truth . . . (166)

Testimony, bearing witness, is an act of manifesting the truth, that is, of repeating what is/was present.[17] The condition of this manifestation is repetition, a doubling, whereby the possibility of *telling* the truth is at once the possibility of *not telling* it, whether by "ruse and/or naïveté," as Derrida remarks of Theuth's testimony, which is to say, whether by lying, perjury, error, mistake, misperception, or by otherwise failing to repeat and thereby to keep one's promise to the other to whom one has sworn, implicitly or explicitly, to tell the truth. A failure that may also be provoked by forgetting or by a lapse into that state of absent-mindedness, "not thinking about it," which affects the principal character, Stéphane Chalier, in Henri Thomas's novel *Le Parjure*, to which Derrida devotes his essay "'Le Parjure,' *Perhaps*: Storytelling and Lying."

Truthful testimony—and one can only believe that there has ever been any such thing—is conditioned by the possibility that it is false. And this possibility is irreducible. If it were not, then testimony would provide the certainty of a proof, and would therefore not be what it is, testimony. To be truly what is called testimony, rather than proof, it must possibly be false, a fiction. With this term of "fiction," however, Derrida does not understand only the contrary of the truthful or the order of falsehood. Fiction would be another name for what Plato calls the simulacrum, and to which he denies the ability to manifest anything but the outer appearance of truth, its repetition. In the modern extension or rather restriction of this determination, fiction has been made largely to coincide with literature in its modern sense, even though neither of these terms is fully covered by the other. Despite this, Derrida will insist that specifically literary fiction and the poetic constitute the *exemplary* site of testimony and therefore for the reflection on it. His three principal texts to date on testimony and bearing witness all take their bearings in literary, poetic compositions: "Aschenglorie," the poem by Celan, Thomas's novel *Le Parjure*, and Maurice Blanchot's *récit*, *The Instant of My Death*.

"Exemplary" here does not mean only "taken as an example of, illustrative." These fictional, poetic texts are as well each singular, exemplary acts *of* testimony, as every such act must be. For every testimony must be exemplary in these two senses: at once replaceable, repeatable, translatable, generalizable, universalizable, on the one hand, and irreplaceable, unrepeatable, untranslatable, singular, on the other. To quote *Demeure*:

> In saying: I swear to tell the truth, where I have been the only one to see or hear and where I am the only one who can attest to it, this is true to the extent

that anyone who *in my place*, at that instant, would have seen or heard or touched the same thing and could repeat exemplarily, universally, the truth of my testimony. . . .[18] The singular must be universalizable; this is the testimonial condition. Simultaneously, at the same instant, in the "I swear, you must believe me," I am claiming, I am demanding, I am postulating the possible and necessary universalization of this singularity: anyone who *in my place*, etc., would confirm my testimony, which is thus both infinitely secret and infinitely public . . . (*Demeure*, 41)[19]

Later on in this same essay, Derrida writes that Blanchot's text "reminds us that the testimonial act is poetic or it is not, from the moment it must invent its language and form itself in an incommensurable performative" (*Demeure*, 83). The testimonial act, the testimonial condition: these designators, we begin to see, are not discriminating a particular classification of acts or kind of condition from others. On the contrary, they generalize the experience and condition of testimony by displacing all the limits thought to confine it and set it apart, for example and exemplarily, from the fictional, poetic act. "Fiction and Testimony," the second title of this essay on Blanchot's *récit*,[20] thereby invokes what is commonly thought to be a pair of mutually excluding terms, according to which belief a testimony cannot present itself as a fiction and a fiction cannot claim to testify. But it does so in order to displace that limit by the necessary inclusion of the *possibility* of fiction in every testimony and thus in every speech act that calls upon the other's belief.

But, then, what is not testimony? "This act of faith is implied everywhere one participates in what are called scenes of bearing witness. And in truth, as soon as you open your mouth. As soon as you open your mouth, as soon as you exchange a look, even silently, a 'believe me' is already involved, which echoes in the other" ("Witnessing," 83–4).

I will conclude by echoing, letting resonate, this echo in the other, in other words, this repetition of the repetition that is an act of testimony "as soon as you open your mouth." At one point in "Poetics and Politics of Witnessing," Derrida recalls, as he has done a number of times, that *Wahrheit*, *vérité*, truth, and so forth say something about keeping, guarding, safekeeping and safeguarding: "the *keeping* of this safekeeping is the movement of *truth* (*veritas*, *verum*, *wahr*, *wahren*, which means to keep; *Wahrheit*: the truth)" ("Witnessing," 80). The German word *Wahrheit* is also set in motion at the beginning of *Demeure*, where Derrida cites Goethe's title, *Dichtung und Wahrheit*, as what he is half-translating, half-displacing by his own title, "Fiction and Testimony." But there is still another, seemingly more distant echo coming from near the end of "Plato's Pharmacy," two pages before a line of periods marks the retreat with Plato, at the end of the day and out of sight of the sun, into the back room of the pharmacy. Before crossing that line, Derrida asks if we can "set off in search of another guard [*une autre garde*]" given that the "pharmaceutical 'system'" so painstakingly analyzed allows nothing to escape its grasp and seems to block all the exits? If this is so, he continues, then "to what general, unnamable necessity are we dispatched [*renvoyés*]? In other words, what does Platonism signify as repetition?" (167–8).

These questions are anything but those of a desperate resignation. On the contrary, they are an extension of the lines we already read at the other threshold of this text, which issue into the space of writing's play with and as repetition:

> Since we have already said everything, the reader must bear with us if we continue on awhile. If we extend ourselves by force of play. If we then *write* a bit: on Plato, who already said in the *Phaedrus* that writing can only repeat (itself), that it "always signifies the same" and that it is a "game." (65)

Near the essay's close, then, we are dispatched, *renvoyés*, that is, sent or referred back to the "general, unnamable necessity" that is the play of repetition *within* the same.[21] The same, which is to say: the other. When it is asked, therefore, if we can "set off in search of another guard," another keeping, safekeeping, or safeguarding of truth, we are in effect already being sent on our way with a referral to the play of the other in the same. For let us play a little and read *une autre garde* not as a noun phrase, but as the cell of a sentence, subject and intransitive verb, and thus of the affirmation: *an other guards*. Such a reading responds to the necessity of this *renvoi* to the other's keeping, an unnamable necessity because truth cannot be given in name in response to the question "What is . . .?" once "writing suspends the question *what is*, which is always, tautologically, the question 'what is the father?'" (146).[22] Rather than another name, this guard is a guarding, and *il faut le faire*, that is, its truth must be made, done, composed, displaced, and we would now add *believed*—or not—if indeed the general necessity to which we are *renvoyés* is also and everywhere that condition called testimonial.

Like everything else, Plato would have already said as much, in his Second Letter, the letter confided to the address of Dionysius and the one Derrida cites just before letting resound the blows from without: "It is a very great safeguard to learn by heart instead of writing. . . . Farewell and believe. Read this letter now at once many times and burn it" (170).

Notes

1. This chapter began as a lecture to the *Collegium Phenomenologicum*, Città di Castello, Italy, in July 2006, convened by Michael Naas, on Derrida's essay "Plato's Pharmacy."
2. See for example, Peter Baker, *Deconstruction and the Ethical Turn* (Gainesville: University of Florida Press, 1995).
3. This syntax can recall, with some delay, the initial cell of Francis Ponge's "Fable"—"*Par le mot* par . . ."—to which Derrida devotes many pages of "Psyche."
4. Although the *OED* documents a use of "compose" in the senses of "to arrange a dispute, conflict of claims, etc. To settle, adjust, arrange **a.** discord or dissension, a dispute, difference, quarrel, war, disturbance, disorder, etc. **b.** contending or rebellious persons, a disturbed district. . . . To arrange (any matter) properly or successfully; to settle," it records no use in this sense with the preposition "with." Johnson, however, was certainly right to sense its lack and supply it.
5. On the question of whether or not this restriction can be sustained, see "Pharmacy," 167–8.
6. See especially the concluding chapter, "Play: From the Pharmakon to the Letter and from Blindness to the Supplement." This title might also be translated: "Play: Concerning the Pharmakon *à la lettre* and Blindness to the Supplement." The two possibilities are playing, undecidably, off of each other. In *Of Grammatology*, Derrida had already deployed the ambiguous syntax of the phrase "de l'aveuglement au supplément" (*Grammatology*, 144).
7. That Derrida could be held up for derision, in the most vulgar version, as an advocate of anything-goes free play is beyond ludicrous. His lesson is incomparably and invariably severe. One need merely consider the fate he reads off for the so-called "pleasure principle" in "To Speculate—on 'Freud'" (*Post Card*).
8. Interlacing, interweaving, *entrelacement* is also one of the key notions for Derrida's reading of Levinas's composition (see "This Work"). For a very fine analysis of Derrida's affinity for textile tropes, see Caroline Rooney, "Deconstruction and Weaving," in *Deconstructions: A User's Guide*, ed. Nicholas Royle (New York: Palgrave, 2000).
9. "The scriptural 'metaphor' thus crops up every time difference and relation are irreducible, every time otherness introduces determination and puts a system in circulation. The play of the other within being must needs be designated 'writing' by Plato . . ." (163).
10. When an initial version of this essay was presented at the *Collegium Phaenomenologicum*, this passing and very conditional reference to "making peace" drew fire from Martin Hägglund, as if I had advanced the idea that the composition between forces of opposition were a peaceful, rather than violent, affair, or as if this possible translation of "coming to terms with" arose necessarily from the wish or the phantasm of perpetual peace (*pace* Kant) and thereby sought to pacify some essential countering drive of deconstructive thought. Perhaps. But if indeed there is only negotiation between conflicting and unequal forces—and I would

agree—nevertheless "peace" must remain one name of what is in play or at stake between them, if only always promised and deferred. At what shall we have arrived if the very name "peace" could no longer even be pronounced, having been utterly forgotten? (For another attempt to read Derrida's negotiation between "war" and "peace," see my "Names of War," *Oxford Literary Review*, 31, 2.)

11. Johnson translates "this displacement . . . is a real and necessary challenge" (104).

12. Gertrude Stein said the same thing, differently of course, in "Composition as Explanation," for example: "The composition is the thing seen by every one living in the living that they are doing, they are the composing of the composition that at the time they are living is the composition of the time in which they are living." In Stein, *Look at Me Now and Here I Am: Writings and Lectures 1909–45*, ed. Patricia Meyerowitz (London and New York: Penguin Books, 1967), p. 24.

13. The expression "il faut le faire" can remind one of a story that Derrida liked to tell and that always cracked him up. A man claiming to be a telepathist had a nightclub act. He would come on stage with his assistant who then proceeded to ask a volunteer from the audience to concentrate on some thought. After a few moments, the assistant would turn to the master and ask him: "Master, can you tell us what this person is thinking?" The telepathist would pause and then reply. "Yes, I can." At which point, his assistant would exclaim to the audience: "Do you hear that, ladies and gentlemen? Il *peut* le faire! He *can* do it!"

14. At least once, Derrida does use the verb "témoigner," but with the sense of "to indicate" or "to signify": "Dieu le roi ne sait pas écrire mais cette ignorance ou cette incapacité témoignent de sa souveraine indépendance" (85–6); "God the king does not know how to write, but that ignorance or incapacity only testifies to his sovereign independence" (76).

15. Johnson translates: "that entire hearing of the trial of writing" (67). When used as a juridical term, *instruction* means the preliminary inquiry or investigation of charges by an examining magistrate, who is called the *juge d'instruction*.

16. The central nerve of Derrida's thinking of testimony, witnessing, perjury, and lying is the very problematic and yet necessary distinction between testimony and proof. "This conceptual distinction is as essential as it is unsurpassable in principle, *de jure*. . . . For the axiom we ought to respect, it seems to me, even though it may be problematized later, is that *bearing witness* is not *proving*. Bearing witness is heterogeneous to producing proof or exhibiting a piece of evidence" ("Witnessing," 75).

17. "Whoever bears witness . . . is someone whose experience . . . attests, precisely, that some 'thing' has been present to him. This 'thing' is no longer present to him, of course, in the mode of perception at the moment when the attestation takes place; but it is present to him, if he alleges this presence, as *re-presented* in memory. At any rate . . . it would be inaccessible, as *perceived* presence, to the addressees receiving the testimony, who are placed in the order of believing or are asked to place themselves there" ("Witnessing," 77–8).

18. This sentence is exemplary of that use of the general first-person indexed

earlier as a trait of Derrida's composition. Moreover, it describes why every "I," at every instant, is subject to this aporetic condition of generalizing singularity.
19. For a remarkable reading of the co-implication of secrecy and testimony in Derrida's thought, see Ginette Michaud, *Tenir au secret* (Paris: Galilée, 2005).
20. It is the second title of the English version only. On this title, see *Demeure*, 15–16.
21. This echo or resemblance between the two thresholds, separated by a hundred pages of the essay, is more than thematic: each stands just before a door to the pharmacy—the front door of the first chapter titled "Pharmacia" and, at the other end, the door to the pharmacy's back room—and each is immediately succeeded by an imperative to repeat: "Let us begin again" (65) and "Let us repeat" (168).
22. And never "what is the mother?" Note, however, the feminine gender mark, which has been neutralized by translation, of the affirmation: *une autre garde*. Only the play of writing can open thinking to an *other* sexual difference, other than the masculine or the paternal.

Chapter 13

The Ear, Who?

Epigraphs

Roderigo: Most reverend signor, do you know my voice?
Brabantio: Not I. What are you?
Roderigo: My name is Roderigo.
Brabantio: The worser welcome:/ I have charged thee not to
haunt about my doors . . .

(Othello, I, i)

. . . about his feet/ A voice clung sobbing till he questioned
it,/ "What art thou?" and the voice about his feet/ Sent up an
answer, sobbing, "I am thy fool . . ."

(Tennyson, Idylls of the King)

The same question—"What are you?", "What art thou?"—posed each
time to a voice, speaking or sobbing, detached from a familiar face,
and thus made strange, unknown, uncanny. As if the questioner had to
doubt that it was indeed *someone's* voice, he asks of it "what" rather
than "who." Calling upon the voice to attach itself again to a name,
an identity, the question might well be addressing a ghost, an "it" not
yet declared to be the ghost of someone or other. *Hamlet*, you recall,
begins with a question thrown out into the night—"Who's there?"—as
Bernardo approaches his fellow watchman.[1] And a few moments later
Francisco takes up the call: "Stand! Who's there?" These sentinels have
been put on edge by, as Barnardo puts it, "What we two nights have
seen"; their question to "who," "who's there?" is something like whis-
tling in the dark, a sound made to reassure themselves that it is indeed
who and not what on approach. And when "it comes again/ In the
same figure like the King that's dead," Horatio's address will have the
same form as Tennyson's King Arthur to the sobbing voice that clung

about his feet: "What art thou that usurps't this time of night . . .?" Like Arthur, Horatio questions the figure—not a detached voice this time but a silent apparition—using the familiar form of address and yet refuses, to him, to thee, to it, the personal interrogative pronoun, calling out not "Who's there?" but "What art thou?" "Stay, speak, speak, I charge thee speak. [*Exit Ghost*]." In the wake of this silent retreating vision, Horatio counsels: "Let us impart what we have seen tonight," and, upon their return the next night with Hamlet, when the ghost's identity and story will unfold from his own mouth, so to speak, the watchers on the rampart question each other in all manner of ordinary what's (Act 1.4): "What hour now?" (l.3), "What does this mean, my lord?" (l.8), "What may this mean . . ." (l.32), "Why, what should be the fear?" (l.45), "And for my soul, what can it do to that . . .?" (l.47), "To what issue will this come?" (l.66).

In the next scene, the beginning of Hamlet's exchange with the Ghost interjects a suspended and ambiguous "What?" between the lines of the apparition's appeal:

Hamlet: Alas, poor ghost!
Ghost: Pity me not, but lend thy serious hearing
  To what I shall unfold
Hamlet: Speak, I am bound to hear.
Ghost: So art thou to revenge when thou shalt hear.
Hamlet: What? (I, 5, ll.5–8)

What is it possible to hear in this monosyllabic question or interjection "What?"? Perhaps impatience to learn what he is bound to hear in a moment, to hear it without delay, in the anticipation that the Ghost has instilled. Or incredulity: Hamlet cannot believe his own ears; has he indeed just heard the ominous word "revenge"? Or even deafness, incomprehension before the sounds the Ghost has made, as if to say "Come again? What did you say?" Finally, perhaps, one may also hear a protest against the precipitation with which his strange interlocutor has bound him through his ear, through his sense of hearing, and thus through his passive reception of the other's words, to a program of bloody revenge even before he has been told what for. For at the point of this interjection, the Ghost has not yet answered Horatio's question "What art thou?" with the claim: "I am thy father's spirit," which is the next line, right after Hamlet's suspended interjection: "What?" To be sure, the previous witnesses have already given Hamlet reason enough to expect not just any ghost. Indeed, when first faced with "such a questionable shape" (I, 4, l.24), he announces a choice of address: "I'll call thee Hamlet,/ King, father, royal Dane" (ll.25–6). But this decision to address a who, indeed to address him by proper name and title, also wavers and he continues, like the watchmen, to refer to the Ghost as "it" ("It will not speak. Then will I follow it" [l.43]; "It waves me forth again. I'll follow it" [l.49]; "It wafts me still. (*To the Ghost*) Go on, I'll follow thee" [l.56]).

"I'll follow it" is followed by "I'll follow thee," which marks a turn toward apostrophe. In that turn, "what" gives way to "who," but perhaps not yet altogether. For a moment later, and as we have just heard, Hamlet says or interjects "What?" upon hearing the Ghost repeat his bound word with the effect that, before he knows it, he is sworn to revenge for what he has not yet been told. "Speak, I am bound to hear," says Hamlet and this reply plays between at least two senses, in the sense of two meanings, one of which has to do with the sense of hearing: on the one hand, "I am bound to hear" responds to the Ghost's demand for "thy serious hearing"; it is the response of a promise, already the form of an oath, swearing to listen, to obey, and not just to hear. But, on the other hand, "I am bound to hear" also says "I cannot fail to, I will necessarily and by necessity have to hear what you will say." Like the sense of smell, hearing is a passive site of reception that the individual will controls only partially and with difficulty. One may close one's eyes and mouth; one may also withdraw from touch, effectively putting an end to the reception of the sensation. But neither nose nor ears can close themselves or cut off sensory contact by themselves. They have no membrane to lower over the orifice or muscle with which to activate closure or withdrawal. They thus remain open and receptive even when one intervenes to stopper them. Hamlet's is a tragedy of this open ear, which is bound to hear, the ear open to the story of the father's ear that is open to the poison of the world. "List, Hamlet, list, O list!" says the Ghost (I, 5, l.22).

|

"(everything comes down to the ear with which you can hear me)." You cannot hear them but this assertion is enclosed between two little ears, the marks of a parenthesis. Jacques Derrida has just cited, in epigraph, a passage in which Zarathustra recounts coming across "an ear! An ear as big as a man!" The immense ear stood "on a frail little stem—but that stem was a man!" From this figure of what Zarathustra calls an "inverted cripple," which is his name for those "who lack for nothing, except having one thing to excess," Derrida begins the second part of his text titled "Otobiographies." This is just one of several titles of his that introduces into the labyrinth of an ear: another is "Tympan," the opening or threshold essay in *Margins of Philosophy*, and, much later, "Heidegger's Ear," the second part of *Politics of Friendship* (omitted from the English translation). But to remain for the moment with *Otobiographies*, in its initial publication, the essay from which I have just quoted appeared in a volume of conference proceedings titled *L'oreille de l'autre*, *The Ear of the Other*, a phrase that also resonates, so to speak, in Derrida's text. For example, already in the parenthetical phrase—"(everything comes down to the ear with which you can hear me)"—where everything comes down to the ear. Which ear? Whose ear? The ear of what? And even we might ask, recalling Zarathustra's strange encounter, the ear, who?

A one who is all ears. This is, in effect, Nietzsche's description of the student in the University apparatus. At one point in his reading of the early text of lectures called *On the Future of Our Educational Institutions*, Derrida summarizes the apparatus Nietzsche describes there in these terms:

> The hypocritical hound [one of Nietzsche's figures for the State] whispers in your ear through his educational systems, which are acoustic or acroamatic apparatuses. Your ears grow larger and you turn into long-eared asses, instead of listening with small, finely tuned ears, and obeying the best master and the best of leaders, you think you are free and autonomous with respect to the State. You open wide the portals of your ears to admit the State, not knowing that it has already come under the control of reactive and degenerate forces. Having become all ears for this phonograph dog, you transform yourself into a high-fidelity receiver, and the ear—your ear which is also the ear of the other—begins to occupy in your body the disproportionate place of the "inverted cripple." (*Ear*, 34–5)

Whereupon, as he has done frequently throughout, Derrida asks his own auditors at an academic lecture if this scenario of so-called "academic freedom" is still the one in which he and they are inscribed. "Is this our scene," he writes. "Is it a question of the same ear? . . . Or rather do we hear ourselves, do we understand each other already with another ear?" These questions are left to hang in the air, or rather to hang on the ear to which they are addressed because, as Derrida then adds: "The ear does not answer" (*Ear*, 35).

The scene, I said, is an academic lecture.[2] When? Where? Who? What? Nietzsche wrote *On the Future of Our Educational Institutions* as seven lectures, of which he delivered the first five in Basel. Slightly more than 100 years later, Derrida delivered "Otobiographies: The Teaching of Nietzsche and the Politics of the Proper Name" at least twice to university audiences, at the University of Virginia and the

Université de Montréal. What is happening when one cites a lecture, that is, a scene of reading, address, audition and reception? And when one cites such a citation, again, "here and now"? The scenes of audition are rolled up within one another; there is always another ear that does not answer. But this abyssal structure is also what allows the question to recur and to resonate again, thirty years later, in the United States still, or 130 years later, or 2,500 years later, prompting one to ask again: "Is this our scene?"

One could continue forever to turn within this labyrinth of the ear. Certainly Derrida never thought to get out of it. The first of its passages he explored led into the structure of what he called "s'entendre parler," whereby meaning-to-say seems to follow a circular path back to the speaker's own ear and thereby to return to its point of departure, which it in fact will never have left. Except that it cannot do so and still be understood to be saying anything at all. The condition of hearing oneself is already the other's hearing, the ear of the other. *S'entendre* says the one and the other at once, untranslatably in Derrida's idiom, with its pronominal construction that is undecidably reflexive and/or reciprocal. And thereby it disseminates, it is disseminated in the letter *s* that Derrida calls elsewhere the most disseminating in the alphabet.[3]

Some years later, "Heidegger's Ear" will tunnel into the condition of *Dasein* that Heidegger calls *Hören*, hearing and especially "hearing the voice of the friend that every *Dasein bei sich trägt*," that every *Dasein* carries near it, by it, with it. But Derrida worries especially these last three words of Heidegger's enigmatic assertion. Its topology, in particular, will draw his questions:

> One wonders what "bei sich tragen" means? Where is an ear? What is the inside and the outside of an ear? What does it mean for an ear to open? What does it mean to *tendre l'oreille* [to stretch out one's ear as one does a hand]? To hear or not to hear? To be deaf, to be *unable* or *unwilling* to hear? . . . Where then is the ear that we lend, as one says, in particular the one we lend to the voice of the friend? What is the ear, in the proper sense if there is one? What is, properly speaking, the ear, the ear as such and in its singularity? ("Oreille," 344)

By "the ear as such and in its singularity," Derrida does not mean primarily its singleness, rather than plurality, or at least duality. For ears do tend to come in pairs, left and right, like eyes, arms, hands, legs, or feet.[4] Elsewhere, in "Heidegger's Hand," which is the second essay in the numbered "*Geschlecht*" series of which "Heidegger's Ear" is the fourth, Derrida interrogates the metonymic reduction of hands to the singular hand, the human hand or the hand of *Dasein* ("Hand," 50).

But the ear's metonymy is left virtually alone here in its singleness, for it is, at least for Heidegger, but the metonymy for the act, so to speak, of hearing. Or rather, it is not a metonymy at all, since hearing, *Hören*, is the condition of having an ear rather than the other way around. Derrida draws this reversal out of the order of Heidegger's existential analytic of *Hören*:

> One will understand what the ear is, the essence and the destination of the ear of *Dasein* beginning from this *Hören* and not the reverse. . . . *Dasein* has an ear and can listen only to the extent that, "bei sich," it carries the friend, the voice of the friend. No ear without friend. No friend without ear. ("Oreille," 356)

Perhaps especially in translation, one can hear how Derrida's formulations here go to some lengths to avoid saying "ears" rather than "ear." For one might think it more natural or idiomatic to use a plural, to write, for example, *Dasein* has *ears* only to the extent that . . ., or else there are no *ears* without friend. In "Heidegger's Hand," the discursive singularization of the hand is linked to the movement of gathering together into a one or a unity that, in all his writings on Heidegger including this one, he uncovers as something like the latter's signature or his *Geschlecht*.[5] In passing, Derrida does indeed recall his own earlier analysis: "for as I have shown on the subject of hands, the passage from the plural or the dual to the singular is here essential" ("Oreille," 355). With the exception of this brief reminder, however, the passage toward the singleness or singularity of the ear is left all but unremarked in "Heidegger's Ear." It is as if the comparison being pointed to between hand and ear were rather more uneasy than suggested, perhaps because something is at work other than the essential movement from plurality to singleness or singularity.[6]

If I keep saying singleness or singularity, it is because I believe that the "something other" may well lodge in the space of this difference. While singleness refers us to a difference from, precisely, plurality, singularity points us in a different direction, toward a different difference, or a different spacing. It is not as a unit of one, rather than two or three, and so on, that singularity counts. For every singularity, in this regard, is uncountable, unaccountable, utterly other than every other. There would be no counting with them at all and thus, finally, neither singular nor plural with which to qualify singularity or singularities. By following out this hesitation between singleness and singularity, we also let ourselves be drawn back to the very beginning of *Politics of Friendship*, the text in which "Heidegger's Ear" occupies but the last third of the French edition.

Already in its "Foreword" and then again in the opening of its first chapter, *Politics of Friendship* raises the question of counting and of counting friends. Each time, this question is opened in one of the only two passages of this long book explicitly marked as carried by more than one voice, as a dialogue, at least, or a polylogue. First, in the "Foreword":

> Unless they come, the friends, in a small number.
> How many are they? How many will we be?
>
> (—Yes in a small number, but what is a small number? Where does it begin and end? At one? At one plus one? Plus one more in the feminine? At each masculine one, at each feminine one? You mean all of them, anyone at all? And democracy, does that count?
>
> —It counts, it counts votes and subjects, but it does not count, it should not count singularities whatever they are: no *numerus clausus* for the arrivants.
>
> —Perhaps it is necessary to calculate still, but otherwise, otherwise with the one and the other.) (*Politics*, ix–x)

And then again, Chapter 1, which opens by citing again the phrase that has never known a first and original citation, the apostrophe that balances its "performative contradiction" between plural address and singular destination:

> "O my friends, there is no friend."
> I am addressing you, am I not?
> How many are we?
> —Does that count?
> . . .
> How many are we?
> – How to count? (*Politics*, 1)

We are brought back to this question of counting friends—can one count them?—because Heidegger, and in his wake Derrida, is concerned with hearing, with lending one's ear to "the voice of the friend." It is the voice—and the friend—whose singularity is borrowed, metonymically, by the figure of the singular ear. Derrida says as much in the opening sentences of "Heidegger's Ear," after the first citation of Heidegger's assertion concerning the "voice of the friend that every Dasein *bei sich trägt*":

> Through the voice that I hear, through this listening, it is the friend himself [and Derrida, *contra* Heidegger, would doubtless add: "the friend herself"] that I hear, beyond his voice but in it. It is the friend that I listen to and carry near me in hearing his voice. Of course, *Dasein* "carries" the friend himself,

but not the friend in his totality, in flesh and bone. It carries him, so to speak, in the hearing of his voice, in the figure of his voice, his metonymic figure (a part for the whole). . . . The question of this metonymy will stay with us throughout. ("Oreille," 343)

It is not, therefore, so much the ear as the friend who has to be counted, each time, as singular. The singularizing metonymic movement follows a path from friend to voice to hearing to ear. When, however, this movement is replaced in the context of *Politics of Friendship* (and we should note the plural of this title), then it is also the seemingly first, original, or proper term of this series of rhetorical substitutions—the friend, hence, the voice of the friend, "der Stimme des Freundes"—whose singularity or singleness begins to tremble under the force of Derrida's reading. For can there ever be only a single friend, a friend in the singular, one who speaks with one, undivided voice and therefore always calls *Dasein* to the gathering—*rassemblement, recueillement*—of Being-in-the-world-with-others? Heidegger would have begun gathering everything together under the name of friend, who is always The Friend, if not the one and only, then the authentic, the true friend, the friend *par excellence*, the friend who is singular above all in the sense conveyed by the general definite article. Between Heidegger and Derrida, who in so many ways are so close here, an irreducible and, ultimately, infinite difference subsists between the one's *rassemblement* and the other's dissemination of friendship, between, on the one hand, the single friend, and on the other, plural, uncountable friends in the singular.

This difference is the difference between, in Derrida's economic shorthand, *quoi* and *qui*, what and who. To see this articulated most clearly, we are once again recalled back close to the beginning of *Politics of Friendship*, where Derrida initiates his trajectory across the corpus of the Western thinking of friendship, which is also a thinking of brotherhood. Rather than to the *Lysis*, Plato's short dialogue on friendship, it is to Aristotle's systematization of the Socratic teaching on the subject that Derrida first turns.

Is not Aristotle in fact the first, in the maieutic tradition of *Lysis*, to be sure (*Lysis, è peri philías*) but beyond it by giving it a directly theoretical, ontological, and phenomenological form, to pose the question of friendship (*peri philías*), of *what* it *is*, *which* and *how* it is, and above all whether it is said in one or in several senses?

It is true that right in the middle of this series of questions, between the one on the being or the being-such of friendship and the one on the possible plurivocity of the saying of friendship, there is the question that in itself is terribly equivocal: *kai tís o phílos*. The question asks *what* the friend is but it also asks *who* is the friend. This hesitation of the language between the *what* and the *who* does not seem to make Aristotle tremble, as if it were finally one and the same interrogation, as if the one enveloped the other, and as if the question "who?" was bound to bow down in advance to the ontological question of the "what?", of the "what is it?".

This implicit subjection of the *who* to the *what* will perhaps call for a question on our part in return—or on appeal. It will not go without protest: in the name of the friend or the name of the name. (*Politics*, 6)[7]

A trace of Aristotle's gesture remains in Heidegger's figure of the voice of the friend. Even if Heidegger does not repeat the conceptual abstraction inaugurating the Western discourse on friendship, and therefore does not, apparently, repeat the subjection of the who to the what, through the singularization of the friend and the voice [*der Stimme des Freundes*], it achieves a similar gathering-under-one-name—friend or voice, the one being represented metonymically through the other—and thus a similar reduction of plural proper names to the single common noun. The protest Derrida announces here, "in the name of the friend or the name of the name," will finally be brought forward through the whole tradition, from Aristotle up to and including, to a certain degree, Heidegger, then beyond. To be sure, Heidegger's friend, however anonymous, remains a who, and its who-ness carries over to his/her voice through the operation of the metonymy. And what is opened at the end of this metonymic chain is called hearing or the ear.

What is opened, I just said. *Hören*, hearing or the ear is a what. Even if it is the possibility of *Dasein*, this opening to the world is in the name of a what. To say "the ear who" is to gesture, with a deformation or malformation of grammar, toward the sort of "inverse cripple" who is all ears or all ear, whom or which Zarathustra mocks. It thereby also recalls the scene of the apparatus of the State's university insofar as its teaching is received by a recording machine: "You open wide the portals of your ears to admit the State, not knowing that it has already come under the control of reactive and degenerate forces. Having become all ears for this phonograph dog, you transform yourself into a high-fidelity receiver, and the ear—your ear which is also the ear of the other—begins to occupy in your body the disproportionate place of the 'inverted cripple.'" Heidegger would have come to know a lot about the "grosse Dummheit" of such a position, the position of whoever (or whatever) did not hear and understand the reactive forces ventriloquizing the voice of the "friend," the forces of the State that issues orders to whatever/whomever is dumb enough to listen and obey. Stupidity, dumbness, was for a long time in English automatically associated with deafness: paradoxically, to be all ears is to be deaf. These associations should suffice to remind us that it is indeed a matter of a *politics* of friendship, or rather of the friend, of the voice(s) of the friend(s) that every *Dasein* carries *bei sich*.

II

What if, however, the essential structure of reception had to be thought otherwise? Not as the relay in an apparatus or machine, but as each time a who the reception of which (or of whom) also *gives to be heard whatever it is possible to understand*? What if what (or who) is called hearing or the ear(s) necessarily shared with this structure the abyssal condition of an irreducibly secret identity, the identity of the ear of the other who lends her/his/its name to the figure of hearing and understanding? The question "The ear, who?" would not necessarily call up first of all Nietzsche's "inverted cripple" or the "hypocritical hound," which overhears all conversations conducted in the sphere of the university's "academic freedom" (listening especially to those voices transmitted or received across a State's borders), even if we must not forget about them. Instead, "the ear, who?" would be asking first of all about the place of whatever/whoever takes place on the condition of being *received*. It is this unlocatable, ultimately secret place of reception that would demand to be called a who, and even by a name, a proper name, and always the same one.

It will perhaps have become apparent where these suggestions are leading, or rather, what or who is drawing them out: *Khōra* is the name, the text so titled by Derrida, and never more audaciously. Khōra, to be sure, is not an ear; still less does it, does she have an ear. Such zoomorphism can itself take or be given place only by the one called Khōra. And yet the one so named cannot but give us also to think of that form of reception called hearing, and its metonymic emblem: the ear. But it is the ear who . . ., and thus a singular ear, "the reference to something which is not a thing but which insists, in its so enigmatic uniqueness, lets itself or causes itself to be called without answering" ("*Khōra*," 97)—not answering, that is, like/as the ear that, or who, does not answer when we ask, for example: "Is this our scene?"

In the work so enigmatically titled *Khōra*, Derrida lets us read the ancient text of *Timaeus* as a bottomless *mise en abyme* of the place of reception of stories, legends, or narratives embedded, that is, *received* one within the other, each one becoming the receptacle of the next. But it is to the place designated by the proper name Socrates that all these embedded, received *récits* are represented as destined, a condition which leads Derrida to remark:

> Socrates is not *khōra*, but he would look a lot like it/her if it/she were someone or something. In any case, he puts himself in its/her place, which is not just a place among others, but perhaps *place itself*, the irreplaceable place. Irreplaceable and unplaceable place from which he receives the word(s) of those before whom he effaces himself but who receive them from him, for it is he who makes them talk. And us, too, implacably. (*"Khōra,"* 97)

The resemblance between Khōra and Socrates is unmistakable from now on, in the wake of the signature on a text titled *Khōra*, even as that resemblance continues to make us talk on all sorts of occasions, including the occasion of academic lectures. And yet something will also have happened by virtue of that signature, something or someone that/who would hear this scene—would receive it, whatever that means—without or before incurring the debt that has bound so many other ears, through the ages, to its implacable logic of reception and destination. To receive without being bound by debt; to receive as a mode of giving, not in order to give back but to give place: that would be the event. Here I cite once again and give ample place to Khōra, the one who, the one which is called by that name.

> *Khōra* receives, so as to give place to them, all the determinations, but she/it does not possess any of them as her/its own. She possesses them, she has them, since she receives them, but she does not possess them as properties, she does not possess anything as her own. She "is" nothing other than the sum or the process of what has just been inscribed "on" her, on the subject of her, on her subject, right up against [*à même*] her subject, but she is not the *subject* or the *present support* of all these interpretations, even though, nevertheless, she is not reducible to them. Simply this excess is nothing, nothing that may be and be said ontologically. This absence of support . . . provokes *and* resists any binary or dialectical determination, any inspection of a philosophical *type*, or let us say, more rigorously, of an *ontological* type. This type finds itself both defied and relaunched by the very thing that appears to give it place. . . . *[I]f there is place*, or, according to our idiom, *place given*, to give place here does not come down to making a present of a place. The expression *to give place* [donner lieu] does not refer to the gesture of a donor-subject, the support or origin of something that would come to be given to someone. (*"Khōra,"* 99–100)[8]

Ordinarily, in an academic lecture, I should now ask to be forgiven for giving too much place to quotation, to what (or to who?) is called a quotation. For it is more or less an expectation of our academic *politesse* that the place of a lecture is reserved for original speech, for the deployment of a single signature. It is this academic *given* of our originality, this measure of our autonomy, that Derrida dislodges, displaces, throughout his oeuvre, into the structure of an originary *reception*, a conditioning "ear" who remains undiscoverable, *introuvable*, even as it calls to be called always by the same name, a proper name, a name that is not certainly that of something or someone. Once again, I give place to *Khōra*:

> Socrates does not occupy this undiscoverable place, but it is the one from which . . . *he answers to his name.* For like/as *khōra* he must always "be called in the same way." And as it is not certain that Socrates himself, this one here, is someone or something, the play of the proper names becomes more abyssal than ever: What is place? To what and to whom does it give place? What takes place under these names? Who are you, *Khōra?* ("*Khōra*," 111)

Like the ear, as the ear, Khōra does not answer.

III

It is time to conclude. I do not know what I have said; I do not know what—or who—has taken place, if anything or anyone. For it is all rolled up in an ear, the other's ear, the undiscoverable ear that or who Jacques Derrida discerns when he bids to sign *Khōra* without passing on the debt incurred to Socrates, as relayed by Plato, then by Aristotle, then by Hegel, then by Nietzsche and Heidegger, to cite only these few proper names of a philosophical inheritance. Nothing less than the end of the indebted ear, the ear that, like Hamlet's, is "bound to hear," the ear who can no longer hear the other for listening to the sound of its own voice or, but it is perhaps the same thing, the voice of the father's ghost. It is nothing less than a place given to a giving-beyond-debt that would take place in the signature Jacques Derrida, which is traced each time in the abyss and the labyrinth of an ear. But, by the same token, it takes or gives place only if and when it will have been received and countersigned as such, as the forgiveness of debt, beginning with the immense debt owed to the one who signed, for example—if indeed one can say "for example" here—a text calling itself and calling to *Khōra*.

In the place of a conclusion and because I can no longer hear myself speak, a long, final passage from another text signed by Jacques Derrida. This time it is apparently not a question of the ear, but of what is here called the ultimate question. This question, Derrida writes, "will not cease, in its many forms, to return and to haunt . . ." I leave you then, as I began, with this ghost resonating in our ears:

> Who forgives or who asks whom for forgiveness, at what moment? Who has the right or the power to do this, "who [to] whom?" And what does the

"who" signify here? This will always be the almost ultimate form of the question, most often of the question insoluble by definition. However formidable it may be, this question is perhaps not the ultimate question. More than once we will be faced with the effects of a preliminary question, prior to this one, which is the question "who" or "what"? Does one forgive *someone* for a wrong committed, for example . . . or does one forgive someone something, someone who, in whatever way, can never totally be confused with the wrongdoing and the moment of the past wrongdoing, nor with the past in general. This question—"who" or "what"—will not cease, in its many forms, to return and to haunt, to obsess the language of forgiveness and this not only by multiplying aporetic difficulties but also by forcing us finally to suspect or suspend the meaning of this opposition between "who" and "what," a little as if the experience of forgiveness (of a forgiveness asked for, hoped for, whether granted or not), as if, perhaps, the impossibility of a true, appropriate, appropriable experience of "forgiveness" signified the dismissal of this opposition between "who" and "what," its dismissal and thus its history, its passed historicity. ("Forgive," 24)

Notes

1. For a very thoughtful and thought-provoking reading of this opening scene on the ramparts, see Thomas Keenan, *Fables of Responsibility: Aberrations and Predicaments in Ethics and Politics* (Stanford: Stanford University Press, 1997), p. 7 ff.
2. This chapter was originally delivered as a keynote lecture at the conference titled "Who or What?—Jacques Derrida," organized by Dragan Kujundžič and held at the University of Florida in October 2006.
3. In his introduction to *Raising the Tone of Philosophy: Late Essays by Immanuel Kant, Transformative Critique by Jacques Derrida* (Baltimore: The Johns Hopkins University Press, 1993), Peter Fenves conducts a probing survey of how Derrida's work has contributed to what Fenves calls "an immense, necessary, and impossible project: to hear with—and along with—the ear of the other" (30); see especially pp. 30–9. For a quite different but no less astute probing of hearing as a lynchpin of Derrida's thought, particularly as regards the university, see Dawne McCance, *Medusa's Ear: University Foundings from Kant to "Chora L"* (Albany: SUNY Press, 2004).
4. On the right/left partition of the body—the animal body but also the body of the institution, for example the university—see "Mochlos," esp. pp. 110–12.
5. On this term and the reasons for which it is left untranslated in the series of essays on Heidegger, see "*Geschlecht*," 7n; on the serialization of the *Geschlecht* essays, see David Farrell Krell, "One, Two, Four—Yet Where Is the Third?", *Epoché* 10, 2 (Spring 2006).
6. In a later passage from the essay, when Derrida reiterates Heidegger's reversal of the ear and hearing, he will use the plural "ears" in formulations very similar to those we've just read: "the ear is not for Heidegger an organ of the auditory sense *with* which we hear. Hearing (*das Hören*), in

the authentic sense, is an assembling, a gathering of one's thoughts and self [*recueillement de soi*] toward the speech that is addressed to us. Hearing gathers beginning from the address and not from the organ of hearing. We hear when we forget our ears and auditory sensations so as to transport ourselves, through them, toward what is said and of which we are a part. In other words, Heidegger reminds us constantly that it is necessary to think *Hören* (hearing) on the basis of listening or lending an ear (*Hörchen*) and not the reverse. . . . He underscores that we do not hear because we have ears; rather we have ears because we hear" ("Oreille," 379).

7. Hélène Cixous also highlights this passage in "The Keys To: Jacques Derrida as a Proteus Unbound," trans. Peggy Kamuf, *Discourse* 30, 1&2 (Winter & Spring 2008), pp. 77–8.

8. The French expression "donner lieu" on which this passage turns would more idiomatically be translated as "to give rise."

Chapter 14

To Do Justice to "Rousseau," Irreducibly

Of Grammatology is a monstrous work. One should say that, if possible, in the best sense, which is to say the sense evoked, now famously, in the last sentences of that book's initial chapter, titled "Exergue":

> Perhaps patient meditation and painstaking investigation on and around what is still provisionally called writing . . . are the wanderings of a thinking that is faithful and attentive to the world that, irreducibly, is coming and that proclaims itself at present, beyond the closure of knowledge. The future cannot be anticipated except in the form of an absolute danger. It is what breaks absolutely with constituted normality and can announce itself, *present* itself only as a sort of monstrosity. (*Grammatology*, 4–5)

Monstrous are "wanderings . . . beyond the closure of knowledge" and it is with just such a wandering, without the security of known and normal compass points, that Derrida makes his way, blindly or monstrously, toward a future for thought and a thought of the future. Wandering, errancy [*errance*] is the name he will claim again, some two hundred pages later, for the "method" he is following, that is, the path toward the exit from "the closure of knowledge," of metaphysics: "[This exiting] proceeds in the manner of an errant thinking on the possibility of itinerary and of method. It affects itself [*s'affecte*] with nonknowledge as with its future and it *ventures out* [s'aventure] deliberately" (162). An errant method, a method of errancy is a flagrant contradiction in terms, a monstrosity that flaunts its aberration by questioning the very possibility of method. Here is a thinker who proclaims, without apology, not only that he is making it up as he goes along but that he is looking for an exit from safe precincts, for the path toward danger, and that, *without knowing it*, he knows a blind spot organizes the reading produced in this way: "And what we call production is necessarily a text, the system of a writing and of a reading, about which we know that they are ordered around their own blind spot. We know this a priori, but only now and with a knowledge that is not one" (164).

Another monstrous provocation: "their own blind spot," "*leur propre tache aveugle*." How can a blind spot be properly attributed? To whom, to what does it belong or return? This formulation is reflecting or repeating the designation of "a sort of blind spot in Rousseau's text" (163), in other words, in the text being read and whose law is being produced by this reading. The Rousseauvian blind spot, namely, the law of the supplement, "the concept of the supplement" (ibid.). Rousseau, as Derrida shows beyond dispute, *names* supplementarity tirelessly, even obsessively, in his theoretical or philosophical texts (*Emile, Essay on the Origin of Languages*) no less than in his autobiographical or literary texts (*The Confessions, The Reveries*). But the law of this naming and the concept governing its compulsive repetition in Rousseau's discourse remains unthought, unnoticed, unread, and *unseen* by the signatory no less than by the generations of scholars or *savants* who have built a house of knowledge on the archive of Rousseau's oeuvre. The blind spot at once belongs and does not belong to the author's signed work; that is, it is undeniably used and properly intended by his discourse, but in order to become legible at all the proper aim of this intention to mean has to deviate through a point it cannot grasp or see and therefore cannot intend. This necessary deviation is therefore *at once* a condition of possibility of proper meaning *and* the condition of its impossibility *as* proper. That the possibility of the properness of any "thing" is conditioned by and as impossibility is what Derrida knows with a knowledge "that is not one" and what his errant thought will remain faithful to in every turn it takes from this point on. It accounts for both the immense diversity across his writings and the incomparable coherence of their wanderings.

But to return to *Of Grammatology*: its deconstruction of property in "the Age of Rousseau" sends tremors across innumerable fault lines and shakes up (and down) the ground of every ontological certainty. This is an enormous claim, befitting the monstrous. To measure it solely within the confines of a reflection on "Derrida's eighteenth century" will certainly fail to do it justice.[1] But then what might count as justice done to a work of this magnitude, one whose impact has only begun to register against such formidable resistance? Perhaps Derrida would say that the justice awaiting his thought will have to be an unraveling around its "own" blind spots, on the order of that which he undertakes with Rousseau's unthought thinking of supplementarity, or again, of Plato's anagrammatic writing of the *pharmakon*. And if this comparison sounds exaggerated, it is still the least one might envision as justice to a thought and a work that, by dint of wandering, would find the exit toward nothing less than a certain *outside* of "Platonism," that is, of the massive and comprehensive structure that raised the curtain on the theater of the West and on its play, in continuous performance since then. One may rightly expect such an unraveling to be delayed for some good while yet, and, even given the acceleration afforded by ever-new technologies of writing, likely to require more than the three centuries separating the appearance of *Grammatology* from that of Rousseau's *Confessions* or *The Essay on the Origin of Languages*. As Derrida writes on the opening page of "Plato's Pharmacy": "The dissimulation of the woven texture can in any case take centuries to undo its web" ("Pharmacy," 64). To be sure, the texture of Plato's web will have resisted its undoing far longer than Rousseau's, but this tends to confirm Derrida's reading of "Rousseau" as largely a repetition, with some important new twists, produced on the stage of the Platonic theater. And, of course, as far as most specialist scholars are concerned, they both continue to resist very well, thank you. The Age of Derrida may have dawned already but, for its contemporaries, it will have remained largely within their blind spot.

Such a figure of doing justice by undoing a text around one of its blind spots (for one cannot assume that there is ever only one)[2] can take us closer to the particularity, even the singularity, of Derrida's "Rousseau," if not his "eighteenth century." For, at first approach, the figure would seem to promise harsh justice indeed, on the order of a judgment, sentence, or condemnation, a justice that is *exacted* by rending the tissue of the corpus rather than justice that is *rendered*, which is to say, returned or given back to the other, here to the name—Rousseau, Plato, Derrida—that stands metonymically for a work and, even beyond that, for an age, an epoch.

In order to hear a rendering rather than a rending as the blind spot comes to light, one has to pay close attention to the ways in which *Of Grammatology* is *situating* Rousseau's text, writing, thought, and, finally or perhaps first of all, his experience. These ways are numerous, but may well all be described as modes of *découpage*: of cutting, separating, partitioning, dividing.[3] It is a matter of setting off thereby different levels or layers of the text from each other by identifying, to some extent, what Derrida calls their "structures of *appartenance*"—that is, their structures of association, belonging, or affiliation. I have already mentioned one such very large structure, "Platonism" or metaphysics, to which Rousseau's texts largely belong through a direct, even if only rarely acknowledged, line of inheritance, in particular as regards the treatment of the question of writing. Within that *découpage*, however, there would be the affiliation between "Rousseau" and other, comparable metonymies, for example, "Warburton," "Condillac," "Hobbes," "Mandeville," "Vico," "Descartes"—but also "Hegel" or "Saussure," which extends the text's layering beyond considerations of its assumed influences or declared polemics.[4]

Besides these declared or more or less legible lines of division, there is what Derrida refers to as the *habitation* of the text being read, that is, the situation of any text in a language and a culture that it inhabits, is habituated to, and reproduces, up to a certain point, by habit, without reflection, this being a condition of the minimal level of its readability.[5] Of this habitual habitation, Derrida remarks, underscoring twice the preposition "in": "the writer writes *in* a language and *in* a logic whose system, laws, and life his discourse by definition cannot dominate absolutely. He uses them only by letting himself, in a certain way and *up to a certain point* [emphasis added], be governed by the system" (158). Up to a certain *point*: this phrase points to a place of *découpage* that must occur if a reading is not to miss, precisely, the point by settling for a repetition of habit that might have occurred in any number of other texts, with other signatures, from different "ages."

One of the many moments at which Derrida recalls the difficulty and necessity of this essential level of *découpage* occurs in the key metadiscursive chapter titled "The Exorbitant. Question of Method" when he is distinguishing his "method" of reading from that of a certain psychoanalysis:

> Such a psychoanalysis [of Jean-Jacques Rousseau] would already have to have located all the structures of belonging [*appartenance*] of Rousseau's text, *everything that is not proper to it*, by reason of the overarching already-thereness of the language or of the culture, everything that is inhabited rather than produced by the writing. *Around the point of irreducible originality of this writing* an immense series of structures, of historical totalities of all kinds are organized; they envelope and cut across each other [*se recoupent*]. If we suppose that psychoanalysis could rightly carry out to completion their *découpage* and their interpretation and that it takes account of the whole history of Western metaphysics which maintains relations of habitation with Rousseau's writing, it would still have to elucidate its own belonging to metaphysics and Western culture. (161; emphases added)

I have underscored two phrases in the above lines because they situate something like the stakes or the point of the daunting enterprise of *découpage* that Derrida challenges psychoanalysis, or any other "method" of interpretation (including the one he is here setting out as his own), to carry out fully. The point would be to be able to situate "the point of irreducible originality of this writing" by cutting away "everything that is not proper to it," a point that would, as it were, remain in the hopper of the reading grid once everything that belongs to other structures of belonging or habitation has been sifted out or cut away. Indeed, the passage just cited continues with an image of reading (or interpretation) as something like a piece of large earth-moving equipment that carries away far more than what it is looking for:

> Let us not pursue this any further. We have already measured the difficulty of the task and the share of failure in our interpretation of the supplement. We are certain that *something irreducibly Rousseauist* is captured there but we have carried off, at the same time, a yet quite shapeless mass of roots, soil, and sediments of all sorts. (ibid.; emphasis added)[6]

Something "irreducibly Rousseauist" would be a "point of irreducible originality." An irreducible point ought to suggest that which cannot be broken down or divided any further; it would be very hasty, however, to understand Derrida's point in a quasi-geometrical sense of indivisibility. For irreducible originality, that point from which the text resists further reduction to some encompassing historical totality or overarching habitation, has also the character or the function of a blind spot and thus of what necessarily *divides* any proper economy (of a self, a subject, a discourse, an intention, etc.) from and within itself. The proper divides (itself) and this is its improperly proper law. And yet, divided and cut off from itself, the irreducible still insists; it beckons to a reading that would not be content to leave undisturbed all those roots and sediments caught up with it, dissimulating its sharp, needle-like point in a haystack of historical, cultural repetitions and habits.

The passage cited above is just one of many comparable moments that surge into view as Derrida proceeds to sharpen ever more finely the irreducible blind spot or point. At this point, the reading of "Rousseau" has only begun, by digging first, as a kind of test drill site, into Jean-Jacques's confessional texts. The "interpretation of the supplement" has thus first situated supplementarity's disconcerting logic—"almost inconceivable for reason" as Rousseau says of his cohabitation with the one he called "Maman," Mme de Warens—in an economy of desire that ruses with substitution, delay, displacement, onanism, guilt, pleasure, nature and its degradation in depravity. Given that Derrida has elected to initiate his reading with the specifically sexual underpinnings of Rousseau's, or rather Jean-Jacques's experience, the warnings about confusing his own "method" (that is, this path being cut through the thicket of three centuries' worth of metaphysical reappropriations of "Rousseau") with those of psychoanalysis seem altogether called-for. And especially in 1967, a year after the much-heralded first publication of Jacques Lacan's *Écrits*, a work whose blind spot Derrida will soon situate in the place of the literary signifier.[7] But these warning remarks about the immense, in fact impossible, task (in French, *tâche*, differentiated only by its circumflex from *tache*, as in *tache aveugle*, blind spot, stain, patch) stand also at the threshold to the reading of the—apparently—nonconfessional, philosophical or theoretical text that is Rousseau's *Essay on the Origin of Languages*, which occupies the much longer second part of the section of *Grammatology* devoted to the "Age of Rousseau." One has, however, also been put on notice that such a distinction—confessional from philosophical, sexually-charged and driven from sexually-neutral or neutralized—is in question from here on out; indeed, the reading of the *Essay* is everywhere shot through with references forward or back to the autobiographical works, *The Confessions, The Reveries, The Dialogues*. Thus, the questioning of these entirely metaphysical distinctions will have begun with Rousseau "himself" (*"c'est la faute de Rousseau . . ."*)—in other words, with his *experience* as writer, thinker, reader, and relay point in the long legacy of Platonism. The question arises not only because the putatively speculative or theoretical writings (the *Essay* above all, but also *Emile, Letter to D'Alembert, The Discourse on the Origin of Inequality, The Social Contract*, etc.) rarely pass on the opportunity to put femininity, "le sexe," in its place far from the stage of serious public matters, as Derrida unfailingly remarks, but above all because Rousseau "chose to live by literary writing" (160), a choice made no less ineluctable by the inflection he gave to the Platonic schema denouncing all the dangers attending such a "life" in writing. Rousseau's experience, in its singularity, of ineluctable textual/sexual supplementarity writes itself across the oeuvre subsumed to his name, to his signature.

It is such an experience—singular, signed, proper, but in irremediable, irreducible, and original rupture with the economic circle of *pure* auto-affection, without alterity—that the dredging machine of reading and interpretation must bring to the surface so as to begin sifting through the roots and sediments in which it has lain buried, for want, perhaps, of a *corresponding* desire that could read it under the haystack of negations.[8] These negations appear to be its "own" but they also resemble and inhabit those of centuries upon centuries of repression. Repression of writing, of desire, of the other, of "woman," of the blind spot, of errancy, and centuries upon centuries, the eighteenth being one more in a series that continues beyond it, approaching closure but still unclosed. But in that century, Rousseau will have cried out *in writing* for justice and articulated this cry or call in his own name (for example, in *Rousseau Judge of Jean-Jacques*) *and* in the general name of "man" (*Discourse on the Origin of Inequality Among Men*). To read "Rousseau" justly, one has to try to hear this articulation so as to respond *in kind*, that is, in and with the supplementary articulation whereby experience is endlessly textualized by differences that alter and space out the selfsame.

Which is why, throughout *Of Grammatology* and without contradicting the concern to cut away everything that does not belong or return to the name, Derrida is no less interested to show how "Rousseau" names, more properly or more legibly than any of his contemporaries, a general, universal condition of experience. What Jean-Jacques in *The Confessions* refers to as "the dangerous supplement" of his onanism, for example, is articulated by Derrida's analysis at precisely the juncture of individual experience and its universal condition: "Auto-affection is a universal structure of experience. Every living being is a potential of auto-affection. And only a being capable of symbolizing, that is to say, of affecting itself, can let itself be affected by the other in general. Auto-affection is the condition of an experience in general" (165).

Rousseau names this condition in another sense as well, that of giving the name to the structure whereby auto-affection requires and thus calls for a supplement in order to "be" (with) itself. But in this very act of naming, Rousseau would have also been at his most blind to what was being said and done *in* his text and *by* his text. And it is this absence from himself, this irreducible blind spot, this condition of writing and being written at once, beyond the pertinence of the opposition of activity to passivity, that calls for justice, which is to say, for the supplement of reading.

At least twice in the course of reading "The Age of Rousseau," Derrida settles provisionally on the notion of "dream" to qualify this state of writing/being written while remaining essentially blind or unconscious. Both passages, however, are clearly articulated around the necessity to produce a new space for thinking experience that does not fall back on metaphysical categories, to which the psychoanalytic concept of dream, in its opposition to waking, consciousness, or vigilance, remains largely hostage. For this reason, the term can be used only provisionally, as a paleonym, or under erasure:

> Using the word and describing the thing, Rousseau displaces and deforms the sign "supplement" in a certain manner, the unity of the signifier and the signified. . . . But these displacements and deformations are regulated by the contradictory unity—itself supplementary—of a desire. As in the dream, in Freud's analysis, incompatibles are simultaneously admitted as soon as it is a matter of satisfying a desire, in spite of the principle of identity or the excluded middle, that is, despite the logical time of consciousness. By using another word than dream, by inaugurating a conceptuality that would no longer be that of the metaphysics of presence or consciousness (which

opposes, still within Freud's discourse, waking and dream), one would thus have to define a space in which this regulated "contradiction" has been possible and can be described. (245)

This new conceptual space would exit the space of metaphysics by permitting an account of *regular* "contradictions," which in their very regularity and regulation overrun the explanatory capacity of conscious logic that wants to exclude any such contradictions as aberrations, anomalies, monstrous. This observable regularity requires and thus calls for a new set of rules, rules that have to be produced as one goes along, inductively and deductively, or rather by thinking always *at* the site of articulation between general structures and their inscription by and as proper names.[9] For this conceptual work, "Rousseau" cannot serve merely as an *example*, replaceable by or reducible to other examples, even as his articulation of supplementarity is not to be accounted for in and of itself, outside the general, universal, and historical conditions Derrida calls *differance*. Rather, it is a matter of *displacing "all the concepts proposed until now with which to think the articulation of a discourse and an historical totality"* (99; emphasis in the original) and of doing so under the impulse given *each time* differently, under a different name and in view of a different displacement, by the inscription of desire in a space like that of dream. For example, and exemplarily, the name of supplement, which will have been (one of) Rousseau's secret proper names.

The last paragraphs of *Grammatology* return to this problem of the word "dream," but this time the movement of displacement toward a new concept is carried by the full impact and impulse of this *inscription* of "Rousseau." This phrase, "the inscription of 'Roussseau,'" must therefore now be understood at once in the active or subjective sense and the passive or objective sense of the genitive: the inscription *of* Rousseau, that is, his inscription both *of* and *by* the text that is offered up to reading in the very movement of supplementarity it describes and submits to.

> To the extent that he belonged to the metaphysics of presence, [Rousseau] *dreamed* of the simple exteriority of death to life, evil to good, representation to presence, signifier to signified, representer to represented, mask to face, writing to speech. But all of these oppositions are *irreducibly rooted* [emphasis added] in that metaphysics. . . . None of the terms of this series, insofar as they are comprehended there, can dominate the economy of differance or of supplementarity. Rousseau's *dream* has consisted of making the supplement enter metaphysics by force.
>
> But what does that mean? Is not the opposition of dream to wakefulness [*la vigilance*] a representation of metaphysics as well? And what must the

dream be, what must writing be, if, *as we now know* [emphasis added], one can write while dreaming? And if the scene of dreaming is always a scene of writing? (315–16)

"As we now know": I am tempted to read this phrase as the echo of one cited earlier in which Derrida, using (as he does throughout *Of Grammatology*) the convention of the first-person plural, points to what "we know a priori, but only now" to be the blind spot ordering the production of this text, "the system of a writing and a reading." How can one know something a priori and yet with delay, "only now"? This delayed effect of knowing is the mark of supplementary differance, of the *irreducible* detour through the other, which is to say, the blind spot. When, in the closing paragraph just cited, Derrida remarks again the *present* of knowing, "as we now know," this delay or detour has not been closed up or closed down but rather *displayed* and *displaced* through the other's text. For having so patiently tracked "Rousseau" through innumerable points of articulation of his discourse with all sorts of general structures, what "we now know" (and "we" *now*, at the end of this work, includes Derrida's readers) has the singular nature of a dream, "the dream of Rousseau," which "has consisted of making the supplement enter metaphysics by force."

Once again, the genitive construction must be given its full play: "the dream of Rousseau" does not let one decide *whose* dream is inscribing the supplement. And it is through this very undecidability that *Of Grammatology* does justice to the one *and the other* "Rousseau," Rousseau as irreducibly the name of more than one, its divisibility being the im-possible condition of its proper reference. The name refers *now*—but a priori it always already did—to a text, that is to say, to an experience *lived as* supplementarity. And this is so not only because Rousseau also chose to write. But because he wrote, and because while writing dreamed incompatible things, it is to the writer's name that is rendered the justice of his immense accomplishment: forcibly displacing the conceptual field of metaphysics from within.

Such a displacement, however, is not yet an exit from that field. The exit had still to be dreamed of when Rousseau wrote and lived, in the "eighteenth century." This delay will now have to be accounted for according to a *differant* historicity. The delayed dream of a new Enlightenment will necessarily have been the dream of (a) monstrosity, that ventures out blindly toward, as we read, "the world that, irreducibly, is coming." But it will also have signaled yet a greater accomplishment, just underway, as the Age of "Derrida" begins to unfold in the blind spot of its history.

Coda

When and if this age ever rounds on itself to try to identify its "own" blind spot, what will it see? This is, of course, a ridiculously premature question since the delay has only begun and the "dissimulation of the woven texture can take centuries to undo its web." In the meantime, there have been relentless attacks on Derrida's work. So far, however, these have not opened up even the smallest breach in that work's incredibly tightly woven—and calculated—fabric. The reason cannot be that no room is left there for discussion, debate, questions, and disagreement. On the contrary, responses are constantly invited and called for.[10] It is rather, I believe, because these bids to dismiss out of court, without a hearing, have precisely the aggressive, even furious character of attack, which is a state that leaves the aggressors utterly incapable of reading. As I have argued above, and differently elsewhere, Derrida is most fundamentally misread when his own work on others' texts (and he is always reading) has been received as destructive, that is, as *rending* rather than *rendering* justice. Love for a text, as Derrida has affirmed more than once, is a necessary condition of reading.[11] Perhaps it is a sufficient condition as well. As to why so many of Derrida's contemporaries believed they *ought not* to love his writing and therefore *ought not* to read it, that is a question on which one can only speculate. But it is also a question I do not believe is going to trouble readers of the future, because such acrimony writes on water where its ripples dissipate in the blink of an eye, in a little interval of blindness.

That said, a tiny opening seems to appear in the very last line of *Grammatology*. It looks to be not deliberate, but instead, although one cannot assert this with any certainty, what is called a lapsus. Bringing his text to a close, and doing so with characteristic courtesy, Derrida leaves the last word to his textual interlocutor of the moment. Hence he cites and gives one to read a passage from *Emile*, in which Rousseau writes this on the subject of dreams and writing:

> the dreams of a bad night are given to us as philosophy. You will say I too am a dreamer; I admit it, but I do what others fail to do, I give my dreams as dreams, and leave it to the reader to discover whether there is anything in them which may prove useful to those who are awake. (316)

The last clauses of this cited passage, which fall on the final lines of the book, in the French edition reads: "je donne mes rêves pour des rêves, laissant chercher [. . .] s'ils ont quelque chose d'utile aux gens éveillés." Where I have inserted an ellipsis in brackets Derrida's quotation has dropped two words from Rousseau's original text, an omission that, as it happens, does not disturb the syntax in French as it might have in English. The two words are, simply: "au lecteur," that is, "to the reader."

To the reader. A blind spot? Perhaps. But whose?

Notes

1. This is a reference to the context in which this essay was originally published: *Eighteenth-Century Studies*, a special issue titled "Derrida's Eighteenth Century."
2. "In certain respects, the theme of supplementarity is no doubt but one theme among others. It is in a chain, carried along by that chain. Perhaps one could substitute something else for it. *But it happens that this theme describes the chain itself, the being-chain of a textual chain, the structure of substitution, the articulation of desire and language, the logic of all the conceptual oppositions taken over by Rousseau*" (*Grammatology*, 163; emphasis in the original).
3. See p. 230 in the original text for a forgrounded use of the term *découpage*.
4. On the crucial *découpage* Derrida effects between "Rousseau" and both "Warburton" and "Condillac," see, for example, p. 272 ff.
5. The term "habitation" is used by Rousseau in *The Confessions* in a passage Derrida has just cited in the previous section: "Besides, I had observed that intercourse with women [*l'habitation des femmes*] distinctly aggravated my ill-health" (156). Derrida's attention to the inscription of sexual difference never flags, here or elsewhere. For example, after citing a passage from *The Letter to D'Alembert* (the text containing some of Rousseau's most furiously misogynistic writing), in which Rousseau elevates his bad experience with "l'habitation des femmes" into the principle that men suffer more than women from their "intercourse," Derrida comments: "The contest is not equal and this is perhaps the most profound meaning of the play of supplementarity" (177).
6. Reading the works of Jean Genet in *Glas*, Derrida employs a similar image to describe his reading "operation": ". . . a sort of dredging machine. From the dissimulated small, closed, glassed-in cabin of a crane, I manipulate some levers and, from afar . . . I plunge a mouth of steel in the water. And I scrape the bottom, hook onto stones and algae there that I lift up in order to set them down on the ground while the water quickly falls back from the mouth" (*Glas*, 204).
7. See Jacques Derrida, "The Purveyor of Truth," in *Post Card*. That a certain psychoanalytic interpretation remains blind to the literary signifier is already asserted explicitly in *Of Grammatology*: "If the trajectory we have followed in the reading of the 'supplement' is not simply psychoanalytic, it is no doubt because the habitual psychoanalysis of literature begins by bracketing the literary signifier as such" (160).
8. On several occasions, Derrida has recalled that his reading of Rousseau as a youth, and especially *The Confessions*, was a determining experience in his

own decision to write. The axes of his identification with Rousseau could be seen as falling along the conventional divisions between philosophy, literature, and autobiography, "genres" that Derrida melds, crosses, and rearticulates with great inventiveness. The confessional genre in particular is one Derrida thoroughly overhauls in *Circumfession.*

9. On the question of the empiricism of his "method," see p. 162.
10. See, in particular, "Afterword." For a very fine analysis of the hostility Derrida's work has encountered, see Marian Hobson, "Hostilities and Hostages (to Fortune): On Some Part of Derrida's Reception," in *Epoché* 10.2 (Spring 2006), pp. 303–14.
11. See the chapter "Deconstruction and Love," in Kamuf, *Book of Addresses* (Stanford: Stanford University Press, 2005).

Chapter 15

The Deconstitution of Psychoanalysis

It is somewhat foolish no doubt to imagine one can circumscribe the extent of Derrida's engagement in writing with psychoanalysis, or with the work of Freud or Lacan or other psychoanalytic thinkers, such as Nicolas Abraham and Maria Torok.[1] While numerous texts might suggest themselves right away as obviously belonging to the classification, there would remain the irradiating effects across an entire oeuvre of what Derrida calls, in his first published essay on Freud, *la percée* or *la trouée freudienne*, the "Freudian breakthrough" ("Freud," 199). In what follows, nevertheless, I have cut out and assembled a set of four distinct texts by Derrida that are "on" psychoanalysis, as we say, but that also share a seemingly contingent feature: they were all initially addressed, in person, to a gathering of psychoanalysts by profession and at their invitation. I have already alluded to the first of these, "Freud and the Scene of Writing," which, as the brief headnote explains, is the "fragment of a lecture delivered at the *Institut de psychanalyse* (Dr. Green's seminar)" ("Freud," 196). The three subsequent texts I have in mind, which each responded to invitations from René Major, are "Du tout," "Geopsychanalysis 'and the rest of the world,'", and "Psychoanalysis Searches the States of Its Soul."[2] What is interesting is this constancy of Derrida's interventions from the place of an outsider invited to address an assembled institution or constitution of analysis. From these four texts I will select only a few traits that are repeated, but also transformed across this corpus.

In "Freud and the Scene of Writing," the situation of address by the putative outsider to the psychoanalytic institution is never brought to the front of the stage or the scene. Indeed, the question of whether psychoanalysis can be thought to stand outside deconstruction (or vice versa) is the framing question of the debate that this lecture sought to open, as Derrida explains in his somewhat telegraphic headnote:

It was a matter then of opening a debate around certain propositions that have been put forward in earlier essays, notably in *Of Grammatology*.

Did these propositions . . . have their place within the field of psychoanalytic inquiry? As concerns that field, where did these propositions stand with regard to their concepts and their syntax? [*Au regard d'un tel champ, où se tenaient-elles quant à leurs concepts et à leur syntaxe?*] ("Freud," 196)

Notice the transformation in the shape of these questions: the first formulation presumes a straightforward topology and asks whether certain propositions belong within or without a given, delimited field, whereas the second opts for a more open form of the question when it asks where those propositions stand "as concerns that field," "au regard d'un tel champ." By "open form" I mean a question that can pose itself to the very constitution or institution of a "field" of inquiry, with the possible effect of opening from within an inquiry into the constitution of such within-ness. Over the next thirty-five years, Derrida will repeatedly remark the situation of his own address to the psychoanalytic institution as occupying this place of a question opening up from within, having been solicited there as the necessary figure of an outside supplement. In "Freud and the Scene of Writing," this structure is demonstrated propositionally or conceptually. In the three later texts, these propositional or conceptual arguments are themselves supplemented, as it were, by the remarking of the condition and situation of address in its first and second persons, the person of the putative or presumed non-analyst, addressing those who, nominally and by profession, are proper analysts. One might also describe this situation of address as a restaging of the scene of "Freud and the Scene of Writing" that, by repositioning the frame set on the discourse, remarks the voice, body, person, and presence of the speaker metonymically in the place of those propositions about which it was asked "Where do they stand as concerns psychoanalysis?"

By 1977, in France, however, the name "psychoanalysis" had long been sundered from any unified institutional referent. It was around that time that the analyst René Major began to convoke discussions among the four different institutional affiliations of French psychoanalysts.[3] These were known as the "Colloques Confrontation" and they also issued in the journal *Cahiers Confrontation*, which continued publication for more than ten years. In this setting Derrida again accepted an invitation to address psychoanalytic practitioners; the published trace of this "confrontation" is the text titled "Du Tout," published in *La Carte postale* in 1980.

It is a rather odd trace, full of inside jokes that turn inside out when animated by this nominal outsider. It is also pretty funny; early on, for example, it compares the scene in which they all find themselves to a

Wild West saloon "into which crowd all sorts of gangs [*bandes*] that are more or less flush with cash, more or less ready for détente, that are looking out of the corners of their eyes from the bar. Certain of them pretend to be playing poker, peacefully, in a corner" ("Tout," 501). As he begins to address them, Derrida rehearses his prior back-and-forth with himself about whether or not he was going to keep the rendezvous or do a no-show, a *faux-bond*, just to make something happen as it surely would have had he stood everyone up ("if you had waited for me and if this place had remained empty for an indefinite amount of time, ten minutes according to one gang, forty-five to fifty according to another, then in that case, if you had waited for me, I am sure something would have happened" ["Tout," 505]).

There was finally, however, something "stronger than me," "plus fort que moi," and as a result there he is, there he was. In this force of the stronger-than-me, one can recognize the pull of what I already pointed to as the metonymic substitution of the body and person of a signatory for the propositions advanced in signed works. "Stronger than me" also signals, in other words, to what is either more or less than a "me" or an ego, even as the movement it impels is the substitution or representation of this ego by the instance of the one who says "I" and "I, me" while addressing himself to others in their and his presence. What is more, this force of the stronger-than-me must be the same, Derrida imagines, for the psychoanalysts: "the psychoanalysts could not avoid inviting me into this place, reserved, until this evening, for the alleged inside of the analytic fold to which I am supposed to be a stranger—neither analyst nor analysand according to the criteria in effect in the code which is the minimal consensus of their four listed groups" (ibid). With this notion of the inevitable invitation from the inside to the supposed or denominated stranger, Derrida formulates a constant in his approach from now on to any similar such invitations.

But to remain a bit longer in this crowded and somewhat tense saloon, the specificity here is the very French and very Parisian atmosphere that is relatively absent from the rest of the corpus I have selected. For in 1977, in Paris, among the four analytic gangs, what had become inevitable was also, Derrida conjectures, the need to find some means to avoid the one or the propositions of the one, the stranger, who had to be invited, inevitably, but perhaps so as better to avoid him or rather those propositions. He asks: "What proves that we have not met this evening, and by appointment, in order to be more certain of avoiding each other? Or of avoiding the texts inscribed on the session's program [the reference here is to *Glas* "and other texts in thematic relation to the theory, movement and institution of psychoanalysis" ("Tout," 498)], of acting as if they had been read because one has kept in one's gaze for two hours, in person, their presumed author, or because one will have spoken of them, of the said texts, so spectacularly?" ("Tout," 506). The analysts in the audience will have begun to realize no doubt that, in this inevitable confrontation, which is to say, perhaps, avoidance, Derrida is attempting to conduct the analysis of a complex set of symptoms of which his own invited presence there is one. "Du Tout" will confront those present at its performance with other symptoms of this avoidance-of-the-stranger that he represents, symptoms that can also take the form of avoiding signed texts by means of their unacknowledged assimilation rather than rejection or repudiation—the "Facteur de la vérité" had appeared just two years earlier and Derrida points to one or two of the more audacious ways Lacan's gang moved quickly to make it appear the master had either written what he had not or not written what he had, all of this as if no one had ever heard of, much less read, "Le Facteur de la vérité" ("Tout," 513–15).

But it is on another front as well, not only on this supposedly external front, that is, between a putative inside and outside of its institution, that Derrida analyzes the condition of a deconstruction of the institution of psychoanalysis. The fault line of the deconstruction falls where the multiple and mutually exclusive, competing institutional formations meet up with that practice among analytic professionals called in French "la tranche," that is, a "piece" or "slice" of analysis, in the later course of one's practice, after the certifying training analysis, a kind of re-certification or updating of one's credentials. Derrida, the stranger, the outsider, asserts that this practice of "what you name, without making a concept or a problem of it, the 'tranche'" ("Tout," 509) has a deconstructive effect from the moment it is possible to "aller faire une tranche"—which is to say, engage a new transference and/or counter-transference (or as he will also write, *tranche*-ference, counter-*tranche*-ference)—by crossing some line supposed to divide the four institutional formations from one another. What is thereby engaged—although not conceptualized or problematized from *within* psychoanalysis—is no less than the deconstruction or deconstitution of the institution of psychoanalysis as a whole, as a *tout*. This consequence follows from the fact that "In France there is not an analytic institution cut into four slices that it would suffice to adjoin in order to complete a whole and to recompose the harmonious unity of a community." Instead:

> Each group—this implication is inscribed in its juridical structure and in its constitutive project—claims to form the only authentic analytic institution, the only one with a legitimate claim to the Freudian inheritance, the only one that develops that inheritance authentically in its practice, didactics, modes

of formation and reproduction. This implies that, at least *de jure*, the three +n other groups are for each group—and one must accept and deal with this consequence—THE outside of psychoanalysis ITSELF when it refers to itself and calls itself by this name. ("Tout," 510; emphasis added)

Because it can *trancher* on other formations, the practice of the *tranche* makes apparent a topology in which the outside and inside of psychoanalysis are finally undecidable; that is, *on ne peut pas y trancher*, one cannot cut the knot and decide. This is, nevertheless, where Derrida's intervention is most trenchant. For, as he underscores more than once, he is making here a *de jure* argument, which unfolds an implication inscribed in a juridical structure and constitutive project. And, as such, "one must accept and deal with its consequence," that is, "*il faut en assumer la conséquence*." This modality of "one must," "il faut" derives its imperative, I venture to say, from an order that cannot be comprehended by psychoanalytic determinations of the genealogy of the law—and here, the text one would need to engage, outside my selected corpus, is "Before the Law" where Derrida's reading of Freud's "Totem and Taboo" voids the hypothesis of the father as origin of the law, of the "law of the law," which is to say, of its imperative (see "Before"). In other words, the name or the no (*le nom ou le non*) of the father cannot, in itself, by itself, *make* the law, make the law of the law. And this is where one must recognize an at least strategic assumption by Derrida in the circumstance of a certain exteriority vis-à-vis psychoanalytic discourse and conceptuality, despite his performative enactment of the undecidable, deconstructing border between the institution's inside and outside. For Derrida also addresses the assembly of the psychoanalytic institution from the place, if not of the law-giver, then of something like the law's necessary *assumption*, a necessity that cannot be accounted for by Oedipal logic. Essentially, then, it is the deconstruction or deconstitution of its own institution that must be assumed if psychoanalysis is to keep the promise of what is called, in "Freud and the Scene of Writing," the "Freudian breakthrough."

That this promise can be betrayed, sent astray, or hijacked is readable as a symptom of institutional pathology. Perhaps Derrida's most unambiguous and forceful display of this symptom's pathology takes place in "Geopsychoanalysis 'and the rest of the world.'" I say it is displayed because it is a certain performance or acting out that this lecture sought to achieve when it was delivered in 1981 to an audience of French and Latin American analysts convoked under no official professional auspices. Once again, before this unofficial, *ad hoc* congress, Derrida explicitly assumes the place of the invited outsider, whose body may be compared to the "foreign body" of the symptom:

I wondered why I had been asked here and what one wanted to ask of me. Why ask me to speak here . . . to say what and to do what. And to whom. . . . My first hypothesis, drawn from my experience, was the following. In this particular psychoanalytic world, in Paris, one seeks to understand as quickly as possible, both as soon and as rapidly as possible, without losing any time, what this foreigner might be saying, this foreign body that belongs to no body, that is not a member, in any capacity, of any of the analytic corporations of the world or of the rest of the world. . . . I say "foreign body" to designate this thing that can neither be assimilated, rejected, interiorized, nor, at the limits of a divisible line between inside and outside, foreclosed. . . . The symptom is always a foreign body and must be deciphered as such; and of course, a foreign body is always a symptom, it always *does* symptom [fait *symptôme*] on the body of the ego, it is a body foreign to the body of the ego. That is what I am doing here: I do symptom, I do the symptom, it's a role I'm playing, if not for each of you, then at least for a certain ego of the analytic institution. And if you want to understand the foreigner or the stranger very quickly . . . then perhaps it's also in order to make the symptom disappear, as quickly as possible, to file away his discourse without delay, in other words, to forget it without ado. ("Geopsych," 320–1)

"Geopsychoanalysis" reads a set of documents around the 1977 revision of the constitution of the IPA, founded by Freud in 1908. The symptom isolated there in all its textual and contextual specificity is the erasure of the name of Latin America. The year is 1977. Argentina's "Dirty War" had gotten underway in 1976 and already there were reports of psychoanalysts colluding, voluntarily or involuntarily, with the torturing regime of the military *junta* (Buenos Aires, it should be noted, is reputed to have a higher number of psychoanalysts per capita than any European or North American city).

But this erasure would be merely symptomatic of a graver destitution of the psychoanalytic "breakthrough" and legacy, a destitution, avoidance, or voiding whose consequences, once again, Derrida insists must be assumed.

On torture, you ought to have essential things to say—and to do. And in particular on a certain modernity of torture, on that of contemporary history and therefore contemporary with psychoanalysis. . . . Does [psychoanalysis] do so? To my knowledge, no . . . Is it not on this point that a properly psychoanalytic intervention ought to be required, at least if there is something "properly psychoanalytic" in this domain? And if there is not, then it would be necessary to draw from this fact the very grave consequence in all its aspects. ("Geopsych," 333)

Once again, we see the assertion of the necessity to draw or *assumer* the consequence. What is being set out here is "a fact or a possibility whose gravity has to give one to think and to act. This possibility makes a symptom, it 'does symptom,'" the symptom of "an inadequation to self as the result of some internal limitation, some occlusion or obstruction that today shapes the analytic cause, its discourse, its clinical and institutional practice" ("Geopsych," 334). That this unanalyzed occlusion has formed around the proper name Freud, which in the IPA's own constitution stands as the only marker of the "properly psychoanalytic," leads Derrida to conclude—"one must conclude," he writes—that

> all those who wish to give themselves the right and the means to develop this kind of question [that is, questions about this proper name, "its relation to science, to thought, to the institution, to the inheritance"], all those who believe in the necessity of drawing institutional consequences must envision a new psychoanalytic *socius*—one that would not necessarily have the structure of a central, national, or international institution, and that would not remain merely a theoretical college as powerless as the League of Nations, whose impotence and whose lack of any power of its own Freud pointed out in 1932 (in a letter to Einstein, 'Why War?'), without, however, asking himself whence a psychoanalytic league of nations might one day draw its own force. ("Geopsych," 339)[4]

This last remark can lead us directly to the fourth text in this corpus, written almost twenty years later, where this passing reference to Freud's exchange with Einstein is expanded into a fuller reading. But first one should underscore how, if the passage just quoted lays out the consequence of the deconstitution or de-institutionalization of psychoanalysis, it does so from premises that are essentially those of one who is playing the role of symptom and foreign body. Although those premises are here telescoped into their minimal traits, they had been developed at length in "To Speculate—on 'Freud,'" published the preceding year, 1980, in *The Post Card*," which interrogates in a different manner the symptom of the institution of psychoanalysis. The "new psychoanalytic *socius*," to be envisioned by "all those who believe in drawing institutional consequences," is thus, in an important sense, modeled on analyses conducted in these and other texts, which one must read without hurrying, which cannot be replaced by early morning lectures from invited outsiders playing the symptom. It is a *socius* of readers of the geopsychoanalytical, geopolitical institutional text who must assume the consequences of that reading and that analysis. Some dozen years later and in yet another context in which Derrida plays the role of outsider, he will give it a name that resonates somewhere between the international movements founded independently and without reference to one another by Marx and Freud.

> The "New International" is not only that which is seeking a new international law through these crimes. It is a link of affinity, suffering, and hope,

a still discreet, almost secret link . . . It is an untimely link, without status, without title, and without name . . . The name of new International is given here to what calls to the friendship of an alliance *without institution* . . . (*Specters*, 85–6; emphasis added)

Our fourth text further plies this space of the New International between its two revolutionary movements. To sketch these very telegraphically, I would point to two aspects that a rereading of "Psychoanalysis Searches the States of Its Soul" might bring to the fore if given the impetus of this selected corpus behind it.

First, of course, would be the answer Derrida himself brings there to his earlier question to the French and Latin American analysts, and through them, to the IPA concerning whether or not there is something "properly psychoanalytic" that would require an intervention in a domain defined by "a certain modernity of torture."

> Let us merely ask ourselves whether, yes or no, what is called "psychoanalysis" does not open up the only way that could allow us, if not to know, if not to think even, at least to interrogate what might be meant by this strange and familiar word "cruelty" . . . Hypothesis on a hypothesis: if there is something irreducible in the life of the living being, in the soul, in the psyche . . . and if this irreducible thing in the life of the animate being is indeed the possibility of cruelty . . . [then t]he only discourse that can today claim the thing of psychical suffering as its own affair would indeed be what has been called, for about a century, psychoanalysis. ("States," 239–40)

Second, there would be a certain call, which was already sounded in "Geopsychoanalysis," to make consequential articulations between psychoanalytic discourse and the domains of the ethical, the political, and the law, especially international law. Or rather, since it cannot be for psychoanalysis *as such* "to evaluate or devaluate, to discredit cruelty or sovereignty from an ethical point of view," then the consequence is not an articulation that follows as a conclusion from premises; it follows rather the route of a necessary discontinuity and indirection, in a word, a leap.

> To cross the line of decision, a leap that expels one outside of psychoanalytic knowledge *as such* is necessary. . . . Is that to say that there is no relation between psychoanalysis and ethics, law, or politics? No, there is, there must be an *indirect* and *discontinuous* consequence. . . . The task, which is immense and remains entirely to be done, both for psychoanalysts and for whomever . . . is to organize that taking account of psychoanalytic reason without reducing the heterogeneity, the leap into the undecidable, the beyond of the possible, which is the object of psychoanalytic knowledge. ("States," 273)

I leave things there, for the moment, in the mid-air of this leap "that expels one outside psychoanalytic knowledge."

Notes

1. This chapter is based on a paper first presented at the American Comparative Literature Association annual conference in May 2008, for a session titled "Jacques Derrida and the Singular Event of Psychoanalysis," organized by Steven Miller.
2. To these might be added "For the Love of Lacan" ("Lacan") and *Archive Fever: A Freudian Impression* (*Archive*), both of which were first delivered as invited lectures on occasions commemorating the Lacanian or Freudian legacy. I leave them aside here because neither occasion was marked by the gathering of a psychoanalytic institution or of psychoanalysts as such, which is what affiliates the four chosen texts.
3. The four groups were: the Société Psychanalytique de Paris, founded in 1926, the Association Psychanalytique de France, which along with Lacan's École Freudienne was formed in 1964 when Lacan's earlier group (the Société Française de Psychanalyse) split in two, and finally, what became known as the Quatrième Groupe, which split off from the École Freudienne in 1969.
4. Two pages earlier, having remarked that the new revision of the IPA's constitution contains a clause allowing for the contingency of a dissolution of the organization, Derrida addresses his listeners out of a conjoined interest in "a radical and ongoing transformation that should one day result in the dissolution of the IPA founded by Freud and in its replacement by something else, something altogether other, whose structure, shape, topology, and map would be essentially different" ("Geopsych," 337).

The Philosopher, As Such, and the Death Penalty

"I will set out from what has long been for me the most significant and the most stupefying—also the most stupefied—fact in the history of Western philosophy."

It would have been sometime around the year 2000 (the same year as the lecture to the Estates General of psychoanalysis) that Jacques Derrida expressed himself in these terms to his interlocutor in the dialogue that, a little while later, will be published with the title *De quoi demain . . .*, *For What Tomorrow . . .* In these sentences, Derrida is categorically and rather uncharacteristically firm in hammering home the superlatives, in naming "the most significant and most stupefying fact, the most stupefied as well in the history of Western philosophy" (*Tomorrow*, 145–6). Upon reading and rereading the superlatives issued by this philosopher who is so stingy, so one says at least, with his positively superlative propositions, I remain stupefied by them. Upon reading and rereading these lines, I hear the slap that his tongue administers to language. I must therefore also set out from this signifying and stupefying blow delivered by means of his language.

Upon rereading these sentences—but remember I am speaking as one who is stupefied—I would say: it is as if Derrida, *as philosopher* (which is what some call him), as if this highly-renowned philosopher (many call him, in the superlative, the greatest philosopher of his age), it is as if Derrida, in the name of philosophers or philosophy as such, were giving (himself) a big smack, delivering a slap to "the history of Western philosophy." This slap is symbolic, one might say, but it is no less stupefying. As if he had felt, at the moment of the gesture, shame for the title of philosopher—often in the superlative—that he is made to bear. As if he had said to himself: OK, then, if I have to wear this superlative, I throw it back, I give it back to language. Take that by way of superlatives, I throw them in your face, since you at least pretend to respect and honor whoever reasons superlatively. And then he hurls the superlatives to the farthest distance, the most stupefying distance, one after the other. In the name of the *philosopher as such*, he slaps his language until its ears ring.

When one continues this stinging quotation, the blow of the "as such," of the *en tant que tel*, may be heard twice. It is a matter then of naming or identifying this superlatively signifying and stupefying fact:

> never, *to my knowledge*, has any philosopher, *as such* [en tant que tel], *in his properly philosophical discourse*, never has any philosophy *as such* [en tant que telle] contested the legitimacy of the death penalty. (*Tomorrow*, 146)

Derrida thus names the stupefying fact first in his most properly philosophical language. Twice, as you heard through the ringing in your ears, there is "as such" in italics. "As such": this is how he designates first the philosopher and next philosophy, who and what. Philosopher, philosophy are general names and not—no longer or not yet—proper names. But proper names of philosophers are going to be called up right away in the next sentence of the passage:

> From Plato to Hegel, from Rousseau to Kant (who was undoubtedly the most rigorous of them all), they expressly, each in his own way, and sometimes not without much hand-wringing (Rousseau) took sides *for* the death penalty.

Whack, whack, whack, whack: the proper names of philosophers *as such* resonate in quantity. But notice that something else is happening when, in the sequence of these sentences, one goes from a general order to the ordered roll call of these proper names. The register shifts from that of a non-act that is proper to philosophy as such (unless it is not already, first of all, proper to the philosopher as such) to an act that is *more* properly political, the act of taking sides, of putting oneself in the balance pro *or* con. First we read that no philosopher, as such—philosopher (still) without proper name—throughout the whole "history of philosophy as such," "has contested the legitimacy of the death penalty." Not to contest is a gesture that refrains from taking sides for *or* against, and it is the gesture, or non-gesture, we read, of the philosophical discourse of the philosopher as such. And this latter is called Plato or Hegel, Rousseau or Kant. As these are no longer simply the names of philosophers, but also of citizens, subjects, persons, fathers, husbands, or friends, that is, names of possible places from which (from whom) to take sides (for *or* against), then clearly the register has shifted to the political order, the order of taking sides *for* (or *against*).

From the fact that the persons named all took sides *for* the death penalty, even as they were also philosophers *as such*, what should one deduce? What happened during the leap that takes its footing on the philosophically solid ground of the "as such" in order to jump with two feet in the direction of the properly political ground of the side taken (for *or* against)? What has to happen so that the one named Assuch (as if it were now a proper name) leaps in the direction of the *for* or *against*, the political terrain where one declares oneself in one's proper name? *Can Assuch leap and keep his name as such?* Does Philosophy, as philosophy that is property of the Assuch family, know how to leap, can it leap without putting its name at risk, without throwing it in its own face?

These are the sorts of questions that leaped to my ears when I played back the record of these sentences and replayed some of the scenes they stage. So as to follow them a little further, I am going to proceed by leaps (still reeling from stupefaction) in the direction of other texts where Derrida puts in play and in the balance the place of the political for the one named Assuch.

The first leap will take us toward that text from the same year, the year 2000, "Psychoanalysis Searches the States of Its Soul," and right away toward, precisely, a series of leaps that are executed across two pages, near the end of the essay. On these same pages, one finds as well several repetitions of the designation "en tant que tel," "as such" (and here I pick up the quotation that was interrupted in mid-leap at the close of the preceding chapter):

> This concept [of indirection] . . . does not signify only detour, strategic ruse, *continuous* transaction with an inflexible force, for example, with the cruelty or sovereign-power drive. . . . [T]his concept of the *indirect* seems to me to take into account, in the mediation of the detour, a radical discontinuity, a heterogeneity a leap into the ethical (thus also into the juridical and political) that no psychoanalytic knowledge *as such* [emphasis added] could propel or authorize. ("States," 273)

The "as such" does not *know* how to leap, it *cannot* leap, having neither the propulsion of a knowing-how-to-leap nor the authorization of a being-able-to-leap. Knowledge, in other words, is stuck in place so long as it awaits the propulsion or the authorization of a knowing-how-to-be-able-to-leap. As such, it will never be able to get off the ground. As "as such," it can only know itself to be properly psychoanalytic or philosophical. "X as X" is the syntax of the proper, which can inscribe only the direct, which cannot, therefore, take account of the indirect, which cannot count on everything that *propels* toward the other in the domain of the ethical-juridical-political. (It would be necessary to think about the *pro-pulsion drive* of this very text, beginning with this word *pulsion* that is so charged in French precisely by psychoanalysis; in other words, it would be necessary to reread it according to the propulsion of this word, following it according to its *pulsion for*, in the direction of or in favor of, while keeping in mind the multiple possibilities of this little word *for* [pour] that Derrida has often underscored, as Hélène Cixous, for one, has reminded us;[1] finally, it would be necessary to reread it for the traces of what-sets-in-motion *for* the other, a forcibly *indirect* propulsion since it cannot know in what sense it is to be understood.)

I skip a little on the page and pick up the quotation further on:

> It is not for the psychoanalyst *as such* [emphasis in the original] to evaluate or devaluate, to discredit cruelty or sovereignty from an ethical point of view. First of all, because he knows that there is no life without the competition between the forces of two antagonistic drives. Whether one is talking about the cruelty or the sovereignty drive [*pulsion*], psychoanalytic knowledge *as such* [emphasis added] has neither the means nor the right to condemn it. In this regard, it is and must remain, as knowledge, within the neutrality of the undecidable. . . .
>
> To cross the line of decision, a leap that expels one [it is thus an expelling propulsion (PK)] outside psychoanalytic knowledge *as such* [emphasis in the original] is necessary. In this hiatus, I would say, the chance or risk of responsible decision is opened beyond all knowledge concerning the possible. (Ibid.)

Repeated three times, twice in italics, the expression "as such" ("en tant que tel"), qualifies what has to remain neutral and in the undecidable, outside decision, outside the leap—thus outside the ethical, political, and juridical, outside the taking of sides without knowing. For there to be a leap, under the impulse of the expelling propulsion, the syntax of the "as such" has to take a detour in the direction of the outside or beyond knowledge; or rather, this propulsion carries one "beyond all knowledge *concerning the possible*." Is a knowledge beyond the possible possible? If Derrida would say no, that does not prevent "felicitous" acts of knowledge, as speech act analysts would say. If, for example, the psychoanalyst believes she knows "that there is no life without the competition between the forces of two antagonistic drives," she knows this as psychoanalyst and, as such, must take this knowledge into account while remaining in the undecidable. But this knowledge or this belief only opens what Derrida refers to here as the "hiatus": the gap, ditch, trench, but also no doubt the impasse, the aporia. On one side and the other of this chasm, it is a matter of aiming at the other side, of taking one's footing on the firm ground of knowing or believing one knows, but then and finally, on one side or other, one cannot know how to leap, one cannot know how to be able to leap because each remains "beyond any knowledge concerning the possible." The hiatus is already there on all sides, in all kinds of knowledge, which can know nothing beyond the possible. It is thus the ground of knowledge that opens beneath one's feet. What is more, on each side there are antagonistic drives, if at least one believes the psychoanalysts when they say what they believe they know. But it is precisely such a taking into account of psychoanalysis as such, as knowledge, that is lacking on the side of the ethico-juridico-political. As the passage continues, Derrida calls clearly for the transformation of the two sides, the one by, but also in view of, *for*, in the direction of, which is to say, in the indirection of the other.

> It is in this place that is difficult to delimit, the space of undecidability and thus of decision opened up by the discontinuity of the indirect, that the translation to come of ethics, law, and politics should *take into account* psychoanalytic knowledge . . . and that, reciprocally, the analytic community should take into account history, notably the history of law. . . . Everything here, it seems to me, remains to be done, on both sides. ("States," 273–4)

This text could keep us for a long time, all the time of a colloquium on "Political Derrida."[2] We could linger over all that is said here about the so-called "performative" but also all that is said about the death penalty, especially the capital punishment still in force in the United States. In the year 2000—the year of that significant anniversary, a superlatively anniversary year according to the "mondialatinized" calendar—it is the figure of the death penalty in all its states of array and disarray but, above all, superlatively United Statesian that provides the link between the two texts by Derrida cited so far. During that same year, Derrida was conducting a seminar with the title "Death Penalty." As philosopher teaching philosophy *as such*, "the history of Western philosophy," this seminar deconstructs, at its weekly rhythm, the capital trait that capital punishment has been throughout this history. It is during this seminar that he discovers and confirms "the most significant and the most stupefying fact—also the most stupefied—fact in the history of Western philosophy." The deconstruction of the traits of what is properly philosophical, which Derrida's seminar carries out under the general title of "Philosophical Institutions," is propelled, one might now say, by the force of a break with philosophy insofar as it is transmitted, as such, by this trait of the support it offers to the maintenance of the death penalty by the state according to national and sovereign law. To break this uninterrupted link, by introducing a wedge *against* this capital trait, is enough to cause the whole institution to tremble, inasmuch as it is in part held up by this link to the sovereign state.

Earlier, the question was asked: what must be deduced from the fact that, as philosophers as such, none of those cited took sides, in his own name, against the death penalty? And if any one had done so, could we say that the effect of such a break would have been limited to philosophy properly speaking and as such? Because it is a matter of breaking with the trait whereby philosophy recognizes itself as such, for that very reason the break or the breach opens in the (in)direction of the other. The break, whose cruel force should not be minimized, lends its propulsion to the leap toward the shore of the political, ethical, juridical. And toward the shore of the psyche and of psychoanalysis whose proper knowledge, if there is one—and this is Derrida's principal thesis in "Psychoanalysis Searches the States of Its Soul"—is or should be cruelty in all its states, all its *états d'âme*. It is this propulsion of the leap, without knowing how, without having the power to do so, without holding some knowledge that can go beyond the possible, it is this non-knowledge of the im-possible that is called deconstruction and that also calls one to think.

Derrida says so nowhere more clearly than in the seminar *The Beast and the Sovereign*. On the question of the deconstruction of sovereignty, one of whose most clearly marked traits is the sovereign right to inflict the punishment of death, he remarks:

> It goes without saying that . . . what I am looking for would be, then, a *slow and differentiated* deconstruction of this logic and the dominant, classic concept of nation-state sovereignty . . . without ending up with a de-politicization, but an other politicization, a repoliticization . . . [T]he rhythm of this deconstruction cannot be that of a seminar or a discourse ex cathedra. This rhythm is first of all the rhythm of what is happening in the world. This deconstruction is what is happening, as I often say, and what is happening today in the world . . . (*Beast*, 75–6)

All those for whom this "slow and differentiated" deconstruction matters can now cite this text, thanks to the publication of Derrida's seminars.[3] *Remains* from now on to read this writing destined to Jacques Derrida's voice. The propulsion of this voice or this writing—the difference remaining at the bottom of what each one understands by death and by this general death penalty—the propulsion of this voice-writing from now on is carried by publication launched toward its future.

Already in view and at work, there is the deconstruction of this superlative fact of the history of Western philosophy: that it has never been able and has never known how, as such, to raise its voice against the death penalty. This is a link of its history, this is one of the proper traits that holds it up and holds it together, holding it to its "as such." Derrida's seminar to come on "The Death Penalty," from which one day it will also be possible to quote and read publicly, has broken and will break again this link, which thereby demonstrates that it is indeed breakable, fallible. It will always have been breakable and yet, as Derrida says in one of his earliest texts, "Plato's Pharmacy," this break, this displacement *"il faut le faire."*[4]

Il faut le faire. Each will understand this affirmation as he or she may. To my ear, today, it signs the propulsive force of deconstruction.

Notes

1. See Hélène Cixous, *Insister of Jacques Derrida*, trans. Peggy Kamuf (Edinburgh: Edinburgh University Press, Galilée, 2006), p. 80.
2. This is an allusion to the original context in which a first version of this chapter was presented: the colloquium "Derrida Politique," in December 2008, at the École Normale Supérieure, Paris, organized by René Major, Marc Crépon, Geoffrey Bennington, and Charles Alunni.
3. *The Beast and the Sovereign*, which is the first volume in the series, was edited by Michel Lisse, Marie-Louise Mallet, and Ginette Michaud.
4. See above, Chapter 12, "Composition Displacement," pp. 141–3, for some commentary on this French expression.

Epitaph

"A New Wave: Scientists Write on Water," reads the Web post headline announcing a "breakthrough" technology:

> A new technology allows researchers to write on water. The AMOEBA (Advanced Multiple Organized Experimental Basin), a circular tank created by Mitsui Engineering at their Akishima laboratory, is able to form letters with standing waves. This remarkable display device consists of fifty water-wave generators surrounding a cylindrical tank five feet wide and a foot deep. The wave generators move vertically to produce cylindrical waves. These "pixels" are about four inches in diameter and one and a half inches in height; these form lines and shapes. The AMOEBA device can form all of the roman alphabet, as well as some kanji characters. Each letter takes about fifteen seconds to produce; Akishima Labs expects to sell the device to amusement parks in a package that combines acoustics, lighting and fountain technology.[1]

Writ large on this remarkable device is the thoroughly prosaic ambition that produced it: to literalize the figure of writing on water by giving it form as literal writing (in letters or characters) on the substance of actual H_2O. More precisely, it is the essentially anti-poetic ambition to close the gap in figuration, to reduce to zero the space that floats the metaphor and carries it virtually wherever experience can leave a trace of its own erasure. One senses that driving the AMOEBA machine is a furiously futile protest against the figure's immemorial value as a reminder of the archive's finitude, its erosion and disintegration—for, along with fire, water is the written archive's greatest enemy. From this perspective, it seems significant that we do not learn at least from this report how long AMOEBA's letters remain readable on the water's surface, as if even the briefest appearance of literal "writing on water" could overcome the import of the figure rather than, and on the contrary, redundantly reconfirming it. With each letter brought to the surface, the machine's inventors cry out "There, see, it can be done!" And done again, and again, and again, by dint of technological reproducibility, which is all that remains but which is absolutely nothing new and, indeed, nothing at all, still less than the nothing of a device for distracting crowds from the morbid idleness of amusement parks.

Nevertheless, AMOEBA does nothing so well as mimic poetic invention, although by reassembling it in a hugely cumbersome, Rube Goldberg-like machine. In the end, however, it must settle for programming possibilities that have been around as long as the single-celled organism invoked by its acronym.[2] Indeed, amoebae, those most elementary of poets, bound up symbiotically, osmotically with their aquatic medium, could doubtless teach these engineers a thing or two about writing in water, about laying down traces of an experience the singularity of which must risk letting itself drown in repetition to become readable for another, if indeed it does before vanishing without a trace.

The figure of writing on or in water says this vanishing, in other words, the appearance of a disappearance. It is an image of the most fleeting form, the persistent repetition of an invention that never waited on "fifty water-wave generators surrounding a cylindrical tank" to be brought to the surface of whatever medium. Many pages ago,[3] we read Melville's own repetition in the passage on wake writing and reading:

> for after being chased, and diligently marked, through several hours of daylight, then, when night obscures the fish, the creature's future wake through the darkness is almost as established to the sagacious mind of the hunter, as the pilot's coast is to him. So that to this hunter's wondrous skill, the proverbial evanescence of a thing writ in water, a wake, is to all desired purposes well nigh as reliable as the steadfast land.

Notice how neatly the phrase "proverbial evanescence" plots the collision of meanings between that which lasts not at all or barely and that which survives through the immemorial citational power of poetic (amoebic, cetacean) traces.

Melville's immediate allusion seems to be not at all ancient since "a thing writ in water" quotes the very phrasing dictated, just thirty years earlier, by John Keats to his friend Joseph Severn for his only epitaph: "Here lies one whose name was writ in water."[4] In iambic pentameter to the end, it comes to stand as the last line of one who had faced "fears that I may cease to be/ Before my pen has glean'd my teeming brain,/ Before high piled books, in charactry,/ Hold like rich garners the full ripen'd grain."[5] According to one of Keats's most recent biographers, it was another friend, Charles Brown, who insisted on supplementing the famously dictated epitaph with a polemical prologue, an act that Brown would later regret as "a sort of profanation."[6] In any case, the line was duly inscribed on the tombstone in Rome's Protestant cemetery. "Writ in water" was thus writ in stone even as Keats's other poetic inventions were entrusted to a medium more durable than granite or marble: proverbial, verbal, word by word repetition.

Keats's invention, like every great invention, churns a wake through the pool of all that had been said and thought before it. The lines upon lines of verse chart new territory out of old, their feet measuring out paths to be followed uncountable times from then on. It is this movement of invention that had to be gone through, however briefly, so as to lay down a path and leave traces of what, until then, had not seemed possible.

Or, as Derrida wrote concerning the necessary displacement of the Platonic legacy, *il faut le faire*. Around the same time, in *Of Grammatology*, he reached for a different image in order to say something similar about the necessity of following a path so as to leave a wake—a *sillage*—in the text. Bracketing the context that calls up this figure (which is an explanation of why, even as this discourse puts transcendentality into question, it must also refer to it), we have to remark the modality of necessity that draws out and traces the wake through the turns of these few sentences (I have added italics to bring this out):

> It is to escape falling back into this naïve objectivism [of Hjelmslevian glossematics] that we refer here to a transcendentality that we elsewhere put into question. It is because there is, we believe, a near side and a far side of the transcendental critique. To do things in such a manner that the far side does not return to the near side is to recognize in this contortion the *necessity* of a *pathway* [*parcours*, Derrida's italics]. This pathway *must* leave a wake [*sillage*] in the text. Without this wake, abandoned to the mere content of its conclusions, the ultra-transcendental text will forever resemble the precritical text to the point that one can mistake the one for the other. We *have to* formulate and meditate upon today the law of this resemblance. What we call here the erasure of concepts *must* mark the places of this meditation to come. (*Grammatology*, 61)

"This pathway must leave a wake in the text." With these words, Derrida spells out a law for what may still come. It is the law or necessity of making one's way through an immense legacy in such a manner as to leave a wake, in other words, a churning through the text of tradition that breaks up its mirror-like appearance, drives contortions through the straits of logic, brings again to the readable surface matter that has sunk out of sight, all the while planting markers by which others may also navigate.[7] As such, it is a law for the other to follow and so that another may read what has been displaced by the engine's impulse.

So, yes, *il faut le faire*: it is necessary, it will have been necessary to do what today, in any today of any present, seems as impossible as writing on water. At the risk, of course, of being drawn into the wake's turbulence.[8]

Notes

1. "A New Wave: Scientists Write on Water," by Bill Christensen, posted: 26 July 2006 11:41 am ET at http://www.livescience.com/technology/060726_water_write.html; consulted 3 March 2010, 11:50 am PST.
2. See Derrida, "Psyche," *passim*, for example: "Thus it is that invention would be in conformity with its concept, with the dominant feature of the word and concept 'invention,' only insofar as, paradoxically, invention invents nothing, when in invention the other does not come, and when nothing comes to the other or from the other. For the other is not the possible. So it would be necessary to say that the only possible invention would be the invention of the impossible. But an invention of the impossible is impossible, the other would say. Indeed. But it is the only possible invention: an invention has to declare itself to be the invention of that which did not appear to be possible; otherwise, it only makes explicit a program of possibilities within the economy of the same" (44).
3. See infra, 9–10.
4. For Keats as well, of course, the figure would have been proverbial. Scholars have suggested sources in Plato, Sophocles, Callimachus, Catullus, Augustine, Shakespeare (*Henry VIII*), and, most likely for Keats who particularly admired them, Beaumont and Fletcher from their 1611 play *Philaster Or: Love Lies A-bleeding*, where it occurs as a curse hurled by the hero at the villain: "Your memory shall be as soul behind you/ As you are living, *all your better deeds/ Shall be in* water writ, but this in Marble:/ No Chronicle shall speak you, though your own,/ But for the shame of men" (V, 3).
5. John Keats, "When I have fears that I may cease to be," in *Complete Poems*, ed. John Stillinger (Cambridge: The Belknap Press of Harvard University Press, 1982), p. 166.
6. Andrew Motion, *Keats: A Biography* (Chicago: University of Chicago Press, 1997), 564–5; the epitaph eventually settled on between Brown and Severn reads: "This Grave contains/ all that was Mortal of/ A YOUNG ENGLISH POET/ Who/ on his death bed/ in the Bitterness of his Heart/ at the Malicious Power of his Enemies/ Desired/ these Words to be engraved/ on His Tomb Stone/ 'Here Lies One Whose Name/ was writ in Water'/ Feb 24 1821." A much earlier biographer, Sidney Colvin, gives a significantly different account of the circumstances that led to the final epitaph: see the epilogue to Colvin's 1917 work, *John Keats: His Life and Poetry, His Friends, Critics and After-Fame*, at http://englishhistory.net/keats/colvinkeats17.html (consulted 3 March 2010 at 10:10 am PST).
7. The French term *sillage* is related to *sillon*, a plowed or planted row of earth.

8. These last pages are indebted to valuable suggestions from Nick Royle and Geoff Bennington. I thank them here, as ever.